Instructor's Manual to Accompany

AN INTRODUCTION TO POETRY

Instructor's Manual to Accompany

AN INTRODUCTION TO POETRY

Fifth Edition

X. J. Kennedy

Dorothy M. Kennedy

Little, Brown and Company

Boston   Toronto

ISBN 0-316-489077

9 8 7 6 5 4 3 2 1

ALP

Published simultaneously in Canada
by Little, Brown & Company (Canada) Limited

Printed in the United States of America

USING THIS MANUAL

Some instructors hold that the proper use for a manual like this is to swat flies. They will be gratified to notice that, with this edition, the manual has been made considerably heftier. But I hope that those who actually read the manual also will welcome its thickening. About a hundred poems new to this edition have been provided with notes, and for many poems that were here already, fresh teaching suggestions and some insights by recent critics have been added. As in the past, the arrangement of this manual follows the order of the contents of An Introduction to Poetry. To help you locate what you're looking for, page numbers appear at the top of pages in this manual. These numbers correspond to the pages of the parent book itself.

Notes are supplied for almost every poem in the book, except for several brief poems that merely illustrate points and two poems that are discussed in the book fairly thoroughly. It has been a joy to include the suggestions and teaching experiences of some in-structors who cared to contribute them. Throughout this manual the intent has been to offer additional questions, background informa-tion, classroom strategies, and some interpretations of the poems that are clear enough--even pig-headed enough--to invite fruitful argument. No one can tell another how to teach, nor would I try. May you continue to view the poems through your own and your stu-dents' eyes and (as James Joyce has cheerfully counseled) "wipe your glosses with what you know."

RENOVATIONS

Besides the addition of a second anthology--the twenty short passages from great (or merely lively) critics--and of the new section "Writing a Poem," this Fifth Edition makes a few changes in organization. The chapter "Saying and Suggesting" now follows immediately after the chapter "Words." Now, if you like, you can go directly from the matters of literal meaning and diction to the matters of denotation and connotation. The matter of evaluating poetry (dealt with in "Telling Good from Bad" and "Knowing Excel-lence"), being hardest, now comes last. In the cabbage-patch of bad poetry (Chapter Fifteen), some stale old stalks have been up-rooted and given a pitch, and a couple of fresh vegetables added.

The sections on writing (now three in number) are all grouped together at the back of the book so the student can find them more
easily.
    Following the advice of many instructors, this edition restores
several old favorites that used to be in previous editions, or
should have been: Hopkins's "Spring and Fall," Frost's "Desert
Places," Meredith's "Lucifer in Starlight," Roethke's "Elegy for
Jane," Waller's "Go, Lovely Rose," Carew's "Ask me no more where
Jove bestows," Hardy's "Ruined Maid," and Boyd's "Cupid and Venus."
At last, there is a hymn in common meter (by William Cowper) facing
Emily Dickinson's "Because I could not stop for Death," so that
Dickinson's debt to hymn-singing will be apparent. Among contempo-
rary poets new to this edition you will find Linda Pastan, Richard
Hugo, Paul Zimmer, Constance Urdang, Ray Young Bear, Ted Kooser,
Jane Kenyon, Etheridge Knight, Galway Kinnell, Margaret Atwood,
David Bottoms, Philip Dow, Amiri Baraka, Wendell Berry, Sterling A.
Brown, Tess Gallagher, Gibbons Ruark, Derek Walcott, Gerald Stern,
Gary Soto, Robert Penn Warren, Tom Wayman, and Willie Nelson. Some
of the long-kept poems in the book have received additional notes
and new questions.

REPRESENTATION

    This edition includes 433 whole poems, including translations:
295 in the body of the book, 138 in the poetry anthology. For anyone interested in the numbers of earlier and later poems included,
here are statistics (with poems dated as in the text—by first
publication or by date of composition if much earlier):

Number of poems before 1700	62
Number of eighteenth-century poems	19
Number of nineteenth-century poems	81
Number of twentieth-century poems before 1960	148
Number of poems 1960–1981	122
Total	432

    For the instructor who wishes to teach a poet's work in
greater depth than a single poem allows, these are the poets most
heavily represented:

Yeats, Emily Dickinson	11 poems each
Frost	10 poems
Whitman	9 poems
William Carlos Williams	8 poems
Shakespeare, Blake, Wordsworth, Hardy, Stevens	7 poems each
Donne, Keats, Housman, Roethke	6 poems each
Tennyson, Cummings	5 poems each
Herrick, Herbert, Hopkins, Eliot, Auden	4 poems each

There are three poems apiece by Milton, Pope, Lawrence, Pound, Dylan
Thomas, Cunningham, Wilbur, Lowell, Jarrell, Levertov, Plath, and
James Wright.

For work by poets who speak for minorities in America, see the selections by Countee Cullen, James Emanuel, Ray Young Bear, Richard Wright, Jean Toomer, James C. Kilgore, Etheridge Knight, Gwendolyn Brooks (two poems), Amiri Baraka, Sterling A. Brown, Langston Hughes (two poems), Dudley Randall, Gary Soto, and the anonymous lyrics "Scottsboro" and "Good Mornin', Blues."

PLAN OF THE BOOK

There is one, but you are not obliged to follow it. Chapters may be taken up in any sequence. Many instructors, for instance, find that a sure-fire chapter to begin with is "Imagery." If, because you skip around in the book, students meet a term unknown to them, let them look it up in the Index of Terms. They will be directed to the page in the book where the term first occurs, and is defined and illustrated.

So that parts of the book may be taught in any order, the sections called "For Review and Further Study" do not review the whole book up to that moment; they review only the main points of the chapter. These sections provide extra material for the instructor who wants to go further into a certain element of poetry. Most contain poems a little more difficult than those poems in the main body of the chapter.

The assumption behind the book is that appreciation of poetry cannot be created, but may be increased. Without trying to usurp the right of instructors to teach poetry in ways after their own hearts, the book offers short discussions of the elements of poetry which students may read for themselves, freeing class time for the study of poems.

TEXTS

Spelling has been modernized (rose-lipped for ros-lip'd) and made American, unless the sound of a word would be changed. But I have left the y in Blake's strange "Tyger" and let Whitman keep his bloom'd on the conviction that bloomed would no more resemble Whitman than a portrait of him in a starched collar would. Untitled poems, except for those that have titles assigned by custom ("The Twa Corbies," "Carrion Comfort"), are identified by their first lines. Chaucer's "Complaint" is given as edited by F. N. Robinson; the poems of Emily Dickinson, as edited by Thomas H. Johnson.

GLOSSES

It would have been simpler to gloss no word a student could find in a desk dictionary, on the grounds that the rummaging of dictionaries is good moral discipline; but it seemed best not to require the student to exchange text for dictionary as many as ten times in reading a single poem. Glosses have been provided for whatever seemed likely to interfere with pleasure and understanding.

Because the slang of the sixties appears to be aging more rapidly than the language of Chaucer, Bob Dylan's song seemed to call for more glosses than it had in the last edition. It remains a great song. But the times, they are a-changing.

ORTHOGRAPHY

The spelling rime is used instead of rhyme, on the theory that rime is easier to distinguish from rhythm.

LIVE POETS

Now that there is a guidebook to poets' whereabouts, there seems no point in trying to include data on setting up poetry readings in this manual. Anyone who wants to order a live poet is advised to send for A Directory of American Poets and Fiction Writers from Poets & Writers, Inc., 201 West 54 St., New York, NY 10019. The price of the 1980-1981 edition is $10.

CREDITS

Dorothy M. Kennedy has made large contributions to this manual in the past, and I am glad now to acknowledge her as its coauthor. Drawing on her experience as a teacher of English at Ohio University and the University of Michigan, and as an editor of a poetry magazine, Counter/Measures, she has written entries for many of these poems; and there is little else in the manual she didn't work over and make better. I continue to take responsibility for the book itself, and also for passages in this manual that inconsistently break out in the first person.

XJK

CONTENTS

1

ENTRANCES

The aim of this chapter is to assure the student that reading
poetry is not going to be entirely different from reading prose,
while setting forth a few ways in which poetry is different.

A. E. HOUSMAN, Loveliest of trees, the cherry now, page 3

Not part of the rough poem Housman began with, the second
stanza was added last. Lines 9-10 originally read: "And since to
look at things you love / Fifty times is not enough." What can be
said for Housman's additions and changes? (These and other manuscript variations are given by Tom Burns Haber in The Making of "A
Shropshire Lad" [Seattle: University of Washington Press, 1966].)

ROBERT FRANCIS, Catch, page 6

Putting a spin on his poem-baseball, hurling high ones and sometimes grounders, the pitching poet keeps the catching reader on his
toes by creating little difficulties, yet once in a while supplies
an instant reward. Most students (though they may paraphrase it
differently) will find this much of Francis's comparison easy to
catch. How does a poet "outwit the prosy"? Playing with swagger
and style, the poet doesn't want to communicate in a dull, predict-
able way, but (being a magician on the mound) will do anything to
surprise, to make poetry a game in which both poet and reader take
joy.
If you skip the chapter "Entrances," or don't discuss "Catch"
at this moment, the poem can be especially useful later in teaching
metaphor, or tone.

LINDA PASTAN, Ethics, page 6

As a student, the narrator, like the others in her class, found
her teacher's ethical puzzler irrelevant. Now the mature woman
pondering the "real Rembrandt" in the museum finds the question
still remote from her vital concerns, but for different reasons.
The approach of her own old age has shown her that nothing lasts,
that with the onflow of years our choices, whatever they may be,
fade into insignificance. Is the theme of the poem carpe diem? No,

1

6-8 (text pages)

for the poet seems not to believe in day-seizing. Is the theme <u>ars longa, vita brevis</u>? No, for both art and life are pitifully brief and temporary. The point, rather, is that all things pass away despite our efforts to hold on to them. In its moving statement of thoughts and feelings, the poem seems essentially lyric rather than narrative. One thing about its story puzzles me though: how many times did the speaker have to repeat that ethics course? She had to sit through the same lesson plan every fall?

In reply to question four, Pastan's language is perceptibly more musical than prose. In particular, she makes beautiful use of alliteration and assonance. Read out loud the poem's last two sentences. Central to "Ethics" is an immense metaphor: old woman, season, earth, painting, and poet become one--all caught in time's fire.

First printed in <u>Poetry</u> for December 1979, "Ethics" was chosen by the poet to represent her in <u>The Poet's Choice</u>, an anthology of poets' own favorite poems edited by George E. Murphy, Jr. (Green Harbor, Mass.: Tendril Magazine, 1980).

DONALD FINKEL, Hands, page 7

Outrageous as Finkel's opening simile may be (the bra with stiched-on hands sounds like a mail-order item advertised in <u>Hustler</u> or <u>True Confessions</u>), it expresses an ancient and honorable view: poetry not only imitates, but embellishes. Aristotle seems to back up Finkel: "If it be objected that the poet's description is not true to fact, the poet may meet the objection if he reply--'But the objects are as they ought to be.'" (<u>Poetics</u>, 25.)

If you want to give students some exercise in paraphrase, let them try to state the sense of the rest of the poem. In lines 5-8, a life without poetry is a dull marriage, and one who lives such a life is like a husband who sees in the world only reflections of his own boredom and impotence. In lines 9-13, the relationship between reader and poem is a lively one that works two ways. A poem is nothing without a reader to respond to it. Like a lover's hands, the poem playfully stirs the reader's emotions; and then, if the reader does accept, both reader and poem will be fulfilled.

ANDREW MARVELL, To His Coy Mistress, page 8

1. There's a grain of truth to this paraphrase, rude though it be. We might question, however, whether Marvell's speaker is trying to hoodwink his loved one. Perhaps he only sums up the terrible truth he knows: that time lays waste to youth, that life passes before we know it. He makes no mention of "romance," by the way--that's the paraphraser's invention. A more nearly accurate paraphrase, taking the three divisions of the poem one by one, might go like this:

2

Lines 1-20: If we had all the room in the world and if we were immortal, then our courtship might range across the globe. My love for you could expand till it filled the whole world and I could spend centuries in praising your every feature (saving your heart for last). After all, such treatment is only what you deserve.

Lines 21-32: But time runs on. Soon we'll be dead and gone, all my passion and all your innocence vanished.

Lines 33-46: And so, while you're still young and willing, let's seize the day. Let's concentrate our pleasure into the present moment. Although we can't make the sun stand still (like Joshua in the Bible), we'll do the next best thing: we'll joyously make time fly.

Now, obviously, any such rewording of this matchless poem must seem a piddling thing. But if students will just work through Marvell's argument part by part, they may grasp better the whole of it.

2. To point out the approximate location of the Humber and the Ganges on the globe of the world (or a simple circle drawn on a blackboard) can drive home the fact that when the poet says world enough, he spells out exactly what he means. A little discussion may be needed to show that in defining "enough" time, Marvell bounds it by events (the conversion of the Jews), numbers the years, and blocks out his piecemeal adoration. Two hundred years per breast is a delectable statistic! Clearly, the lover doesn't take the notion of such slow and infinitely patient devotion seriously.

3. Both Marvell and Housman in "Loveliest of trees" are concerned with the passage of time; they differ on what needs to be done about it. Marvell urges action; Housman urges filling one's youth with observed beauty. Of these two expressions of carpe diem theme, Housman's seems the more calm and disinterested!

4. In lines 37-44, Marvell's point seems that time works a gradual, insidious violence. It is like a devouring beast (slow-chapped), holding us in its inexorable jaws. Some students will find the imagery odd, even offensive in a love poem: birds of prey (who want to eat, not be eaten), the cannonball of strength and sweetness that batters life's iron gates. Violence is not the speaker's counsel, but urgency. His harsh images lend his argument intensity and force.

5. This fifth question presents an easy dichotomy, but of course Marvell's speaker is both playful and serious. In making clear the tone of the poem, a useful poem for comparison is Marlowe's "Passionate Shepherd" (page 343). What are the two speakers' attitudes toward love? Marvell's seems more down-to-earth, skeptical, and passion-driven: a lover in a fallen world, not (like Marlowe's shepherd) a lover in a pastoral Eden.

6. How is Marvell's masterpiece disturbing? Answers will be unpredictable! To me, it's the concreteness of the poem that startles and disturbs, with its imagery of time's hurrying chariot and that slow-chapped beast that consumes us all. The poem is an amazingly physical evocation of love and longing: Marvell does not separate the soul from the body that perspires.

3

If later on, in teaching figures of speech, you want some great lines for illustrations, turn back again to this inexhaustible poem. There's hyperbole in lines 7-20, understatement ("But none, I think, do there embrace"), metaphor, simile, and of course the great personification of chariot-driving time.

Telling a class that Marvell was a Puritan usually shakes up their overly neat assumptions. Some may be surprised to learn that one can be a Puritan and not necessarily be puritanical.

2

LISTENING TO A VOICE

TONE

THEODORE ROETHKE, My Papa's Waltz, page 10

Jay Parini would disagree. In his Theodore Roethke: An American Romantic (Amherst: University of Massachusetts Press, 1980), he finds that in "My Papa's Waltz" the boy "clings to his father for dear life, terrified by his physical power." "Which is to miss the point completely," protests John Lucas, reviewing Parini's book in the TLS for February 6, 1981. For the mature poet, looking back,

> recognizes how his timidity of spirit must have been a kind
> of death to his father, a terrible drag on his vitality.
> "Such waltzing was not easy." In substituting the trite
> phrase about clinging on for dear life for Roethke's finely
> judged one about hanging on like death, Parini quite fails
> to note how, for once at least, Roethke makes good use of
> cliché rather than being used by it.

As Alan Seager discerns in his biography of Roethke, The Glass House (New York: McGraw-Hill, 1968, pp. 23-26), the mature Roethke seems to have felt a certain guilty resentment against his father, a sense of how (as an awkward, chubby, bookish, and sensitive child) the young poet had failed to make the old man proud of him.

"My Papa's Waltz" may have had its genesis in a wish-fulfilling dream. After his father's death, Roethke wrote a memoir (calling himself "John"): "Sometimes he dreamed about Papa. Once it seemed Papa came in and danced around with him. John put his feet on top of Papa's and they'd waltz. Hei-dee-dei-dei. Rump-tee-tump. Only babies expected dreams to come true." (Quoted by Seager, page 24.)

COUNTEE CULLEN, For a Lady I Know, page 11

From Cullen's first book, Color (1925), this is one of a series of twenty-nine epitaphs. Compare it with another brief poem that makes a biting social comment: Sarah N. Cleghorn's "The Gold Links" (page 25). Cleghorn's poem seems angrier; the tone of Cullen's poem seems to be wry amusement at stupidity.

Cullen's early biography is sparsely documented. Raised by his grandmother until he was eleven, he was then adopted by the Reverend

Frederick A. Cullen, pastor of a Methodist church in Harlem, who
gave the future poet not only a name but a new life of books and
conversation. Famed as the leading poet of the Harlem Renaissance,
Cullen suffered a decline in reputation when militant black critics
of the 1960s reevaluated his work and found it wanting in anger and
social consciousness. But his wit can bite, as it does in "For a
Lady I Know"; and Houston A. Baker has rightly called much of his
work an "ironical protest . . . against economic oppression" in his
short study of Cullen, A Many-colored Coat of Dreams (Detroit:
Broadside Press, 1974).

ANNE BRADSTREET, The Author to Her Book, page 12

The "rags" (line 5) worn by this bastard brat of a book may
have been the first edition's abundance of typographical errors.
Although Anne Bradstreet patiently revised her work, she did not
live to see her "brat" appear in better dress. This poem prefaced
the Boston edition published in 1678, six years after the poet's
death.
    Robert Hutchinson, in the introduction to his edition of Poems
of Anne Bradstreet (New York: Dover, 1969) gives a concise account
of the book's publication. Evidently the author's family, proud of
her poetry, felt that it deserved more notice than New England could
then give. The Reverend John Woodbridge, Mrs. Bradstreet's brother-
in-law, took with him to England the manuscript of the collection.
London at the time had sixty printers; New England, one--and so it
must have been difficult, even then, to print poetry in America.
"The fact," notes Hutchinson, "that Herrick's Hesperides had just
appeared in England while the latest venture of Samuel Green, the
Cambridge, Massachusetts, printer, was a revision of The Bay Psalm
Book to rid it of its crudities, gives an indication of the intel-
lectual distance between the two countries."

WALT WHITMAN, To a Locomotive in Winter, page 13

EMILY DICKINSON, I like to see it lap the Miles, page 14

Though both of these great nineteenth-century Americans take
almost the same subject, in tone and in form the two poems differ
as sharply as opera differs from chamber music. (Some students
might argue that the mutual subject isn't a moving locomotive, but
the poets' praise of it. While seeing a real similarity, they would
be missing the distinction between subject and tone.) Whitman
addresses his machine in awe and exultation. In lines 14-19 he
practically prays to it (almost like Henry Adams on bended knees
before the dynamo in his Education). Dickinson is evidently more
playful in her affectionate view of the locomotive as a great beast.
It is horselike in that it neighs and has a stable, but it isn't
quite a horse: it crawls and hoots. Both poets, incidentally, see
not only a locomotive, but a whole train. Dickinson's seeing it

"chase itself" suggests cars trying to catch their locomotive as they roll downhill. Dickinson's allusion to Boanerges means no more, I think, than that the locomotive is a servant, and is thunderous.

Whitman's poem is full of diction from music: <u>recitative</u>, <u>beat</u>, <u>ringing bell</u>, <u>notes</u>, <u>chant</u>, <u>harp</u>, <u>piano</u>, <u>trills</u>. The locomotive embodies poetry, too, in its <u>metrical</u> pant and roar, and in its ability to serve the Muse. The word <u>recitative</u> indicates the form the poem will be cast in. In Italian opera, to which Whitman was devoted, Rossini had introduced the use of the full orchestra to accompany the recitative, the passage of half-sung, half-spoken declamation; and it may be that, as Robert D. Faner has argued, such recitative was a basic model for Whitman's poetry. "The recitative, highly rhythmic and emotional, punctuated by instrumental accompaniment with thrilling effect, and in its chanted delivery giving the impression of the rhythms of speech, he found well adapted to the bulk of his work, which he thought of as a sort of bardic chant." (<u>Walt Whitman & Opera</u> [Carbondale, Ill.: Southern Illinois University Press, 1951], p. 234.)

JOHN MILTON, On the Late Massacre in Piemont, page 14

Sorrow, wrath, and hatred seem mingled in this powerful sonnet. Milton sees the Waldenses as true primitive Christians. They had broken with Rome in the twelfth century, refusing to accept rituals and dogmas which, they thought, had been too recently decreed. Protestant Europe was outraged at the massacre. As Cromwell's secretary, Milton was instructed to write letters of protest to the Duke of Savoy, the Catholic King and Cardinal of France, and other heads of state. His own indignant prayer to a wrathful God has, as William Riley Parker has said, "the awesome sound of a great wave pounding against a wall."

THE PERSON IN THE POEM

RANDALL JARRELL, A Sick Child, page 16

Lonely and bored, the child is tired of his own imaginings. He longs for something colossal and unthinkable to take him by surprise. He wishes that creatures from another world would arrive and make him their pet--the very wish of grown-up Gottfried Rosenbaum in Jarrell's novel Pictures from an Institution (1954), as Suzanne Ferguson points out in The Poetry of Randall Jarrell (Baton Rouge: Louisiana State University Press, 1971).

In the imaginary conversation, the mailman seems ashamed that his game of make-believe has been spurned, but he hasn't understood the child's terrible longing to be surprised. By understanding the child, by so perfectly detailing the child's mental games, by conveying the child's longing in simple language that bursts into a kind of desperate outcry at the end, Jarrell clearly shows his own profound sympathy.

18-20 (text pages)

WILLIAM WORDSWORTH, I Wandered Lonely as a Cloud, page 18

To point out the distance between art and reporting, it may be helpful to read Wordsworth's poem aloud--at least parts of it. In their rhythm, lines such as "Fluttering and dancing in the breeze" and "Tossing their heads in sprightly dance" make the motion of the daffodils come alive. By comparison, Dorothy Wordsworth's record of the incident ("the rest tossed and reeled and danced") seems merely excellent prose.

Actually, Wordsworth's sister was a distinguished poet in her own right, as Hyman Eigerman demonstrates in The Poetry of Dorothy Wordsworth (New York: Columbia University Press, 1940), an anthology of passages from the journals arranged into formally open verse.

PAUL ZIMMER, The Day Zimmer Lost Religion, page 19

Like Tom Wayman, author of "Wayman in Love" (page 384), Paul Zimmer writes usually comic, sometimes touching poems featuring a central character who bears his own last name. If Zimmer in this poem is the poet and not a fictitious character, then the speaker may be the mature Zimmer, looking back through his own younger eyes. The "old days" mentioned in line 8 would seem an even earlier time when, as a schoolboy, Zimmer assisted at Mass. Now (as an adolescent?) he has come to doubt--but he still takes a boyish view, expecting Christ "like the playground bully" to punish him. The last two lines seem the mature Zimmer's view. Only the grown-up are ready for Christ. Without knowing the actual Zimmer's present convictions, we can assume that the mature poet speaks either as a believer or as one with a deepened respect for belief.

For more Zimmer poems, see The Zimmer Poems (Washington, D.C., and San Francisco: Dryad Press, 1976). The world in which the character Zimmer moves often seems dreamlike.

RICHARD HUGO, In Your Young Dream, page 20

Unless you were ever a traveling basketball player who loved a woman now married to someone else, the you in the poem isn't you. It may well be the poet. But by relating this dream in the second person (and in the present tense) Hugo gains for his poem a certain immediacy.

What makes this narrative convincingly dreamlike? Years drop away. The other player is "vaguely seen." With the precipitous haste and defiance of space that characterize dreams, the woman--at the will of "you"--is suddenly transported to "your room." (But she is "surrounded by children"--hardly a situation that invites seduction!)

A question which may be useful even if the class has yet to grapple with symbols is: what do the missing nets suggest? (The central character's feelings of emptiness and frustration, perhaps?)

For more of Hugo's "you" poems, see his collection from which "In Your Young Dream" is taken: 31 Letters and 13 Dreams (New York: Norton, 1977).

WILLIAM CARLOS WILLIAMS, The Red Wheelbarrow, page 21

Evidently many readers have found it easy to admire this poem without feeling a need to know the circumstances in which it was written. For a fairly recent appreciation see Louis Untermeyer, The Pursuit of Poetry (New York: Simon and Schuster, 1969), p. 25. Untermeyer views the poem as a kind of haiku that makes us aware of glories in commonplaces. A more sharply critical estimate is that of Roy Harvey Pearce in his fine essay "Williams and the 'New Mode'" in The Continuity of American Poetry (Princeton: Princeton University Press, 1961), pp. 335-348. Pearce charges the poem with sentimentality: "At its worst this is togetherness in a chicken-yard." However, in Pearce's view, the poem also has a better aspect: what "depends" is the poet's vocation as a poet. He needs common objects in order to write poems, and the objects in turn need him to imagine them into poetry.

If the librarian is right about the situation in which the poem was written (see page 32), "The Red Wheelbarrow" seems to me a better poem than I had realized: a kind of prayer, a work of compassion. However, that the poem fails to give us an intimation of the reasons for the poet's feelings (and of why we ought to share them) does expose it to Pearce's accusation that it is sentimental. Whatever the instructor's opinion, the merits and demerits of the poem can be a lively topic for class discussion.

IRONY

W. H. AUDEN, The Unknown Citizen, page 23

For making students better aware of irony, Auden's familiar satire remains as dependable as any poem I know. Little seems to have dated in it, other than the praise of the citizen for adding five children to the population. Students are usually good at seeing that, unlike the unknown soldier, the citizen is all too thoroughly identified; and that nevertheless, his true nature and inmost wants remain unknown. Meaty questions for discussion naturally arise: what are the premises of such a society? It seems dedicated to the proposition that to conform to a norm is the highest virtue--any individual traits, of course, being an annoyance to statisticians. What is a "Modern Man"? One with animal needs, but no aspirations. The epitaph, often overlooked, is worth dwelling on: it tells us at once that the unknown citizen is only a number, and that bureaucrats keep track of him--and incidentally, like the rest of the poem, the epitaph is in rime.

"The Unknown Citizen" is one of six poems in this chapter in which we hear a voice obviously not the poet's. (The others are the ones by Jarrell, Betjeman, Urdang, Stephens, and Blake.)

9

24-26 (text pages)

JOHN BETJEMAN, In Westminster Abbey, page 24

Cadogan Square was an especially fashionable London address around the turn of the century, and the fact that the speaker owns stocks (line 30) also indicates her style of life. Her mind, however, is ordinary: her ideals seem bounded by drugstore novels and by plumbing that works properly.

Students usually have a fine time picking out the easy contradictions in the lady's beliefs: that the Lord may allow bombs to hit German women, but not English women; that He protects whites more dutifully than blacks; that it is all very well for the "gallant blacks" to die, but let the Empire remain united; that democracy and class distinction go hand in hand.

The speaker's attitude seems to be: "let God wait upon my convenience." To call His word a <u>treat</u> reduces Scripture to the importance of candy. That Betjeman first printed this ironic blast at smug, hate-mongering chauvinism in the midst of World War II strikes me as a brave and large-minded plea for genuine Christian charity.

SARAH N. CLEGHORN, The Golf Links, page 25

What a great epigram!--no verbal irony in it, just matter-of-fact notation of a social condition that seems ironic in the extreme. As Robert Frost said, in his introduction to Cleghorn's autobiography <u>Threescore</u> (1936), "There is more high explosive for righteousness in the least little line of Sarah Cleghorn's poem about the children working in the mill . . . than in all the prose of our radical-bound-boys pressed together under a weight of several atmospheres of revolution." (The conservative Frost didn't like Marxists, but he called Cleghorn "a saint and a reformer" anyway.) For a more recent tribute, see Irving Dilliard, "Four Short Lines," <u>The Nation</u> 222 (April 10, 1976), pp. 444-445.

In Stanley Kunitz and Howard Hayward's <u>Twentieth Century Authors</u> (New York: Wilson, 1942), in an article on Cleghorn that apparently she helped write, there is an explanation for the gap of twenty years that intervened between her early books and her later ones. "This was caused by the fact that her socialism and pacifism made editors and publishers reluctant to use her later writing, and partly by the fact that in middle age she became a teacher." Among her other works is a novel, <u>The Spinster</u> (1916), and a last collection, <u>Poems of Peace and Freedom</u> (1945).

CONSTANCE URDANG, The Miracle-Factory, page 26

An ordinary boy being taken to see his father's dingy place of work, the speaker--unlike the poet--seems unaware that there is anything out of the ordinary in a miracle factory. Irony comes not only from the discrepancy between the speaker's point of view and the poet's, but between the actual run-down, drafty, and soot-covered factory and its magical function. The boss seems an

10

ordinary boss—but who knows? Other apparent ironies are in the
remark, "You got to . . . make them believe in it!" (exactly the
kind of remark a manufacturer of, say, toothpaste might make) and
in the detail that the old building is "taller than God."

Poet and novelist Constance Urdang lives in Saint Louis. "The
Miracle-Factory" is from her collection The Lone Woman and Others
(University of Pittsburgh Press, 1980).

THOMAS HARDY, The Workbox, page 27

Dramatic irony is present in the discrepancy between the carpenter's limited knowledge and the reader's growing conviction that
the wife knew John much better than she cares to admit. Her phrase
"mere accidental things" contains verbal irony, and in general the
whole speech in lines 25-28 is a verbal irony. Cosmic irony may be
operating too (and one is sure that it is, knowing Hardy) in the
Fate or chance that caused the carpenter to select a piece of poor
John's coffin out of all pieces of wood in the world.

To me, the situation in the poem had seemed like that in James
Joyce's "The Dead": the wife, by remembering a young man who died
of love for her, has a bleak realization that she might have known
a joyous life had she married him instead. However, Albert Furtwangler and his students at Mount Allison University found other
possible levels of irony, as he kindly wrote to report. For Professor Furtwangler, "The Workbox" is marred by an excess of irony
that runs too deep: "it remains fascinating in the long run more
as a puzzle than as a clear disclosure of character." Among other
readings he considered the two following, which he thinks overin-
genious and yet consistent with the poem.

The husband, aware of his wife's past, has contrived his present
as a cunning torture for her. "He seems to offer it in love, but
takes pleasure in drawing out his wife's confused replies . . . thus
trapping her in her own hypocrisy."

The husband knows his wife's history; and she knows that he
knows it. "But they coexist uneasily with each other by exercising
an elaborate fiction of ignorance."

What will you and your students decide?

J. O. Bailey sees in this poem the "ballad-like theme of the
lover who died of grief when his beloved married another." Like
traditional English and Scottish ballads, the poem has a question-
and-answer structure and ends in a surprise. (See The Poetry of
Thomas Hardy [Chapel Hill: University of North Carolina Press,
1970].) Compare "The Workbox" in these respects with "Bonny Barbara
Allan" (page 110) and "Edward" (page 280).

28-29 (text pages)

FOR REVIEW AND FURTHER STUDY

JOHN BERRYMAN, Life, friends, is boring. We must not say so, page 28

Students might find it helpful to know that in The Dream Songs the central character maintains a running dialogue with voices he hears in his head—some (like his mother's) real, others imaginary. Perhaps reflecting Henry's indecision, the language of the poems varies wildly and includes baby talk ("peoples bore me"), poetic clichés ("tranquil hills"), slang ("a drag"), and dialect.

The mother's statement seems confused because it doesn't exhort her son to have Inner Resources, it exhorts him to keep his boredom concealed. Inner Resources are capitalized to show how important they appear to the mother; achilles takes a small letter to show that Henry thinks little of him.

For indirect light on Berryman's poem, see "Some Instances of Boredom" in Robert Martin Adams, Nil: Episodes in the literary conquest of void during the nineteenth century (New York: Oxford, 1970). The mother in Berryman's poem expresses an attitude that Adams finds prevalent among the English: "To confess oneself bored is, as it were, to confess oneself without inner resources and perhaps even ungrateful before the gift of God; it flies in the face of the crucial Puritan doctrine of the calling. We are supposed to know, by intimate inspiration, what to do in this world—if we don't there must be something wrong with us." And yet (Adams continues) such boredom has been viewed by philosophers from Pascal to Kierkegaard as a necessary dissatisfaction that comes before a religious awakening.

Robert Pinsky finds parallels between this poem and Matthew Arnold's poem "Self-Dependence," in The Situation of Poetry (Princeton: Princeton University Press, 1976), pp. 35-36.

Exercise: Telling Tone, page 28

RICHARD LOVELACE, To Lucasta, page 29

WILFRED OWEN, Dulce et Decorum Est, page 29

"To Lucasta" may refer to an actual parting. During the Puritan Revolution of 1642-45, Lovelace fought in the service of Charles I. Students will readily see the poet's theme that Honor (duty to God and King) takes priority over duty to Lucasta; the tone of the poem may give them greater difficulty. The closing line makes a serious affirmation: Honor for Lovelace is not an "old lie," but a creed. Neither grim nor smug, the poem also has wit and loving tenderness. The witty second stanza seems almost comic in its figures of speech: having renounced Lucasta's nunlike chastity and calm, the speaker will now go whet his sword upon the body of someone wilder.

Owen's theme is apparent: death in battle is hideous, no
matter what certain ignorant poets say about it. For us, there
seems irony in the fact that Owen himself was to be killed in action
in November 1918 while leading troops across the Sambre Canal in
France. Although in a wartime letter he called himself "a conscientious objector with a very seared conscience," Owen in this
poem does not question that to die for one's country may be necessary. His attitude is overpowering disgust--with the butchery of
war, with those who idealize it.

JAMES STEPHENS, A Glass of Beer, page 30

     The high regard of the Irish for the magical powers of speech
has given them a long and glorious tradition of poetic cursing. In
the ancient tales of the Ulster sage, we read of kings who wouldn't
go to battle without an accompanying druid: a poet-priest charged
with pronouncing magnificent metrical curses upon the enemy. Who
knows?--in the pubs of Stephens's native Dublin, curses like the
one in "A Glass of Beer" may well have seemed ordinary, even mild.
     Although the speaker--some frustrated drinker hard up for cash
--is in a towering rage at the barmaid who denied him, the tone of
Stephens's poem is not anger but high amusement. There is irony,
too, in the obvious contrast between the speaker's stupendous hyperboles and the puny occasion for them. Save this poem, if you like,
for teaching figures of speech.
     There is hardly a better modern poem, however, for reminding
students that the feelings expressed in poetry aren't always positive. A poem may be written in rage or chagrin, as well as in love
or joy. This seems an essential truth, and one that I have tried to
demonstrate at some length in Tygers of Wrath: Poems of Hate,
Anger, and Invective (Athens, Ga.: University of Georgia Press,
1981), an annotated anthology showing the tradition of dark emotion
in British, Irish, and American poetry from the Middle Ages to the
present. Naturally, in this tradition, "A Glass of Beer" holds an
honored place.

JONATHAN SWIFT, On Stella's Birthday, page 30

     Swift's playfully tender birthday gift kids Stella about her
size, but artfully turns a dig into a compliment. Imagining her
split in two, he declares that even half of her would surpass any
other whole woman. For most students, the only difficult lines will
be 7-8. Swift's argument seems to be that, while Stella has lost
much of the slender beauty she had at sixteen, she hasn't greatly
declined in total worth, for an increase in her mental gifts (among
them wit) has amply compensated.

WILLIAM BLAKE, The Chimney Sweeper, page 31

Set next to Cleghorn's "Golf Links," Blake's song will seem larger and more strange; and yet both poets seem comparable in their hatred of adults who enslave children. "The Chimney Sweeper" resembles Jarrell's "A Sick Child" mainly in its child's-eye point of view. Though Blake is not a child, he obviously shares Tom Dacre's wish that the chimney sweepers be freed from their coffin-like chimneys, washed clean, and restored to childhood joys. The punning cry "'weep! 'weep! 'weep!" is the street cry of the sweepers, sent through London to advertise their services. Compare the tone of this poem to that of Blake's "London"; the anger is similar, but in "The Chimney Sweeper," a poem also touching and compassionate, anger is not stated outright, but only implied.

Music to "The Chimney Sweeper" has been supplied by Allen Ginsberg, who sings the resulting song on Songs of Innocence and Experience (MGM recording FTS 3083), assisted by Peter Orlovsky.

3

WORDS

LITERAL MEANING: WHAT A POEM SAYS FIRST

Why a whole section on literal meaning? The need first occurred to me in a conversation with Robert Reiter and David Anderson
of Boston College. Professor Reiter, who had been using the book
in a previous edition, told me that, while it was well to encourage
students to read poetry for its suggestions, his students tended to
go too far in that direction, and sometimes needed to have their
attentions bolted down to the denotations of words on a page. Early
in a poetry course, the problem seemed especially large--"I try not
to let them look for any symbols until after Thanksgiving!" Mr.
Anderson had felt the same difficulty. In teaching Donne's "Batter
my heart" sonnet, he had had to argue with students who couldn't see
how, in a poem of spiritual aspiration, Donne possibly could be referring to anything so grossly physical as rape. They needed to see
the plain, literal basis of Donne's tremendous metaphor, that they
might then go on to understand the poet's conception of sanctifying
grace.

With these comments in mind, the publishers sent a question-
naire to more than 100 instructors who had used the book, asking
them (among other questions) whether they felt the need for more
emphasis on denotation. All who replied said that they would welcome such an emphasis (in addition to the old emphasis on connotation)--all, that is, except for one instructor (God help him) who
reported that he couldn't persuade his students ever to rise above
the level of the literal, if indeed he could get them to rise that
far.

Most instructors like to discuss imagery fairly early. They
will find nothing to hinder them from taking the chapter on imagery
ahead of this one. Another procedure would be to defer "Imagery"
until after having discussed both denotation and connotation--taking
in sequence the present chapter, "Words," and Chapter 4, "Saying and
Suggesting."

WILLIAM CARLOS WILLIAMS, This Is Just to Say, page 34

Dr. Williams once recalled that this poem was an actual note
he had written to his wife--"and she replied very beautifully. Unfortunately, I've lost it. I think what she wrote was quite as
good as this." (Conversation with John W. Gerber and Emily M.

Wallace in <u>Interviews with William Carlos Williams</u>, ed. Linda Wel-
shimer Wagner [New York: New Directions, 1976].)
   For parodies of this famous poem, see Kenneth Koch's "Variations on a Theme by William Carlos Williams" in <u>Contemporary American Poetry</u>, ed. A. Poulin (Boston: Houghton Mifflin, 1980), and
other anthologies.

KNUTE SKINNER, The Cold Irish Earth, page 36

   Skinner is an American poet who lives most of each year in
Killaspuglonane (pronounced the way it looks, with the accent on
POOG), a village of about 200, near Liscannon Bay in the west of
Ireland. This poem is one of several recollections of Irish country
life in his book <u>A Close Sky over Killaspuglonane</u> (Dublin: Dolmen
Press, 1968; second edition, St. Louis: Burton International Ltd.,
1975). The Hag's face is a rock formation in the Cliffs of Moher
(or Mohee), in whose crevices members of the IRA once hid from the
British.
   The familiar phrase, of course, is "to become wet to the bone."
Every image in the poem indicates that it is to be taken literally.

HENRY TAYLOR, Riding a One-Eyed Horse, page 36

   Henry Taylor comments in a letter: "I like the question about
the one-eyed horse; the answer is, of course, both."
   The poem was first published in <u>Practical Horseman</u>.

ROBERT GRAVES, Down, Wanton, Down!, page 37

   This poem can be an astonisher, especially if students haven't
read it in advance. One freshman group I sprang it on provided a
beautiful gamut of reactions: from stunned surprise to hilarity.
At first, most didn't know quite what to make of the poem, but they
soon saw that its puns and metaphors point to details of male and
female anatomy; and in catching these, they found themselves looking
to literal meanings, and I was glad. After further discussion, they
decided (as I further exulted) that the poem, however witty, makes
a serious point about the blindness of lust. To get at this point,
I had asked them to sum up the contrast Graves is drawing between
Love and Beauty and the wanton's approach to them.
   The title (and opening line) echo a phrase from Shakespeare in
a passage about eels being rolled into a pie (<u>King Lear</u>, II, iv,
118-123):

   Lear: O me, my heart, my rising heart! But down!
   Fool: Cry to it, nuncle, as the cockney did to the eels when
      she put 'em i' th' paste alive. She knapped 'em o' th' cox-
      combs with a stick and cried, "Down, wantons, down!" 'Twas
      her brother that, in pure kindness to his horse, buttered his
      hay.

One instructor at a community college in New Jersey has reported an embarrassing experience. One morning, not having had
time to prepare for class, he introduced this poem without having
read it first. "What's it about?" he queried, and someone in the
class replied, "An erection." "WHAT?" he exploded. "Come on, now,
let's look at it closely . . ." But as he stared at the poem before
him, a chill stole over him. Luckily, he was saved by the bell.

PETER DAVISON, The Last Word, page 38

The tangible side of Davison's central metaphor--that to part
with a lover is to chop off her head--is plainly enforced by lines
9-13: painful physical actions that end with the k-sound of an
abrupt crack in nick . . . creak . . . block.

DAVID B. AXELROD, Once in a While a Protest Poem, page 38

The crucial word in this disturbing poem is silicone, a substance injected into flat bosoms to make them buxom, in order to
put up a false front--like those sympathies we merely pretend to
feel. Carefully cropped by someone in an advertising agency, the
breast of the starving woman (like a breast treated with silicone)
is artificially changed and becomes abstract. Although the photograph is supposed to rouse our sympathies (and our contributions),
it often has the opposite effect of making us callous. To the poet,
it seems meant to "toughen us" (as silicone toughens the bosoms of
Playboy bunnies?); it seems meant to "teach us to ignore."

MILLER WILLIAMS, On the Symbolic Consideration of Hands and the
Significance of Death, page 39

Living hands being so often on the move, the mourners asso-
ciate dead hands with the motions of life, and so can't believe the
evidence in front of them. But the nuns, who have to look long and
intently at each lifeless bone to carve rosaries, have no such
illusions. Miller Williams announces his poem with a deliberately
long, gaseous title, and then, as if to twit readers who expect the
poem to be full of large abstractions too, chooses words as simple
as possible (all but ten of them monosyllables). Implied in the
poem, maybe, is the advice that if we (like the nuns) want to know
reality, we had best believe our eyes, and switch off our symbol-
izers.

JOHN DONNE, Batter my heart, three-personed God, for You, page 39

On Donne's last line: the literature of mysticism is full of
accounts of spiritual experience seen in physical terms; and any
students who wish to pursue the matter might be directed, for

instance, to the poems of St. John of the Cross (which have been splendidly translated by John Frederick Nims).

John E. Parish has shown that Donne's poem incorporates two metaphors, both worn and familiar: the traditional Christian comparison of the soul to a maiden and Christ to a bridegroom, and the Petrarchan conceit of the reluctant woman as a castle and her lover as an invading army. Donne brilliantly combined the two into a new whole. In lines 1-4, the sinner's heart is like a walled town, fallen to Satan, the enemy. Now God the rightful King approaches and knocks for entrance. But merely to knock won't do--the King must break open the gates with a battering ram. The verbs in these lines all suggest the act of storming a citadel, "and even blowe may be intended to suggest the use of gunpowder to blow up the fortress." ("No. 14 of Donne's Holy Sonnets," College English 24 [January 1963], pp. 299-302.)

"The paradox of death and rebirth, the central paradox of Christianity" is (according to A. L. Clements in another comment) the organizing principle of the poem. To illustrate the paradox of destroying in order to revive, Donne employs two sorts of figurative language: one, military and destructive; the other, marital and uniting. ("Donne's 'Holy Sonnet XIV,'" Modern Language Notes 76 [June 1961], pp. 484-489.)

Both the Clements and the Parish articles are reprinted, together with four other discussions of the poem, in John Donne's Poetry, edited by Clements (New York: Norton, 1966).

I have always found it hard to talk for long about rhythm in poetry without citing the opening lines of "Batter my heart." Both in meter and in meaning, they must be among the most powerful lines in English poetry.

THE VALUE OF A DICTIONARY

RICHARD WILBUR, In the Elegy Season, page 41

Rich in imagery, this early Wilbur poem makes a revealing companion piece to Keats's "To Autumn" (page 337). But unlike Keats, the speaker in Wilbur's poem accepts the season neither with mind (which gazes backward, remembering summer) nor with body (which strains ahead, longing for spring). The poem is also wealthy in allusions. Perhaps the "boundless backward of the eyes" echoes Shakespeare's Tempest: "the dark backward and abysm of time." The goddess heard climbing the stair from the underworld is Persephone. I am indebted to Donald Hill's reading of the poem in his study Richard Wilbur (New York: Twayne, 1967).

A brief glossary of etymologies:

potpourri: rotten pot (denotation: an incongruous mixture)
revenance: a return (denotation: the return of a spirit after death)
circumstance: condition that surrounds
inspiration: a breathing in

conceptual: taking in (denotations: perceived, apprehended, imagined)
commotion: co-motion, moving together (a wonderful word for what a bird's wings do!)
cordial: pertaining to the heart (cor in Latin)   (Denotations: friendly, stimulating.)
azure: lapis lazuli

Exercise: Catching Allusions, page 43

CID CORMAN, The Tortoise, page 43

J. V. CUNNINGHAM, Friend, on this scaffold Thomas More lies dead, page 43

HERMAN MELVILLE, The Portent, page 43

JOHN DRYDEN, Lines Printed Under the Engraved Portrait of Milton, page 44

Corman's allusion to the Aesop fable has to be caught, if students are to see his metaphor. Inexorable time is the tortoise that keeps plodding onward. The hare is haste--or more specifically, a man trying to win his race with time, but given to fits of delay and laziness.

Cunningham's epigram also states a metaphor: it likens two famous separations decreed by Henry VIII. Separation of the Body (the Church of England) from the Head (the Pope) is like the decapitation of More, who had opposed it.

Melville's symbolic poem also refers to an execution: the hanging of James Brown on December 2, 1859, for seizing the arsenal at Harpers Ferry, where the Shenandoah River meets the Potomac. Captured by Robert E. Lee, Brown suffered a wounded scalp, concealed by a cap he wore to the gallows. Melville, seeing the swinging corpse with its long beard as a comet with a streaming tail, refers to the ancient belief that comets and meteors are omens of war or catastrophe--as students may recall from Shakespeare's Julius Caesar. Melville's recognition of the portent proved right, of course: Union troops were soon to go into battle singing "John Brown's Body."

According to Dryden, Homer plus Dante equals Milton. The rightness of the equation comes from the fact of all three having been the authors of epics, or (if The Divine Comedy isn't an epic) poems of enormous scope.

JOHN CLARE, Mouse's Nest, page 44

The connection between the final couplet and the rest of the poem is one of metaphor. Small trickles of water that "scarce could run" are newborn mice; "broad old cesspools," their mother.

44-45 (text pages)

Milton Klonsky has praised the poem in his recent anthology of graphic and pictorial poetry, Speaking Pictures (New York: Harmony Books, 1975). He admires "the cinematic flow of Clare's imagery, with each picture flashing by to be replaced by the next before its own afterimage has completely faded." This comment might be discussed--do students agree that Clare's poem seems cinematic and contemporary?

A few facts of Clare's heart-breaking life might interest students. Born into grinding poverty, the son of a field laborer in Northamptonshire, Clare enjoyed brief fame for his Poems Descriptive of Rural Life (1820). Lionized by Coleridge and other London literati as an untutored genius, he was then forgotten. The latter half of his life was spent in lunatic asylums, where he wrote some remarkable lyrics and (under the delusion that he was Lord Byron) a continuation of Don Juan. Theodore Roethke, whose work shows a similar delight in close-up views of living creatures, has paid tribute (in his poem "Heard in a Violent Ward") to "that sweet man, John Clare."

LEWIS CARROLL, Jabberwocky, page 45

"Jabberwocky" has to be heard aloud: I usually ask a student to read it, alerting him or her in advance to prepare it, and offering tips on pronunciation. ("The i in slithy is like the i in slime; the a in wabe, like the a in wave.")

Although Carroll added chortled to the dictionary, not all his odd words are invented. Gyre of course means "to spin or twist about"--it is used as a noun in Yeats's "Sailing to Byzantium" and "The Second Coming." Slithy (sleazy or slovenly), rath (an earthen wall), whiffling (blowing or puffing), and calloo (an arctic duck that winters in Scotland, so named for its call) are legitimate words, too, but Carroll uses them in different senses. Frabjous probably owes something to frab, a dialect word meaning "to scold, harass, or nag"--as Myra Cohn Livingston points out in her anthology O Frabjous Day! (New York: Atheneum, 1977).

Writing in 1877 to a child who had inquired what the strange words meant, Carroll replied:

I am afraid I can't explain "vorpal blade" for you--nor yet "tulgey wood"; but I did make an explanation once for "uffish thought"--it seems to suggest a state of mind when the voice is gruffish, the manner roughish, and the temper huffish. Then again, as to "burble": if you take the three verbs "bleat," "murmur" and "warble," and select the bits I have underlined, it certainly makes "burble": though I am afraid I can't distinctly remember having made it that way.

(Uffish suggests oafish, too.)

Students can have fun unpacking other portmanteau words: gimble (gamely, gambol); frumious (which Carroll said is fuming plus <u>furious</u>); <u>vorpal</u> (<u>purple</u>, <u>voracious</u>); <u>galumphing</u> (<u>galloping</u> in <u>triumph</u>), and so on. Some of these suggestions I owe to Martin Gardner, who supplies copious notes on the poem (as well as translations of it into French and German) in <u>The Annotated Alice</u> (New York: Bramhall House, 1960).

WALLACE STEVENS, Metamorphosis, page 46

A possible meaning of <u>metamorphosis</u> is a sudden change undergone by an insect or a tadpole in the process of maturing. But I think Stevens implies by the falling sky (dead and lying with the worms) and the hanged street lamps that the year is decaying, not changing for the better, but undergoing (as <u>Webster's New World Dictionary</u> puts it) "a transformation, especially by magic or sorcery."
Language is, in a sense, also decaying rapidly. The name of the month of October is transformed, too, into a birdcall.
"Niz--nil--imbo" is a corruption of "November." It contains the words <u>nil</u> (nothingness) and <u>limbo</u>.
The first definition: "a sudden twist, turn, or stroke." The season makes such a sudden turn, and so does language. A worm is a "pretty quirk" in that it is physically twisted; also, it happens to appear unexpectedly (in flesh suddenly dead, or in fall fruit become overripe).

J. V. CUNNINGHAM, Motto for a Sun Dial, page 47

In mathematics, a <u>function</u> is a variable quantity or factor; a <u>constant</u> is an invariable. Like the sun dial whose shadow depends on the shifting sun, the value of a function depends on that of another quantity or other quantities.

WORD CHOICE AND WORD ORDER

JOSEPHINE MILES, Reason, page 49

Only the reference to Gary Cooper's horse makes this perpetually fresh poem seem at all dated. (Cooper made many Western films, among them <u>High Noon</u>.)

HUGH MacDIARMID, Wheesht, Wheesht, page 50

MacDiarmid, the most eminent twentieth-century poet to write in Scots, is often compared with Burns; and for another brief love lyric at least partly in dialect, students might be asked to compare "John Anderson my jo, John" (page 255).

THOMAS HARDY, The Ruined Maid, page 52

In a London street, an innocent girl from Dorset encounters a friend who has run away from life on the farm. Now a well-paid prostitute, 'Melia calls herself <u>ruined</u> with cheerful irony. That this maid has been made, it would seem, has been the making of her. Hardy, of course, is probably less stricken with awe before 'Melia's glamorous clothes than is the first speaker. As the <u>ain't</u> in the last line indicates, 'Melia's citified polish doesn't go deep.

For a sequel to "The Ruined Maid," see "A Daughter Returns" in Hardy's last collection of poetry, <u>Winter Words</u>. With "dainty-cut raiment" and "earrings of pearl," a runaway daughter returns to her country home, only to be spurned by her father for having lost her innocence.

E. E. CUMMINGS, anyone lived in a pretty how town, page 53

Trained in the classical languages, Cummings borrows from Latin the freedom to place a word in practically any location within a sentence. The first two lines are easy to unscramble: "How pretty a town Anyone lived in, with so many bells floating up [and] down." The scrambling is artful, and pedestrian words call attention to themselves by being seen in an unusual order.

The hero and heroine of the poem are anyone and noone, whose names recall the pronoun-designated principals in Cummings's play <u>Him</u>—hero Him and heroine Me. Are they Everyman and Everywoman? Not at all: they're different, they're strong, loving individuals whom the poet contrasts with those drab women and men of line 5, "both little and small," who dully sow <u>isn't</u> (negation) and reap <u>same</u> (conformity). Unlike wise noone and anyone, the everyones and someones of line 17 apparently think they're really somebody.

In tracing the history of anyone and noone from childhood through their mature love to their death and burial, Cummings, I think, gives us a brief tour through life in much the way that Thornton Wilder does in <u>Our Town</u>. But not all readers will agree. R. C. Walsh thinks that, in the last two stanzas, anyone and noone do not literally die but grow into loveless and lifeless adults, whose only hope of rejuvenation is to have children (<u>Explicator</u> 22 [May 1964], no. 9, item 72). But it seems to me unlike Cummings to make turncoats of his individualists. Bounded by the passage of the seasons, the rain, and the heavens, the mortal lives of anyone and noone seem concluded in their burial. But in the next-to-last stanza they go on sleeping in love and faith, dreaming of their resurrection.

JAMES EMANUEL, The Negro, page 54

<u>The-ness</u> is the white viewing the black as a stereotype (some of whose features are illustrated in the second stanza). <u>A-ness</u> is the view that hasn't prevailed: of the black as an individual.

RICHARD EBERHART, The Fury of Aerial Bombardment, page 55

Dr. Johnson said that technical language is inadmissible to
poetry, but in the case of Eberhart's poem, I find it hard to agree.
We do not need to know the referents of "belt feed lever" and "belt
holding pawl" in order to catch the poet's meaning. Indeed, he evidently chooses these terms as specimens of a jargon barely compre-
hensible to the unlucky gunnery students who failed to master it.
At a reading of his poems in public, Eberhart once remarked that he
had added the last stanza as an afterthought. The tone (it seems
to me) remains troubled and sorrowful but shifts from loftiness and
grandeur to matter-of-fact. This shift takes place in diction as
well: from the generality of "infinite spaces," "multitudinous
will," "eternal truth," and "the Beast" in man's soul down to "Names
on a list," "lever," and "pawl." The poem is a wonderful instance
of a poet's writing himself into a fix--getting snarled in unanswerable questions--and then triumphantly saving the day (and his poem)
by suddenly returning with a bump to the ordinary, particular world.
    A good poem to set beside Eberhart's poem for class discussion
is Thomas Hardy's "Channel Firing" (page 322), another speculation
into why God allows men to kill one another. See comments on
Hardy's poem in this manual, page 131.

Exercise: Different Kinds of English, page 55

ANONYMOUS, Carnation Milk, page 55

A. R. AMMONS, Spring Coming, page 56

WILLIAM WORDSWORTH, My heart leaps up when I behold, page 56

WILLIAM WORDSWORTH, Mutability, page 56

GEORGE STARBUCK, Verses to Exhaust My Stock of Four-letter Words,
page 57

ANONYMOUS, Scottsboro, page 57

    Students won't need much help to see that "Carnation Milk" is
unschooled speech; that Ammons combines technical terms with colloquial speech (nice); that Wordsworth's diction in "My heart leaps
up" is plain and unbookish (except perhaps for natural piety),
while his language in the famous "Mutability" sonnet is highly
formal--not only in diction, but in word order (Truth fails not);
and that "Scottsboro" is a song in the speech of a particular culture (and by the way, wonderful in its power to express).
    About Ammons: compare Richard Eberhart's "The Fury of Aerial
Bombardment" (page 55) in its use of technical terms, and ponder
Dr. Johnson's opinion. What would Johnson have thought of "Spring
Coming"? (Probably: "Sir, Ammons wrote no language, and no man
can utter it.")

On the difficult "Mutability" (if anyone wants to read it for its sense): Geoffrey Durrant suggests that "the tower sublime" may refer to the Bastille in his excellent discussion of the poem in Wordsworth and the Great System (Cambridge, Eng.: Cambridge University Press, 1970), pp. 82-85. For other poems on the theme of mutability, try "Ozymandias" (page 263) and "Ode on a Grecian Urn" (page 335).

For Starbuck, a four-letter word isn't an obscenity, but an unusual word in which four letters (all the same) stand in a row. In brilliant light verse, he supplies a showcase for four such words.

Repercussions from the Scottsboro case seem without end. In October 1976, the state of Alabama granted a full pardon to Clarence Norris, last survivor of the nine "Scottsboro boys," after he had spent fifteen years in prison (five on death row) and thirty-one years as an escaped fugitive. In 1976, after the televised showing of a dramatization, "Judge Horton and the Scottsboro Boys," both alleged rape victims unsuccessfully brought suit against NBC for libel, slander, and invasion of their privacy. (The last of these suits was dismissed in July 1977.)

4

SAYING AND SUGGESTING

JOHN MASEFIELD, Cargoes, page 60

Much of the effect of Masefield's contrast depends on rhythms
and word-sounds, not just on connotations. In stanza two, the poet
strews his lines with dactyls, producing ripples in his rhythm:
diamonds, emeralds, amethysts, cinnamon. In the third stanza,
paired monosyllables (salt-caked, smoke stack, Tyne coal, road-rails,
pig-lead, firewood) make for a hard-hitting series of spondees. Internal alliteration helps the contrast, too: all those m-sounds in
the dactyls; and in the harsher lines "Dirty British coaster with a
salt-caked smoke stack, / Butting," all the sounds of the r, the t,
and the staccato k.
    "Cargoes" abounds with lively, meaningful music--and yet Mase-
field is generally dismissed nowadays as a mere balladeer--a jog-
trot chronicler of the lives of the poor and unfortunate. In naming
him poet laureate, George V (it is said) mistakenly thought him a
hero of the working class; and unluckily for his later fame, Masefield, like Wordsworth, enjoyed a long senility.

WILLIAM BLAKE, London, page 61

Blake at first wrote, "I wander through each dirty street, /
Near where the dirty Thames does flow." For his equally masterful
revisions of the poem's closing lines, see page 234 in the chapter
"Alternatives."
    Tom Dacre's dream has a basis in reality: in Blake's time,
sweeps were often sent up chimneys naked, the better to climb
through narrow spaces (and thus saving the expense of protective
clothing). Martin K. Nurmi points out this fact in his essay,
"Fact and Symbol in 'The Chimney Sweeper' of Blake's Songs of Innocence" (Bulletin of the New York Public Library, 68 [April 1964],
pp. 249-256). "Naked immersion in soot, therefore, is Tom's normal
state now, and naked white cleanliness is its natural opposite."
    If Blake were to walk the streets of an American city today,
would he find any conditions similar to those he finds in "London"?
Is this poem merely an occasional poem, with a protest valid only
for its time, or does it have enduring applications?

WALLACE STEVENS, Disillusionment of Ten O'Clock, page 63

Stevens slings colors with the verve of a Matisse. In this
early poem, he paints a suggestive contrast between the pale and
colorless homeowners, ghostlike and punctually going to bed at ten
and, on the other hand, the dreams they wouldn't dream of dreaming;
and the bizarre and exotic scene inside the drunken head of our disreputable hero, the old seafarer. Who in the world would wear a
beaded sash or ceinture? (A Barbary pirate? An Arabian harem-
dancer?) Ronald Sukenick has made a terse statement of the poem's
theme: "The vividness of the imagination in the dullness of a
pallid reality" (Wallace Stevens: Musing the Obscure [New York:
New York University Press, 1967]). Another critic, Edward Kessler,
has offered a good paraphrase: "Only the drunkard, the irrational
man ('Poetry must be irrational' [Opus Posthumous, page 162]), who
is in touch with the unconscious--represented here, and often elsewhere, by the sea--can awake his own passionate nature until his
blood is mirrored in the very weather." (Images of Wallace Stevens
[New Brunswick: Rutgers University Press, 1972].)
While they will need to see the contrast between pallor and
color, students might be cautioned against lending every color a
particular meaning, as if the poem were an allegory.
Stevens expressed further disappointment with monotonous
neighbors in a later poem, "Loneliness in Jersey City," which seems
a companion piece to this. In Jersey City, "the steeples are empty
and so are the people," who can't tell a dachshund from a deer.
Both poems probably owe some of their imagery to Stevens's days as
a struggling young lawyer, living in rooming houses in East Orange,
New Jersey, and Fordham Heights, in New York City.

GUY OWEN, The White Stallion, page 64

There is a beautiful ambiguity in lines 4-5: we are not certain whether the stallion is a miracle to the boy or vice versa.
Both are miracles to each other, it seems, but grammatically,
miracle refers to the speaker. Line 6 makes it clear that the
stallion is looking right at him.

SAMUEL JOHNSON, A Short Song of Congratulation, page 64

"You have heard in the papers how Sir John Lade is come to
age," wrote Dr. Johnson to his friend Mrs. Thrale in 1780. "I have
enclosed a short song of congratulation, which you must not shew to
anybody." Lade, Mrs. Thrale's nephew, was to fulfill Johnson's expectations. After a seven-year binge, he married a courtesan,
Laetitia Darby, and ran through the rest of his fortune. He is the
same Lade who (according to Mrs. Piozzi's Anecdotes of Dr. Johnson)
once called across a drawing-room, "Mr. Johnson, would you advise
me to marry?" only to be told, "I would advise no man to marry, Sir,
who is not likely to propagate understanding."

TIMOTHY STEELE, Epitaph, page 65

"Silence is golden"--but Sir Tact is obviously a coward, afraid to speak his mind. This epigram is included in Steele's first collection of poems, Uncertainties and Rest (Baton Rouge: Louisiana State University Press, 1979).

RICHARD SNYDER, A Mongoloid Child Handling Shells on the Beach, page 66

Snyder elaborates his metaphor with beautiful economy: the "unbroken children," those without handicaps, are like surf at the sea's edge, also like seabirds that skim the beach and the water. Bright as they are, there is something superficial about them, in contrast to the mongoloid child. Slow and deliberate as deep ocean currents, she is both "broken" (like the shells she fondles) and at the same time whole. As she hums her return-message to the sea, she is calm and serene, possessing a sober happiness.

To discuss: should the poem now be retitled "A Child with Down's Syndrome Handling Shells on the Beach"? Would that be as effective?

GEOFFREY HILL, Merlin, page 66

There is an incantatory quality to this poem that makes me think it is Merlin speaking; but then, nearly all of Geoffrey Hill's richly suggestive and highly formal poems tend to sound this way. The dead who might "come together to be fed" recall the souls encountered by Odysseus in the underworld, to whom he fed blood. Once, the towers of Camelot sheltered Arthur and his associates; now, only the pointed tents of piled-up cornstalks (or perhaps growing cornstalks, flying their silklike pennants) stand over the city of the dead.

WALLACE STEVENS, The Emperor of Ice-Cream, page 67

Choosing this poem to represent him in an anthology, Stevens once remarked, "This wears a deliberately commonplace costume, and yet seems to me to contain something of the essential gaudiness of poetry; that is the reason why I like it." (His statement appears in Fifty Poets: An American Auto-Anthology, ed. William Rose Benét [New York: Duffield and Green, 1933].)

Some students will at once relish the poet's humor, others may discover it in class discussion. I try to gather the literal facts of the situation before getting into the poem's suggestions. The wake or funeral of a poor old woman is taking place in her own home. The funeral flowers come in old newspapers, not in florist's fancy wrappings; the mourners don't dress up, but wear their usual street clothes; the refreshments aren't catered but are whipped up in the kitchen by a neighbor, a cigar-roller. Like ice cream, the refreshments are a dairy product. Nowadays they would probably be a sour cream chip-dip; perhaps in 1923 they were blocks of Philadelphia cream cheese squashed into cups for spreading on soda crackers. To a correspondent Stevens wrote that fantails refers not to fans but to fantail pigeons (Letters [New York: Knopf, 1966], p. 341). Such embroidery seems a lowbrow pursuit: the poor old woman's pathetic aspiration toward beauty. Deal furniture is cheap. Everything points to a run-down neighborhood, and to a woman about whose passing nobody very much cares.

Who is the Emperor? The usual guess is Death. Some students will probably see that the Emperor and the muscular cigar-roller (with his creamy curds) suggest each other. (Stevens does not say that they are identical.) Ice cream suggests the chill of the grave--and what besides? Today, some of its connotations will be commonplace: supermarkets, Howard Johnson's. To the generation of Stevens, ice cream must have meant more: something luxurious and scarce, costly, hard-to-keep, requiring quick consumption. Other present-day connotations may come to mind: sweetness, deliciousness, childhood pleasure. Stevens's personal view of the ice cream in the poem was positive: "The true sense of Let be be the finale of seem is let being become the conclusion or denouement of appearing to be: in short, ice cream is an absolute good" (Letters, p. 341). An absolute good! The statement is worth quoting to students who have doubts about the poet's attitude toward ice cream--as did an executive of the Amalgamated Ice Cream Association, who once wrote to the poet in perplexity (see Letters, pp. 501-502). If ice cream recalls sweet death, still (like curds) it also contains hints of mother's milk, life, and vitality.

On a visit to Mount Holyoke, I was told that, as part of an annual celebration, it is customary for the trustees and the seniors to serve ice cream (in Dixie cups) to the freshman class at the grave of Mary Lyon, founder of the college. In a flash I remembered Stevens's poem, and embraced Jung's theory of archetypes.

ROBERT FROST, Fire and Ice, page 68

In his first line, Frost probably refers to those who accept the Biblical prophecy of a final holocaust; and in his second line, to those who accept scientists' forecasts of the cooling of the earth. I never can teach this poem without admiring that final suffice. A magnificent understatement, it further shows the power of a rime to close a poem (as Yeats said) with a click like a closing box.

5

IMAGERY

EZRA POUND, In a Station of the Metro, page 69

Pound recalled that at first this poem had come to him "not in speech, but in little splotches of color." His account is reprinted by K. K. Ruthven in A Guide to Ezra Pound's Personae (1926) (Berkeley: University of California Press, 1969). Students might like to compare this "hokku-like sentence" (as Pound called the poem) with the more suggestive Japanese haiku freely translated on pages 75-77.

TANIGUCHI BUSON, The piercing chill I feel, page 69

Harold G. Henderson, who translates this haiku, has written a good terse primer in An Introduction to Haiku (Garden City, N.Y.: Anchor Books, 1958). Most of Henderson's English versions of haiku rime like this one; still, the sense of the originals (as far as an ignorant reader can tell from Henderson's glosses) does not seem greatly distorted.

WALLACE STEVENS, Study of Two Pears, page 71

The "opusculum paedagogum" isn't a couple of pears, but the "Study of Two Pears" itself. In short-clipped lines, this methodical poem flatly sets forth lessons. Lesson the first is that metaphors for pears must be swept away; particular pears are excellent in themselves, worthy to behold, and mere comparisons cannot do them justice. As usual, Stevens has great faith in the reliability of the senses. Compare this poem with "Thirteen Ways of Looking at a Blackbird" (page 189), in which Stevens again insists on the wisdom of paying attention to particulars of the physical world.

THEODORE ROETHKE, Root Cellar, page 72

Probably there is little point in spending much time dividing imagery into touches and tastes and smells; perhaps it will be enough to point out that Roethke's knowledgeable poem isn't all picture-imagery. There's that wonderful "congress of stinks," and the "slippery planks" are both tactile and visual. Most of the language in the poem is figurative, most of the vegetation is

29

rendered animal: bulbs like small rodents, shoots like penises, roots like a forgotten can of fishing worms. Roethke doesn't call the roots lovely, but obviously he admires their tough, persistent life.

ELIZABETH BISHOP, The Fish, page 73

This poem is made almost entirely of concrete imagery. Except for wisdom (line 63) and victory (66), there is no very abstract diction in it.

Obviously the speaker admires this stout old fighter. The image "medals with their ribbons" (line 61) suggests that he is an old soldier, and the "five-haired beard of wisdom" (line 63) suggests that he is a venerable patriarch, of whom one might seek advice.

The poor battered boat has become magnificent for having the fish in it. The feeling in these lines is joy: bilge, rust, and cracked thwarts are suddenly revealed to be beautiful. In a way, the attitude seems close to that in Yeats's "Sailing to Byzantium" (page 260), in which the triumphant soul is one that claps its hands and louder sings for every tatter in its mortal dress. The note of final triumph is sounded in "rainbow, rainbow, rainbow!" (line 75). The connotations of rainbow in this poem are not very different from the connotations often given the word by misty-eyed romantic poets such as Rod McKuen, but I think we believe Bishop because of her absolutely hard-eyed and specific view of the physical world. (She even sees the fish with X-ray imagination in lines 27-33.)

Anne Stevenson says in Elizabeth Bishop (New York: Twayne, 1966):

It is a testimony to Miss Bishop's strength and sensitivity that the end, the revelation or "moment of truth," is described with the same attention to detail as the rest of the poem. The temptation might have been to float off into an airy apotheosis, but Miss Bishop stays right in the boat with the engine and the bailer. Because she does so, she is able to use words like "victory" and "rainbow" without fear of triteness.

Because the fish has provided her with an enormous understanding, the speaker's letting it go at the end seems an act of homage and gratitude.

Compare "The Fish" with the same poet's richly imaged "Filling Station" (page 291).

The poet reads this poem on a recording, The Spoken Arts Treasury of 100 Modern American Poets, vol. 10 (SA 1049).

RAY YOUNG BEAR, grandmother, page 75

The poet's images take us through at least four kinds of imagined sense-experience. The speaker sees, feels, smells, and hears
--in that order. His grandmother, as the final simile makes clear,
stirs and impresses him, rouses him to life.
    Ray Young Bear, a young native American poet, lives in Tama,
Iowa. This poem is from his first collection, Winter of the Sala-
mander (New York: Harper and Row, 1980).

ABOUT HAIKU

    Basho's frogjump poem (page 77) may well be the most highly
prized gem in Japanese literature; in Japanese there exists a three-
volume commentary on it.
    For an excellent discussion of the problems of teaching haiku,
and of trying to write English ones, see Myra Cohn Livingston's
When You Are Alone/It Keeps You Capone: an approach to creative
writing with children (New York: Atheneum, 1973), pp. 152-162.
Livingston finds it useful to tell students a famous anecdote.
Kikaku, a pupil of Basho, once presented his master with this specimen:

        Red dragonflies--
        Tear off their wings
        And you have pepper pods.

As a haiku, said Basho, that's no good. Make it instead:

        Red pepper pods--
        Add wings
        And you have dragonflies.

    A moment of triumph, such as all teachers of poetry hope for
but seldom realize, has been reported in a letter to XJK from Professor Maurice F. Brown, Department of English, Oakland University,
Rochester, Michigan:

        Last year, teaching W. C. Williams in an "invitational"
    course for a week, I began with "Red Wheelbarrow" . . . and
    a student hand went up (class of 100): "That's not a poem!
    That's junk. What if I say, 'Here I sit looking at a black-
    board while the sun is shining outside.' Is that a poem?"
        It was one of those great teaching moments . . . and I
    did a quick count and wrote it on the board:

        Here I sit looking
            At a blackboard while the sun
        Is shining outside.

Not only a poem . . . a perfect haiku.

31

76-79 (text pages)

RICHARD BRAUTIGAN, Haiku Ambulance, page 76

This is a Zen poem poking fun at overly thoughty attempts to write Zen poems. Its satire does not seem in the least applicable to the successful haiku-in-English of Gary Snyder, Paul Goodman, and Raymond Roseliep.

FOR REVIEW AND FURTHER STUDY

JEAN TOOMER, Reapers, page 78

This ominous poem, with its contrasts between sound and silence, possibly contains a metaphor. The black field hands are being destroyed by something indifferent and relentless, much as the trapped rat is slain under the blade. (Or, as in "Scottsboro," as a cat stalks a "nohole mouse"?)

A grandson of P. B. S. Pinchback, the black who served for a short time during Reconstruction as acting governor of Louisiana, Toomer had only a brief public career as a writer. His one book, Cane (1923), which experimentally combined passages of fiction with poetry, helped to spearhead the Harlem Renaissance. "Reapers" is taken from it.

GERARD MANLEY HOPKINS, Pied Beauty, page 78

The point of question 5 is that if Hopkins's images were sub-tracted, his statement of theme would disappear as well. Rough paraphrase of the poem: God is to be praised not only for having created variegation, but for creating and sustaining contrasts and opposites. In lines 5-6, tradesmen's tools and gear, like the plow that pierces the soil and cuts it to pieces, strike through the sur-face of raw materials, to reveal order and inner beauty that had lain concealed. "Counter, original, spare, strange" seems an apt description of Hopkins's poetry, but I doubt he intended it.

Students probably will not yearn for background on the poet's notions of instress and inscape, nor on the theological sources of the poem; but if you do, see John Pick, Gerard Manley Hopkins, Priest and Poet, 2nd ed. (Oxford: Oxford University Press, 1966), pp. 53-56.

JOHN KEATS, Bright star! would I were steadfast as thou art, page 79

Unlike Petrarchan poets, Keats isn't making the star into an abstraction (Love); he takes it for a visible celestial body, even though he sees it in terms of other things. His comparisons are so richly laden with suggestions (star as staring eye, waters as priestlike), that sometimes students don't notice his insistent negations. The hermit's all-night vigil is not what Keats desires.

32

He wants the comfort of that ripening pillow, and (perhaps aware of
his impending death) envies the cold star only its imperishability
--oh, for unendurable ecstasy, indefinitely prolonged! Compare
this to Keats's "To Autumn," in which the poet finds virtue in
change.

Many readers find the last five words of the poem bothersome.
Students might be asked, does Keats lose your sympathy by this
ending? If so, why? If not, how would you defend the ending?
(I can't defend it, myself; it seems bathetic, almost as self-
indulgent as Shelley's lines in "Indian Serenade":

> Oh, lift me from the grass!
>   I die! I faint! I fail!
> Let thy love in kisses rain
>   On my lips and eyelids pale.

--but Keats is better than that.)

CARL SANDBURG, Fog, page 79

Like Pound's "In a Station of the Metro," Sandburg's celebrated
minipoem is all one metaphor, all imagery. Not closely detailed, it
seems vague when set next to Eliot's agile fog-cat in "Prufrock."
Eliot can depict even fog without vagueness; evidently cats are
right up his alley. Students also might enjoy a look at his Old
Possum's Book of Practical Cats.

Experiment: Writing with Images, page 80

To write a poem full of images, in any form, is probably easier
for most students than to write a decent haiku. (On the difficulties of teaching haiku writing, see Myra Cohn Livingston, cited
under "About Haiku" above.) Surprisingly, there is usually at
least one student in every class who can't seem to criticize a poem
to save his neck, yet who, if invited to be a poet, will bloom or
at least bud.

WALT WHITMAN, The Runner, page 80

Try reading "The Runner" without the adverbs lightly and par-
tially. Does the poem even exist without those two delicate modi-
fiers?

T. E. HULME, Image, page 80

Hulme's poems seem always to have been brief. In his own collection Personae, Ezra Pound took two pages to include "The Complete
Poetical Works of T. E. Hulme" (in which "Image" does not appear).

33

80-81 (text pages)

Pound remarked, "In publishing his Complete Poetical Works at thirty, Mr. Hulme has set an enviable example to many of his contemporaries who have had less to say."

WILLIAM CARLOS WILLIAMS, The Great Figure, page 80

Is the figure a symbol? It looks like one--such intent concentration upon a particular. In an otherwise static landscape, only the 5 moves. It's the one moving thing, as in the eye of the blackbird in Stevens's "Thirteen Ways." As far as I can see, however, the 5 has no great meaning beyond itself. Williams just rivets our attention on it and builds an atmosphere of ominous tension. The assumption, as in "The Red Wheelbarrow," is that somehow the figure has colossal significance. But "The Great Figure" is a much more vivid poem than "Wheelbarrow," and it contains no editorializing ("So much depends"). Like the poems in the section on "Literal Meaning," it's useful for discouraging students from spelling out colossal significances.

ROBERT BLY, Driving to Town Late to Mail a Letter, page 81

No doubt the situation in this poem is real: Bly, who lives in frequently snowbound Madison, Minnesota, is proprietor of The Seventies Press, and emits hundreds of letters. Compare this simple poem to Frost's "Stopping by Woods on a Snowy Evening," which also has a speaker who, instead of going home, prefers to ogle snowscapes.

GARY SNYDER, Mid-August at Sourdough Mountain Lookout, page 81

In brief compass, Snyder's poem appeals to the mind's eye (with smoke haze, pitch glows on fir cones, rocks, meadows, and the imagined vista at the end), the sense of moisture (after five days rain), of hot (three days heat) and of cold (snow-water from a tin cup). The swarms of new flies are probably both seen and heard.
For more background to this poem and to Snyder's work in general, see Bob Steuding, Gary Snyder (Boston: Twayne, 1976). A fictional portrait of Snyder appears in Jack Kerouac's novel The Dharma Bums (New York: Viking, 1958).

H. D. [HILDA DOOLITTLE], Heat, page 81

Heat becomes a tangible substance in this imagist poem, whose power resides mainly in its verbs, all worth scrutiny.

34

TED KOOSER, Beer Bottle, page 82

More than imagery, by the way, makes this small poem effective.
The simile like a cat thrown off of a roof to kill it seems particularly exact. In line 13, dazzled suggests not only that the bottle
reflects sunlight, but also that it seems surprised, stricken with
awe at having arrived in the ditch unbroken. Notice, too, the
visual shape of the poem: skinny and upright in appearance, like
its subject.

Kooser is an insurance underwriter in Lincoln, Nebraska. In
1980 the University of Pittsburgh Press brought out Sure Signs, his
new and selected poems. Like "Beer Bottle," all tend to be short,
precise, and free from pretentiousness.

6

FIGURES OF SPEECH

WHY SPEAK FIGURATIVELY?

ALFRED, LORD TENNYSON, The Eagle, page 84

For a hostile criticism of this poem see Robert Graves, "Technique in Poetry," On Poetry: Collected Talks and Essays (New York: Doubleday, 1969), pp. 402-405. Graves finds Tennyson's fragment unable to meet the minimal requirement that a poem should make good prose sense. He complains that if the eagle stands on its hands then its wings must be feet, and he ends up by rewriting the poem the way he thinks it ought to be. Though his remarks are fascinating, Graves reads the poem too literally.

A recent critic has suggested that this poem is a product of Tennyson's hopeless nearsightedness. Celebrating the eagle's 20-20 zoom-lens vision and ability to see a fish from high up, Tennyson yearns for a goal he could not attain: "optical inclusiveness." (See Gerhard Joseph, "Tennyson's Optics: The Eagle's Gaze," PMLA 92 [May 1977], no. 3, pp. 420-427.)

WILLIAM SHAKESPEARE, Shall I compare thee to a summer's day?, page 84

HOWARD MOSS, Shall I compare thee to a summer's day?, page 85

Shakespeare's original--rich in metaphor, personification, and hyperbole--means more, of course, than Moss's tongue-in-cheek desecration. The only figure of speech in Moss's rewrite is the simile in line one, and even that is denegated ("Who says?"). Moss manages to condense 113 great words to 78, a sonnet to a mere thirteen lines. It took a poet skilled in handling rimes to find such dull ones.

Shakespeare's nautical metaphor in line 8 may need explaining: a beautiful young person is a ship in full sail; accident or age can untrim the vessel. Compare this metaphor to "Bare ruined choirs where late the sweet birds sang" ("That time of year," page 364).

METAPHOR AND SIMILE

RICHARD WILBUR, A Simile for Her Smile, page 87

Despite the title, it may be necessary to point out that the detailed and extended comparison that occupies Wilbur's poem isn't between the smile and the approach of a riverboat, but between the latter and the speaker's <u>experience</u> of his loved one's smile, or his anticipation of it, or his memory of it.

The graceful ingenuity of this poem, in which the simile is made so explicit, recalls earlier metaphysical poetry. Compare Wilbur's simile with Donne's figure of the two parted lovers in "A Valediction: Forbidding Mourning" (page 305), or to Edmund Waller's central metaphor in "On a Girdle" (page 95).

ALFRED, LORD TENNYSON, Flower in the Crannied Wall, page 87

Why does Tennyson say "what God and man is" instead of "what God and man <u>are</u>"? Apparently, this isn't faulty grammar, but higher pantheism. God and man is One.

SYLVIA PLATH, Metaphors, page 88

Students usually are prompt to see that the central fact of the poem is the speaker's pregnancy. The speaker feels herself to be a walking riddle, posing a question that awaits solution: what person is she carrying? The <u>nine syllables</u> are like the nine months of gestation. All the metaphors refer to herself or to her pregnancy, except those in lines 4-5, which refer to the unborn baby: growing round and full like an apple or plum, seeming precious as ivory (and with ivory skin?), fine-timbered in sinew and bone like a well-built house.

The tone of the poem is clear, if complicated. Humor and self-mockery are evident in the images of elephant and strolling melon. In the last line, there is a note of wonder at the inexorability of gestation and birth: <u>the train there's no getting off</u>.

A lively class might be asked to point out any possible connection between what the poem is saying about the arbitrary, fixed cycle of pregnancy and its form--the nine nine-syllable lines.

JANE KENYON, The Suitor, page 89

This economical poem moves from simile to simile: (1) <u>like the chest of someone sleeping</u> (steadily rising and falling); (2) <u>like a school of fish</u> (flashing their pale bellies); and (3) <u>like a timid suitor</u> (hesitant, drawing back, reluctant to arrive).

Jane Kenyon is a young poet who lives in Danbury, New Hampshire. "The Suitor" is from her first collection, <u>From Room to Room</u> (Cambridge, Mass.: Alice James Books, 1978).

37

89-91 (text pages)

EMILY DICKINSON, It dropped so low-in my Regard, page 89

The whole poem sets forth the metaphor that someone or something the speaker had valued too highly proved to be like a silver-
plated item (a chafing-dish? a cream pitcher?) that she had mis-
taken for solid silver. Its smash revealed that it was made of
cheap stuff.

In another version, lines 5-6 read: "Yet blamed the Fate that
fractured--less / Than I reviled myself." Students may be asked
which version they prefer, and why they prefer it. (Personally, I
much prefer reviled to denounced because of its assonance--the sound
of the i--and its alliteration--the l in reviled and self. Besides,
fractured seems a more valuable word than flung: it gets across the
notion of something cracked or shattered, and its r sets up an alliterative echo with the words entertain, ware, and silver.)

RUTH WHITMAN, Castoff Skin, page 89

Apparently crawled away means that the old woman died, leaving
her body behind as a snake sheds a useless skin. Paper cheek seems
a fine evocation of snakeskin. The simile in line 2 ("small as a
twig") also suggests stiffness and brittleness.

DENISE LEVERTOV, Leaving Forever, page 90

The man seems glad to go: stones rolling away suggests the
shedding of some great weight, or possibly even a resurrection (an
echo of the rolling away of the stone from the Easter tomb?). But
in the woman's view the mountain seems like someone rejected and
forlorn. The woman's view, expressed in a metaphor and given force
by coming last, seems stronger than the man's simile.

Another question: is the poet right to repeat away, way,
away, away? The sound reverberates with a terrible flat monotony,
it is true--but apparently that is the effect necessary.

Exercise: What Is Similar?, page 90

No one instructor's method is necessarily of use to another,
but let me suggest that this exercise be run through rapidly. I
wouldn't give students much time to ponder, but would briskly call
on people, and if anyone I called on hesitated for long, I would
skip to someone else. Give them time to cogitate about these items,
and they are likely to dredge up all sorts of brilliant, reached-
for similarities between each pair of things--possibly logical, but
having nothing to do with the lines. Immediate flashes of understanding are the goal of this particular exercise, not ponderous
explication. Do this one for fun, and so it might be; do it slowly
and seriously, and it could be deadly.

OTHER FIGURES

JAMES STEPHENS, The Wind, page 91

As a birthday present to Stephens, James Joyce once translated this poem into five other languages (French, German, Latin, Italian, and Norwegian). These versions are reprinted in Letters of James Joyce, ed. Stuart Gilbert (New York: Viking, 1957), pp. 318-319.

Exercise: Paradox, page 93

CHIDIOCK TICHBORNE, Elegy, Written with His Own Hand, page 93

Tichborne was only eighteen years old when put to death in the Tower of London, along with six others who took part in the unsuccessful Babington conspiracy against Queen Elizabeth. "One must admit the possibility that these verses were written by some other poet, rather than by the protagonist himself," note J. William Hebel and Hoyt H. Hudson in Poetry of the English Renaissance (New York: Appleton-Century-Crofts, 1929). Set to music by a later composer, the "Elegy" was sung as a madrigal.

On the subject of puns, students familiar with Hamlet and other classics of the Bard may be asked to recall other puns of Shakespeare (besides the celebrated lines about golden lads and girls, quoted on page 94). If such a discussion prospers, Dr. Johnson's well-known observation in his preface to Shakespeare's works may provide an assertion to argue with:

> A quibble is to Shakespeare what luminous vapors are to the traveler: he follows it at all adventures; it is sure to lead him out of his way, and sure to engulf him in the mire. . . . A quibble is the golden apple for which he will always turn aside from his career or stoop from his elevation. A quibble, poor and barren as it is, gave him such delight that he was content to purchase by it the sacrifice of reason, propriety, and truth. A quibble was to him the fatal Cleopatra for which he lost the world, and was content to lose it.

GEORGE HERBERT, The Pulley, page 94

The title may need clarification. Man's need for rest is the pulley by which eventually he is drawn to rest everlasting. The pulley Herbert has in mind is probably not horizontal (like the one with a clothesline), but the vertical kind rigged to hoist a heavy weight. Despite the puns the tone of the poem is of course devoutly serious, Herbert's concern in it being (in the view of Douglas Bush) "to subdue the wilful or kindle the apathetic self."

Lines 2-10, on the "glass of blessings" and its contents, set
forth a different metaphor. As Herbert's editor F. E. Hutchinson
(Works [Oxford: Oxford University Press, 1941]) and others have
remarked, "The Pulley" seems a Christian version of the story of
Pandora. At her creation Pandora received gifts from all the gods,
mostly virtues and graces--though Hermes gave her perfidy. In some
tellings of the myth, Pandora's gift-box (or vase) held not plagues
but further blessings. When she became curious and opened it, they
slipped away, all except one that lay at the bottom--hope.

Herbert's poem, in its fondness for the extended metaphysical
conceit, invites comparison with Donne's metaphor of the compasses
in "A Valediction: Forbidding Mourning" (page 305). If the instructor cares to discuss metaphysical poetry, "The Pulley" may be
taken together with Herbert's "Redemption' (page 210) and "Love"
(page 326). ("Easter Wings" (page 194) raises distracting considera-
tions and may be left for a discussion of concrete or graphic poetry.)
Other metaphysical poems by Waller and Roethke immediately follow
"The Pulley" in this chapter. (See note on Roethke's poem below.)
Other poems of Donne and of Emily Dickinson can be mentioned. For
recent poems that contain extended conceits see Wilbur's "A Simile
for Her Smile," also in this chapter, and Alan Dugan's "Love Song:
I and Thou" (page 306).

It is a problem, of course, how deeply to become embroiled in
metaphysical poetry, if one wants to do so at all. Personally, I
try to encourage students to see that poets of the seventeenth century had certain habits of thought strikingly different from our
own; but that some of these habits--like the fondness for startling
comparisons of physical and spiritual things--haven't become extinct.
Perhaps the closest modern equivalent to the conceits of Herbert and
Donne may be found in fundamentalist hymns. I like to quote for
students two earlier twentieth century illustrations:

> If you want to watch old Satan run
> Just fire off that Gospel gun!

and

> My soul is like a rusty lock.
> Oh, oil it with Thy grace!
> And rub it, rub it, rub it, Lord,
> Until I see Thy face!

(The first example is attributed to a black Baptist hymn-writer;
the second, to the Salvation Army, according to Max Eastman in
Enjoyment of Laughter [New York: Simon and Schuster, 1936], p. 79.)
An even more recent illustration, probably influenced by funda-
mentalist hymns, is a country and Western song recorded in 1976 by
Bobby Bare, "Dropkick me, Jesus" ("through the goalposts of life").

EDMUND WALLER, On a Girdle, page 95

    Another way to enter this poem might be to ask:
    1. In what words does the poet express littleness or constric-
tion? (In the "slender waist," the rime confined/bind, "pale which
held," "narrow compass," bound.)
    2. In what words does he suggest vastness and immensity?
(With any luck, students will realize that the entire poem demonstrates the paradox stated in lines 9-10.)
    There may be another pun in line 6: deer.
    What is the tone of "On a Girdle"? Playful and witty, yet
tender. You can have fun with this poem by asserting an overly
literal-minded reading: somewhere in the world, isn't there probably some ruler who wouldn't abdicate just to put his arms around
her? If the speaker rejects all the sun goes round, where will that
put him and his loved one? If students have trouble objecting to
such quibbles, remind them of the definition of a figure of speech.
That should help. An overstatement isn't a lie, it's a means of
emphasis.
    Compare this to another love poem full of hyperbole: Burns's
"Oh, my love is like a red, red rose," at the end of this chapter.

THEODORE ROETHKE, I Knew a Woman, page 96

    Both outrageous puns occur in line 15. In question two, the
three lines quoted contain overstatement or hyperbole. The speaker's
reference to his whole being as old bones is synecdoche. "Let seed
be grass, and grass turn into hay" are not metaphors, but literal
events the speaker hopes for--unless you take the ripening of the
grass to be the passage of time. Metaphors occur also in the
sickle and the rake, and in calling lovemaking mowing.
    "I Knew a Woman" shows Roethke's great affection for meta-
physical poetry in its puns, its brief conceits (sickle and rake),
and its lovely image out of geometry--"She moved in circles, and
those circles moved." Two metaphysical poets of the seventeenth
century come immediately before Roethke in this chapter: Herbert
and Waller. Here's a good chance to dwell on metaphysical poetry,
or at least to mention it. (See the notes on Herbert's "Pulley,"
above.)
    For more outrageous puns, compare Robert Graves's "Down, Wan-
ton, Down!" (page 37).

FOR REVIEW AND FURTHER STUDY

ROBERT FROST, The Silken Tent, page 97

    Although the word as in the opening line might lead us to ex-
pect a simile, "The Silken Tent" is clearly an immense metaphor,
comparing woman and tent in a multitude of ways. What are the
ropes or cords? Not merely commitments (or promises to keep) to

41

friends and family, but generous sympathies, "ties of love and thought," on the part of a woman who cares about everything in the world.

While paying loving tribute to a remarkable woman, the poem is also a shameless bit of showing off by a poet cocksure of his technical mastery. Managing syntax with such grace that the poem hardly seems contrived, Frost has sustained a single sentence into an entire sonnet. "The whole poem is a performance," says Richard Poirier, "a display for the beloved while also being an exemplification of what it is like for a poem, as well as a tent or a person, to exist within the constrictions of space ('a field') and time ('at midday') wherein the greatest possible freedom is consistent with the intricacies of form and inseparable from them" (Robert Frost: The Work of Knowing [New York: Oxford, 1977], pp. xiv-xv). Poirier points out, too, that the diction of the poem seems biblical, perhaps echoing "The Song of Songs" (in which the bride is comely "as the tents of Kedar") and Psalm 92 (in which the godly "grow like a cedar in Lebanon"). Not only does the central cedar pole signify the woman's spiritual rectitude, it points toward heaven.

In teaching this poem, one can quote Frost's remark to Louis Untermeyer, "I prefer the synecdoche in poetry, that figure of speech in which we use a part for a whole." In 1931 Frost recalled that he had called himself a Synecdochist back when other poets were calling themselves Imagists, "Always, always a larger significance. A little thing touches a larger thing." (Quoted by Elizabeth Shepley Sergeant, Robert Frost: The Trial by Existence [New York: Holt, Rinehart and Winston, 1960], p. 325.)

JAMES C. KILGORE, The White Man Pressed the Locks, page 98

White body (the suburbs) holds black body (the inner city) in a tight grip, as if squeezing the life out of it. Students may be asked to spell out the connotations of certain well-loaded words and phrases. Why is the body in line 3 darkening? (Because more and more blacks are gathering in the inner city?) And blighted suggests both disease and the familiar phrase "urban blight." In the bloodstream, white corpuscles act as aggressive devourers. Possibly the hugging white arms suggest the commuter's wife and children, to whom he speeds home—but from the black poet's point of view in this poem, they appear sinister.

OGDEN NASH, Very Like a Whale, page 98

Nash's meandering lines and forced rimes may have been inspired by the work of Mrs. Julia A. Moore, the self-styled "Sweet Singer of Michigan" (1847-1920); but any number of quasi-literate poets could have shown him the way. Compare these lines (running on for as long as necessary, then riming like a screech of trampled brakes) by the bard of Dundee, William McGonagall (1830-1902) on "The Tay Bridge Disaster":

Oh! ill-fated Bridge of the Silv'ry Tay,
I must now conclude my lay
By telling the world fearlessly without the least dismay,
That your central girders would not have given way,
At least many sensible men do say,
Had they been supported on each side with buttresses,
At least many sensible men confesses,
For the stronger we our houses do build,
The less chance we have of being killed.

Exercise: Figure Spotting, page 100

RICHARD WILBUR, Sleepless at Crown Point, page 100

In Wilbur's implied metaphor, promontory and wind are to each other as bull is to matador.

ANONYMOUS, The fortunes of war, I tell you plain, page 100

There are two instances of metonymy: wooden leg (being wounded) and golden chain (being decorated). This couplet was current in England at the time of the Crimean War.

ROBERT FROST, The Secret Sits, page 100

Besides its personification of the sitting Secret, Frost's poem contains an implied metaphor. To dance round in a ring is to make futile efforts to penetrate a secret—merely going around in circles.

MARGARET ATWOOD, You fit into me, page 100

The first two lines state a simile. In the second couplet, hook and eye turn out (to our surprise) to be puns.

ROBERT GRAVES, Love Without Hope, page 101

Love isn't a noun, of course; it's a verb in the imperative. Apparently the point of the poem is: what a grand, unselfish sacrifice!

JOHN ASHBERY, The Cathedral Is, page 101

Slated is a pun.

101-102 (text pages)

ETHERIDGE KNIGHT, For Black Poets Who Think of Suicide, page 101

To search in <u>sweet dark caves</u> and <u>hunt for snipe / Down psychic trails</u> seem metaphors (for "indulging in sentimental thoughts of death" and "looking for Freudian symbols," maybe?). Lines 9-12 introduce four more metaphors. The poem ends in synecdoche: <u>marching feet</u> suggest an advancing army.
One black poet who thinks of suicide, at least in the title of his poem on page 290, is Amiri Baraka. In lines 1-2 perhaps Knight recalls a white poet who took his own life: Hart Crane, who leaped to his death from a steamship, wrote <u>The Bridge</u>.

W. S. MERWIN, Song of Man Chipping an Arrowhead, page 101

The poem contains an apostrophe to the chips of flint or stone. That the chips are <u>little children</u> is also a metaphor; so is <u>the one you are hiding</u>--the emerging arrowhead.

ROBERT BURNS, Oh, my love is like a red, red rose, page 101

Figures of speech abound in this famous lyric: similes (lines 1-2, 3-4), a metaphor (<u>sands o' life</u>, 12), overstatements (8 and 9, 10), and possibly another overstatement in the last line.
See other professions of love couched in hyperbole, among them Waller's "On a Girdle" (page 95), Roethke's "I Knew a Woman" (page 96), Marvell's "To His Coy Mistress" (page 8), and Auden's "As I Walked Out One Evening" (page 287). Are the speakers in these poems mere throwers of blarney, whom no woman ought to trust?
For a discussion of this poem that finds more in it than figures of speech, see Richard Wilbur, "Explaining the Obvious," in <u>Responses</u> (New York: Harcourt Brace Jovanovich, 1976). Burns's poem, says Wilbur, "forsakes the lady to glory in Love itself, and does not really return. We are dealing, in other words, with romantic love, in which the beloved is a means to high emotion, and physical separation can serve as a stimulant to ideal passion." The emotion of the poem is "self-enchanted," the presence or absence of the lady isn't important, and the very idea of parting is mainly an opportunity for the poet to turn his feelings loose. Absurd as this posture may be, however, we ought to forgive a great songwriter almost anything.

7

SONG

SINGING AND SAYING

Most students who wrote comments about this book in its last edition said that this chapter was the one that most appealed to them. "It shows that poetry isn't all found in books," was a typical comment; and many were glad to see song lyrics that they knew.

Even if there is not time for a whole unit on song, the instructor who wishes to build upon this interest can use at least some of this chapter to introduce the more demanding matters of rhythm, sound, and form (treated in Chapters 8, 9, and 10). Some instructors take the tack that lyric poetry begins with song, and so begin their courses with this chapter, supplemented by folk ballads elsewhere in the text.

BEN JONSON, To Celia, page 104

Students may not know that in line 2 I will pledge means "I will drink a toast." Also, I would not change for thine (line 8) in modern English becomes "I would not take it in exchange for yours."

To demonstrate that "To Celia" is a living song, why not ask the class to sing it? Unfortunately, you can no longer assume that the tune is one that everybody knows, so you may need to start them off.

ANONYMOUS, The Cruel Mother, page 105

Some versions of this ballad start the narrative at an earlier point in time, with a woman discovering that she is pregnant by the wrong man when she is about to marry another. See Alan Lomax's notes to The Child Ballads, vol. 1 (Caedmon TC 1145), which record contains an Irish version.

If the instructor cares to discuss the bottomless but student-spellbinding topic of archetypes, this ballad will serve to illustrate an archetype also visible in the stepmother figure of many fairy stories. (See the cursory discussion in the text on pages 221-223.)

108-111 (text pages)

EDWIN ARLINGTON ROBINSON, Richard Cory, page 108

PAUL SIMON, Richard Cory, page 108

This pair sometimes provokes lively class discussion, especially if someone in the class maintains that Simon converts Robinson into fresh, modern terms. Further discussion may be necessary to show that Robinson's poem has a starkly different theme.

Robinson's truth, of course, is that we envy others their wealth and prestige and polished manners, but if we could see into their hearts we might not envy them at all. Simon's glib song does not begin to deal with this. The singer wishes that he too could have orgies on a yacht, but even after he learns that Cory died a suicide, his refrain goes right on, I wish that I could be Richard Cory. (Live rich, die young, and make a handsome corpse!)

Some questions to prompt discussion might include:

1. In making his song, Paul Simon admittedly took liberties with Robinson's poem. Which of these changes seem necessary to make the story singable? What suggestions in the original has Simon picked up and amplified?

2. How has Simon altered the character of Richard Cory? Is his Cory a "gentleman" in Robinson's sense of the word? What is the tone of Simon's line, He had the common touch? Compare this with Robinson: he was always human when he talked. Does Robinson's Cory have anything more than Power, grace and style?

3. In the song, what further meaning does the refrain take on with its third hearing, in the end, after the news of Cory's suicide?

4. What truth about life does Robinson's poem help us see? Is it merely "Money can't make you happy" or "If you're poor you're really better off than rich people"? Does Simon's narrator affirm this truth, deny it, or ignore it?

BALLADS

ANONYMOUS, Bonny Barbara Allan, page 110

Despite the numerous versions of this, the most widespread of all traditional ballads in English, most versions keep the main elements of the story with remarkable consistency. American versions tend to be longer, with much attention to the lovers' eventual side-by-side burial, and sometimes have Barbara's mother die of remorse, too! Commentators since the coming of Freud have sometimes seem Barbara as sexually frigid, and Robert Graves once suggested that Barbara, a witch, is killing Sir John by sorcery. An Irish version makes Barbara laugh hideously on beholding her lover's corpse.

To show how traditional ballads change and vary in being sung, a useful recording is The Child Ballads, vol. 1 (Caedmon TC 1145), containing performances collected in the field by Alan Lomax and Peter Kennedy. Six nonprofessional singers are heard in sharply different versions of "Barbara Allan," in dialects of England, Scotland, Ireland, and Wales.

WOODY GUTHRIE, Plane Wreck at Los Gatos (Deportee), page 114

In most of this song and in its refrain, the singer's point of
view is that of a sympathetic commentator, but in stanzas 2-4 the
point of view changes and the singer becomes one of the deportees.
Read in print, some of Guthrie's lines seem feeble (such as 25-26),
and yet a tremendous metaphor informs the whole song. The fall to
death of the wetback pickers is like the fall of leaves from the
trees whose fruit they picked. By implication, the waste of human
life is like the spoilage of fruit shown in the opening lines.
Teaching this song, the instructor can touch back on the matter
of didactic poetry (discussed in the text on pages 4-5), or can
place Guthrie's protest in a tradition of poems that side with
victims, along with Blake's "The Chimney Sweeper," Cleghorn's "Golf
Links," Jarrell's "Death of the Ball Turret Gunner," and many more.

JOHN LENNON and PAUL McCARTNEY, Eleanor Rigby, page 115

"Eleanor Rigby," I think, is a poem. Although swayed by the
superstition that priests are necessarily lonely because celibate,
Lennon's portrait of Father McKenzie and of Eleanor have details
that reflect life. Both music and words contain an obvious beat,
and if students pick out those syllables in long lines 4 and 7, 14
and 17, and 24 and 27, they will be getting into the subject of
meter. (Each of the lines contains a stressed syllable followed by
four anapests.)

FOR REVIEW AND FURTHER STUDY

Exercise: Songs or Poems or Both?, page 116

AUGUSTUS MONTAGU TOPLADY, A Prayer, Living and Dying, page 116

ANONYMOUS, Fa, mi, fa, re, la, mi, page 117

ANONYMOUS, The silver swan, who living had no note, page 117

ANONYMOUS, On Top of Old Smokey, page 118

ANONYMOUS, Good Mornin', Blues, page 118

WILLIE NELSON, Heaven and Hell, page 119

Of these six songs, only "Fa, mi" seems unreadable: its words
do little more than fill up a tune.
Toplady's immortal hymn retains some power even if merely read
on the page, especially in its original version. Students may be
asked why eye-strings break is better poetry than the modernization
eyelids close, or asked which wording they prefer. Toplady was an
ordained minister of the Established Church in England, a bitter

opponent of the Wesleys, and a hymnist who expressed a passionate and emotional Calvinism. That he composed the hymn after being caught in a thunderstorm and taking refuge under a cliff is one of many apocryphal tales about is composition. Some of the lore and history of "Rock of Ages" have been collected by Theron Brown and Hezekiah Butterworth in The Story of the Hymns and Tunes (New York: American Tract Society, 1906). Confederate General J. E. B. Stuart called for it to be sung as he lay dying; Prince Albert whispered it to Victoria on his deathbed; the steamer London went down in the Bay of Biscay in 1866 while the doomed passengers belted it out; Armenian Christians sang it while being massacred in Constantinople.

Comparing the two madrigals, the instructor can raise the question, "Why is 'The silver swan' a memorable poem while 'Fa, mi' isn't?" With luck and a little prompting, students may see that poetry isn't mere musical noise: poems say something. They also tend to contain figurative language such as the metaphor unlocked her silent throat and the apostrophe to death; and interesting sounds--the subtle silver / living and other alliterations. What, by the way, is a "swan song"? Some students may need an explanation.

"On Top of Old Smokey" and "Good Mornin', Blues" are strong poems, their abstractions rendered solid. At the end of Leadbelly's song, the blues becomes a living creature--a mean hunting dog.

Willie Nelson's "Heaven and Hell" is surprisingly metaphysical! What sense do students make out of front tracks and back tracks? (Does the singer feel like a moving train leaving a freezing wasteland and headed for refreshing waters? Nelson has a fine ear, and his lyric gains richness from internal rime (back track), alliteration, and sonorous repetition. A Texas-born country-and-western singer and composer, Nelson hit the big time in 1975 with his album Red Headed Stranger. He starred in the 1980 movie Honeysuckle Rose.

8

SOUND

SOUND AS MEANING

ALEXANDER POPE, True Ease in Writing comes from Art, not Chance,
page 121

Nowadays, looking at the pages of an eighteenth-century book
of poetry, we might think the liberal capitalization and use of
italics merely decorative. But perhaps Pope wished to leave his
readers little choice in how to sound his lines. Most of his typographical indications seem to me to make sense--like a modern stage
or television script with things underlined or capitalized, lest the
actors ignore a nuance.

Line 12 is deliberately long: an alexandrine or twelve-syl-
lable line that must be spoken quickly in order to get it said within the time interval established by the other shorter, pentameter
lines.

WILLIAM BUTLER YEATS, Who Goes with Fergus?, page 123

Originally a song in Yeats's play The Countess Cathleen, this
famous lyric overflows with euphony. Take just the opening question
(lines 1-3): the assonance of the various o-sounds; the initial
alliteration of w, d, and sh; the internal alliteration of the r in
Fergus, pierce, and shore--musical devices that seem especially
meaningful for an invitation to a dance. The harsh phrase brazen
cars seems introduced to jar the brooding lovers out of their rev-
eries. Unless you come right out and ask what brazen cars are (I
have found), a few students will not realize that they are brass
chariots. (In ancient Ulster, such chariots were sometimes used
for hunting deer--though how you would drive one of them through
the deep woods beats me.)

If you discuss meter, what better illustration of the power of
spondees than And the WHITE BREAST of the DIM SEA?

The last line of the poem, while pleasingly mysterious, is
also exact. The personification dishevelled wandering stars makes
me think of beautiful, insane, or distracted women with their hair
down: Ophelia in Olivier's film Hamlet. That they are wandering
recalls the derivation of the word planet: Greek for "wanderer."
In what literal sense might stars look dishevelled? Perhaps in
that their light, coming through the atmosphere (and being seen

49

through ocean spray) appears to spread out like wild long hair.   For
comparable figures of speech, see Melville's "The Portent" (page 43),
in which John Brown's beard is a meteor; and Blake's "Tyger" (page
292), in which the personified stars weep and throw spears.

Exercise: Listening to Meaning, page 124

JOHN UPDIKE, Winter Ocean, page 124

FRANCES CORNFORD, The Watch, page 124

WILLIAM WORDSWORTH, A Slumber Did My Spirit Seal, page 124

EMANUEL diPASQUALE, Rain, page 125

   Onomatopoeia is heard in Updike's underline{scud-thumper} and underline{pusher}
(echoing the boom and rush of the waves), and is heard even more
obviously in Cornford's watch-ticks.   In diPasquale's lines, the
underline{s}-sounds fit well with our conception of rain, and underline{hushes} is an
especially beautiful bit of onomatopoeia.   By the way, diPasquale's
poem is especially remarkable in view of the fact that the poet,
born in Sicily, did not learn English until he was sixteen.
   For another winter ocean to compare with Updike's, also heavy
on alliteration, turn to Pound's "The Seafarer" (page 352), a translation of an old English poem.   (Probably Updike was trying to write
a poem that would sound like Old English poetry.)
   In Wordsworth's Lucy poem, sound effects are particularly no-
ticeable in the first line (the soporific underline{s}'s) and in the last two
lines (the droning underline{r}'s and underline{n}'s).   If students go beyond the sound
effects and read the poem more closely, they might find problems in
the first stanza.   Is the poet's slumber a literal sleep or a figurative one?   That is: is Wordsworth recalling some pleasant dream
of Lucy (whether the living Lucy he used to know, or the dead Lucy
in Eternity), or is he saying that when she was alive he was like a
dreamer in his view of her?   If so, he was deluded in thinking that
she would always remain a child; he had none of the usual human
fears of death or of growing old.   However we read the poem, there
is evidently an ironic contrast between the poet's seeing Lucy (in
stanza one) as invulnerable to earthly years, and his later view
that she is affected, being helplessly rolled around the sun once
a year with the other inanimate objects.   And simple though it
looks, the poem contains a paradox.   The speaker's earlier dream or
vision of Lucy has proved to be no illusion but an accurate fore-
shadowing.   Now she is a "thing," like rocks and stones and trees;
and she cannot feel and cannot suffer any more from time's ravages.

ALLITERATION AND ASSONANCE

A. E. HOUSMAN, Eight O'Clock, page 126

The final struck is a serious pun, to which patterns of alliteration begun in the opening line (st . . . st, r), and continued
through the poem, have led up. The ticking effect of the clock is,
of course, most evident in The clock collected.
Compare Housman's strapped and noosed lad with the one in Hugh
Kingsmill's paradox of Housman (page 241); and this lad's cursing
his luck with what Terence has to say about luck in "Terence, this
is stupid stuff" (page 329).

ROBERT HERRICK, Upon Julia's Voice, page 127

Julia, apparently, is singing; for the lutes provide accompaniment. At beginning and end, this brief poem is particularly
rich in music: the sibilance of so smooth, so sweet, so silv'ry;
and the alliteration (both initial and internal) of the m and l
sounds in the last line.
The second line seems a colossal hyperbole, meaning, "Julia,
your singing is sweet enough to make the damned in Hell forget to
wail." In Herrick's poems, such flattery is never out of place.
This is the quality of Herrick's work--a lovely deliberate absurdity
--I've tried to echo (feebly) in a two-line parody:

When Vestalina's thin white hand cuts cheese,
The very mice go down upon their knees.

JANET LEWIS, Girl Help, page 127

A sensitive comment on this poem is that of the poet's husband,
Yvor Winters:

There is almost nothing to it, really, except the rich
characterization of a young girl with her life before her
and the description of a scene which implies an entire way
of life. The meter is curious; one is tempted to call it
irregular three-beat accentual, but it seems to be irregular
iambic trimeter. On the second basis, the first line starts
with a monosyllabic foot, and the fourth line has two feet,
both iambic. But wide and broom are almost evenly accented,
and both are long; if one is moved by this to choose the
accentual theory, her is too lightly accented to count,
although it would count as the accented syllable of an
iambic foot. There are a few other such problems later in
the poem. But there is no problem with the rhythm; the
fourth line virtually gives us the movement of the broom,
and the seventh and eighth give us the movement of the girl;
the movement of the poem is that of indolent summer in a

51

127-133 (text pages)

time and place now gone; the diction, like the rhythm, is
infallible.

Winters (1900-1968)--see his own poem on page 389--wrote this
analysis in Forms of Discovery (Denver: Alan Swallow, 1967),
p. 332.
    Janet Lewis, known for The Wife of Martin Guerre, The Trial of
Soren Qvist, and other novels, has lately brought out her Poems Old
and New: 1918-1978 (Athens, Ohio: Swallow Press/Ohio University
Press, 1981). The volume includes recent work.

Exercise: Hearing How Sound Helps, page 128

    Wyatt's version surpasses Surrey's for me, especially in Wyatt's
opening line with its remarkable use of assonance--a good instance
of the way long vowel-sounds can slow our reading of a line and make
us linger over it. The initial alliteration and internal alliteration in these first two lines help besides. In its rhythm, Surrey's
version sounds a bit singsong by comparison. The inverted word
order in the last line seems awkward.

ALFRED, LORD TENNYSON, The splendor falls on castle walls, page 128

    If read aloud rapidly, this famous lyric from Tennyson's The
Princess will become gibberish; and the phrase Blow, bugle, blow, a
tongue-twister. But if it is read with any attention to its
meaning, its long vowels and frequent pauses will compel the reader
to slow down. Students may want to regard the poem as mellifluous
nonsense, but may be assured that the poem means something. In
fact, it is based on a personal experience of the poet's. Visiting
the lakes of Killarney in 1848, Tennyson heard the bugle of a boat-
man sound across the still water, and counted eight distinct echoes.
A scar (line 9) is a rocky crag or bluff. The splendor falls is
the poet's attempt to convey his experience in accurate words.

RIME

ROBERT FROST, Desert Places, page 132

    Some possible answers:

    1. Terrible pockets of loneliness.
    2. The word snow, occurring three times. Other o-sounds occur
in oh, going, showing, no, so, home. The l of lonely is echoed by
alliteration in looking, last, and lairs.
    3. It makes me feel a psychic chill! Yet the feminine rime
lightens the grim effect of what is said and gives it a kind of
ironic smirk.

WILLIAM BUTLER YEATS, Leda and the Swan, page 133

The deliberately awful off-rime up / drop ends the sonnet with an appropriately jarring plop as the God-swan discards the used Leda and sinks into his postejaculatory stupor.
Other questions that can be raised:

  1. What knowledge and power does Yeats refer to in line 13?
  2. Do the words staggering (line 2) and loosening (line 6) keep to the basic meter of the poem or depart from it? How does rhythm express meaning in these lines? (It staggers on staggering and loosens on loosening.)
  3. Compare this peom to Donne's sonnet "Batter my heart" (page 39). Is the tone of Yeats's sonnet--the poet's attitude toward this ravishing--similar or dissimilar?

For an early draft of the poem, see Yeats's Memoirs, ed. Denis Donoghue (New York: Macmillan, 1973), pp. 272-274.

GERARD MANLEY HOPKINS, God's Grandeur, page 134

Students who think Hopkins goes too far in his insistence on rimes and other similar sounds will have good company, including Robert Bridges, Yeats, and Yvor Winters. Still, it is hard not to admire the euphony of the famous closing lines--that ingenious alternation of br and w, with a pause for breath at that magical ah!--and the cacophony of lines 6-8, with their jangling internal rimes and the alliteration that adds more weight to smeared, smudge, and smell. For Hopkins, of course, sound is one with meaning; and the cacophonous lines just mentioned are also, as John Pick has pointed out, "a summary of the particular sins of the nineteenth century." For a brilliant demonstration that sound effects in Hopkins's poetry have theological meaning, see J. Hillis Miller, The Disappearance of God (Cambridge, Mass.: Harvard University Press, 1963), pp. 276-317. Miller finds the poet's theory revealed in his sermons and journals: "Any two things however unlike are in something like"; therefore, "all beauty may by a metaphor be called rhyme."
In the text, it seemed best not to bury the poem under glosses, but to let the instructor decide how thoroughly to explicate it. Here are a few more glosses in case they seem necessary:

  1. charged: as though with electricity. 3-4: It gathers . . . ooze of oil / Crushed: God's grandeur will rise and be manifested from the world that man has abused, even as oil rises and collects from crushed olives. 4. reck his rod: obey his law. 7. man's smudge: the blight of smoke and ugliness cast over the countryside by factories and mines. As a student for the priesthood in North Wales and as a parish priest in London and Liverpool, Hopkins had known the blight intimately. Another suggestion in the phrase: nature is fallen and needs to be redeemed, like man, who wears the smudge of original sin. 10. deep down things: Hopkins

omits the preposition in before things. Tightly packing a poem, he
sometimes drops small words like a man composing a telegram against
a word-limit. 11. last lights off the black West went: when the
English church broke from Rome at the Reformation? 12. morning
. . . springs: The risen Christ is like the sun at dawn. Eastward
is the direction of Jerusalem, also of Rome. (Hopkins cherished
the hope that the Church of England and the Pope would one day be
reconciled.) 13-14: bent / World: Perhaps because of its curva-
ture the earth looks bent at the horizon; or perhaps the phrase is
a transferred epithet, attributing to the earth the dove's bent-over
solicitude. (And as the world seems to break off at the horizon,
line 13 breaks at the word bent.) 14. broods: like a dove, traditional representation of the Holy Ghost.

For still more suggestions, see Pick, Gerard Manley Hopkins,
Priest and Poet, 2nd ed. (Oxford: Oxford University Press, 1966),
pp. 62-64; Paul L. Mariani, Commentary on the Complete Poems of
Gerard Manley Hopkins (Ithaca, N.Y.: Cornell University Press,
1970); and (not least) the poet's "Pied Beauty."

A sonnet by Wordsworth (page 218) also begins "The world is,"
and Hopkins no doubt knew of it. In their parallel (though different) complaints against trade and commerce, the two deserve to
be compared. Both poets find man artificially removed from nature:
this seems the point of Hopkins's observation in lines 7-8 that
once soil was covered (with grass and trees) and feet were bare;
now soil is bare and feet are covered. Clearly we have lost the
barefoot bliss of Eden; but in answer to Wordsworth, one almost
expects Hopkins to cry, "Great God! I'd rather be a Christian."
(Wordsworth by world means "worldliness.")

EMILY DICKINSON, The Soul selects her own Society, page 134

Door / more is the one exact rime in the poem. Gate / Mat and
One / Stone are slant rimes--at the end, the latter provides a particularly hollow and reverberating off-note. Other couplings
(Society / Majority, nation / attention) sound roughly like feminine
rimes, but seem too far out to be called slant rimes. (Quasi rimes,
perhaps?) Although falling where we expect rimes, pausing and
kneeling seem not to rime at all.

In general, when a poet follows a line with another line mark-
edly shorter, the shorter line receives the larger share of our
attention--it is as though it had been underlined. (See, for
instance, Eliot's "Prufrock," lines 8-9 and 118-119.) Dickinson's
poem is built entirely of such long-and-short pairs. In the last
stanza, wherein the shorter, even-numbered lines have dwindled to
two syllables, both syllables taking full stresses, the effect is
powerful. Colossal emphasis is placed upon Like Stone, which shuts
the door of the poem.

Two interpretations of this cryptic poem seem likely; and students might be asked whether, like the Soul, they care to Choose
One, or perhaps to come up with another:

1. The chosen One is poetry. The Soul has selected it as the sole object of her attention, and decisively spurns other society. Biographical conjecture tends to support this view: by 1862, about when the poem was written, Dickinson had given up trying to publish her work. Feeling her creative powers at their height, she more frequently shunned society, apparently in order to devote her concentrated energies to her poetry. This poem "can be taken as a motto for her own guidance" in her now-decided way of life. (This is the opinion of Thomas H. Johnson in Emily Dickinson: An Interpretive Biography [Cambridge, Mass.: Harvard University Press, 1955].)

2. The One is God, whose society the Soul has selected over that of men. Her low Gate is her tombstone; her Mat, the grass on her grave. The Valves of her attention are the avenues of her senses, now closed in death and become (like stone) impenetrable.

READING AND HEARING POEMS ALOUD

Here is a fresh comment by William Stafford on why certain poets read their poems with apparent carelessness. Poets spend their energies in writing poems and are not effective public speakers. Unlike the Russian poet Voznesensky, a great performer, Stafford remarks,

> . . . most of the poets I know would feel a little guilty about doing an effective job of reading their poems. They throw them away. And I speak as one who does that. It feels fakey enough to be up there reading something as though you were reading it for the first time. And to say it well is just too fakey. So you just throw it away.

(Interview in The Literary Monitor, 3, 1980, no. 3/4.)

This comment raises provocative questions for discussion. What is the nature of a poetry reading? Should it be regarded as a performance, or as a friendly get-together?

For a symposium on poetry readings, with comments by Allen Ginsberg, James Dickey, Denise Levertov, and twenty-nine other poets, see Poets on Stage (New York: Some/Release Press, 1978); available as a paperback from Small Press Distribution, 1636 Ocean View Ave., Kensington, CA 94707, for $3.50.

Exercise: Reading for Sound and Meaning, page 137

MICHAEL STILLMAN, In Memoriam John Coltrane, page 137

WILLIAM SHAKESPEARE, Full fathom five thy father lies, page 137

EBENEZER ELLIOTT, On a Rose in December, page 138

A. E. HOUSMAN, With rue my heart is laden, page 138

T. S. ELIOT, Virginia, page 138

GALWAY KINNELL, Blackberry Eating, page 138

In Michael Stillman's tribute to the great jazz saxophonist, coal train is not only a rich pun on Coltrane's name, it also becomes the poem's central image. The poet has supplied this comment:

> One thing about that poem which has always pleased me--beyond its elegiac strain--is the way the technique of the lines and phrases corresponds to a musical effect on Coltrane's playing. He was known for his ability to begin with a certain configuration of notes, then play pattern after pattern of variations. The repetition of "Listen to the coal . . . listen to the . . . listen to . . . listen" was one way to capture a feature of his playing. The image of the coal train disappearing into the night comes, particularly, from a place on the James River, west of Richmond, where I happened to be when I heard of Coltrane's death. Like all jazz musicians, I felt the loss very deeply.

Shakespeare's song contains an obvious illustration of onomatopoeia (the bell's sound), obvious alliteration in the f-full first line, and (less obviously) internal alliteration (note the r and n sounds), and assonance galore. Like a drowned man's bones, ordinary language becomes something "rich and strange" in this song.

Ebenezer Elliott's two-line lyric is packed not only with meaning but also with music. Work through its alliteration and assonance--or have a student do so at the blackboard--by circling each repeated vowel sound or consonant, then joining them with lines. An intricate structure of sound binds the poem together like the strands of a spiderweb. A self-educated poet like John Clare, Elliott is best (but little) remembered for his Corn-Law Rhymes. There is a choice of his work in W. H. Auden's Nineteenth-Century Minor Poets (London: Faber, 1967).

Housman's better known lyric will reward the same sort of scrutiny, not that a class will sit still for much scrutiny of this sort!

Eliot's "Virginia" is an experiment in quantitative verse, according to George Williamson (A Reader's Guide to T. S. Eliot [New York: Noonday, 1957]). You might read aloud "Virginia" and Campion's quantitative "Rose-cheeked Laura" (page 154), and ask the class to detect any similarity. Ted Hughes has written of "Virginia" with admiration. How is it, he wonders, that Eliot can create so vivid a landscape without specific images? "What the poem does describe is a feeling of slowness, with a prevailing stillness, of suspended time, of heat and dryness, and fatigue, with an undertone of oppressive danger, like a hot afternoon that will turn to thunder and lightning" (Poetry Is [New York: Doubleday, 1967]).

Galway Kinnell, reading his poems at Bentley College on
March 17, 1981, read "Blackberry Eating," vigorously, with special
attention to the two long one-syllable words <u>squinched</u> and <u>strengths</u>.
"They're the longest one-syllable words I could find," he remarked.
"Nine letters long. If I had known any one-syllable words of ten
or eleven letters, I would have put them in instead."

9

RHYTHM

STRESSES AND PAUSES

In the first section of this chapter, rhythm is discussed with as few technicalities as possible. For the instructor wishing to go on to the technicalities, the second part of the chapter, "Meter," will give the principles of scansion and the names of the metrical feet.

Except for one teacher at the University of Michigan, James Downer, who would illustrate the rhythms of Old English poetry by banging on his desk for a drum, I have never known anyone able to spend whole classes on meter without etherizing the patients. Meter, it would seem, is best dealt with in discussing particular poems.

Exercise: Appropriate and Inappropriate Rhythms, page 142

The rollicking anapests of Poe and Eliza Cook seem inappropriate, ill-suited to the poets' macabre subject matter. Cook, by the way, is the author of another wretched specimen, "The Old Arm-Chair" (page 256).

Tennyson's monosyllabic words, further slowed by pauses, convey not only the force of the tide, but its repetitiousness.

The rhythms of these lines by Shakespeare and Greg Keeler seem suitably rollicking.

GWENDOLYN BROOKS, We Real Cool, page 145

The poet might have ended every line with a rime, as poets who rime usually do:

We real cool.
We left school.

The effect, then, would have been like a series of hammer blows, because of so many short end-stopped lines and so many rimes in such quick succession. But evidently Gwendolyn Brooks is after a different rhythm. What is it? How to read the poem aloud? Let members of the class take turns trying, and compare their various oral interpretations. If you stress each final We, then every syllable in the poem takes a stress; and if, besides, you make even

a split-second pause at every line-break, then you give those final
We's still more emphasis. What if you don't stress the We's, but
read them lightly? Then the result is a skipping rhythm, rather
like that of some cool cat slapping his thighs.

After the class has mulled this problem, read them Gwendolyn
Brooks's own note on the poem (from her autobiography Report from
Part One [Detroit: Broadside Press, 1972], p. 185):

> The ending WEs in "We Real Cool" are tiny, wispy,
> weakly argumentative "Kilroy-is-here" announcements. The
> boys have no accented sense of themselves, yet they are
> aware of a semi-defined personal importance. Say the "We"
> softly.

Kilroy, as students may need to know, was a fictitious--even
mythical--character commemorated in graffiti chalked or penciled by
U.S. soldiers wherever they traveled in World War II. KILROY WAS
HERE was even scrawled in the sands of Anzio. A small testimonial
that the graffitist is a person.

As a student remarked about the tone and theme of this poem,
"She doesn't think they're real cool, she thinks they're real fool--
to die so young like that."

Brooks has recorded her own reading of the poem for The Spoken
Arts Treasury of 100 Modern American Poets, vol. 13 (SA 1052).

ROBERT FROST, Never Again Would Birds' Song Be the Same, page 145

He is Adam. In line 9, you say "as MAY be," because the iambic
rhythm wants you to. The effect of Frost's closing string of sixteen monosyllables is quietly powerful, in keeping with his final
understatement. Much of our pleasure in those lines comes from
hearing ordinary, speakable phrases so beautifully accommodated.

Sometimes teachers and critics try to account for the unique
flavor of Frost's language by claiming that it is all a matter of
his vocabulary. But what rural words are there in this poem, a
poem as Yankee-sounding as they come, despite some highly literate
diction ("Admittedly an eloquence")? No, what makes the lines
memorable is that they embody what Frost called the "sound of
sense." He was convinced that certain phrases, customarily spoken
with feeling, have a pattern of intonation so distinctive that we
can recognize them and catch their meaning even if we hear only the
drone of them from behind a closed door. (See Frost's explanations
and illustrations in Selected Letters, ed. Lawrence Thompson [New
York: Holt, Rinehart and Winston, 1964], pp. 79-81 and 111-113.)

Reading this poem to an audience in Ann Arbor in March 1962
when he was 88, Frost delivered its closing line with the air of a
slowball pitcher hurling a flawless third strike into the catcher's
glove to retire the side. The audience caught it and burst out
clapping.

Pope's line of monosyllables, by the way, doesn't seem dull
either.

146-149 (text pages)

BEN JONSON, Slow, slow, fresh fount, keep time with my salt tears, page 146

O sounds slow the opening line, whose every word is a mono-syllable. Further slowing the line, eight of the ten monosyllables take heavy beats. "Drop, drop, drop, drop" obviously racks up still more stresses, as do the spondees that begin lines 4, 5, and 6. The entire effect is that we are practically obliged to read or sing the poem slowly and deliberately--as befits a lamentation.

ROBERT LOWELL, At the Altar, page 146

ALEXANDER POPE, Atticus, page 147

Even though both poems are in rimed couplets and in iambic pentameter, they differ sharply in their general, overriding kinds of rhythm. This difference is mainly because of Lowell's casting his breathless poem almost entirely in run-on lines, and because of Pope's custom of usually ending each graceful line with a word that also completes a unit of syntax. Lowell's nonstop lines keep running on, like his speaker's berserk car, and keep running on even after the car has crashed into the altar, like a drunken man's revved-up mind. (It is odd that the priest doesn't pause at this loud interruption, but keeps right on mumbling.) Pope's famous dissection of Addison is performed in couplets like locked boxes, each box neatly packed with whole units of syntax--dependent clauses, things in series, antitheses.

For a definition of the heroic couplet and a brief discussion of it, direct students to pages 163-164.

Exercise: Two Kinds of Rhythm, page 148

SIR THOMAS WYATT, With serving still, page 148

DOROTHY PARKER, Résumé, page 149

These two poems differ in rhythm: Wyatt compels a heavy pause only at the end of every quatrain, while Dorothy Parker end-stops every line. Students may be shown that pauses and meanings go to-gether. Both poems are cast in two sentences, but Wyatt develops one uninterrupted statement throughout the entire poem (in sonnet fashion: first the summary of the speaker's problem in the opening three stanzas, then the conclusion beginning with "Wherefore all ye"). "Résumé," as its punctuation indicates, makes a new self-con-tained statement in every line.

A question on meaning: must light verse necessarily be trivial in its theme? State Parker's theme in "Résumé." Surely, it isn't trivial. At least in theme, the poem seems comparable to Hamlet's soliloquy, "To be or not to be. . . ."

After <u>Not So Deep as a Well</u>, her collected poems of 1936,
Dorothy Parker brought out no more poetry collections. "My verses,"
she insisted to an interviewer. "I cannot say poems. Like every-
body was then, I was following in the exquisite footsteps of Miss
Millay, unhappily in my own horrible sneakers." (<u>Writers at Work</u>:
<u>The</u> Paris Review <u>Interviews</u>, first series [New York: Viking, 1959].)
Parker's wit, acerbic and sometimes macabre, is as clear from
"Résumé" as it is from her celebrated remark on being informed that
Calvin Coolidge had just died: "How do they know?"

METER

I used to think of a meter as a platonic ideal norm from which
actual lines diverge, but J. V. Cunningham's essay "How Shall the
Poem be Written?" changed my mind. Metrical patterns (in the abstract) do not exist; there are only lines that poets have written,
in which meters may be recognized. "Meter," declares Cunningham,
"is perceived in the actual stress-contour, or the line is perceived as unmetrical, or the perceiver doesn't perceive meter at
all." (<u>The Collected Essays of J. V. Cunningham</u> [Chicago: Swallow
Press, 1976], p. 262.)

MAX BEERBOHM, On the imprint of the first English edition of "The
Works of Max Beerbohm," page 150

John Updike has paid tribute to this brilliant bit of fluff:

The effortless a-b-a-b rhyming, the balance of "plain" and
"nicely," the need for nicety in pronouncing "iambically"
to scan--this is quintessential light verse, a twitting of
the starkest prose into perfect form, a marriage of earth
with light, and quite magical. Indeed, were I a high priest
of literature, I would have this quatrain made into an amulet
and wear it about my neck, for luck.

("Rhyming Max," a review of Beerbohm's collected
verse reprinted in <u>Assorted Prose</u> [New York: Knopf,
1965].)

THOMAS CAMPION, Rose-cheeked Laura, come, page 154

Campion includes this famous lyric in his polemic <u>Observations
on the Art of English Poesie</u> (1602), in which he argues that English
poets ought to adopt the quantitative meters of Greek and Latin.
"This cannot be done in English," says John Hollander, "with its
prominent word stress, save by assigning Latin vowel lengths to the
written English, and simply patterning what amounts to a typographical code which cannot be heard as verse. . . . 'Rose-cheekt Lawra'
is therefore merely an unrhymed English trochaic poem, perfectly

61

plain to the ear." (Introduction to <u>Selected Songs of Thomas Campion</u>, selected by W. H. Auden [Boston: David R. Godine, 1973].)

WALTER SAVAGE LANDOR, On Seeing a Hair of Lucretia Borgia, page 155

In first printing Landor's poem in 1825 in the <u>New Monthly</u>, Leigh Hunt explained, "A solitary hair of the famous Lucretia Borgia . . . was given me by a wild acquaintance who stole it from a lock of her hair preserved in the Ambrosian Library at Milan." (Lord Byron very well could have been the wild acquaintance.) According to Hunt, when he and Landor had met in Florence, they had struck up a conversation over the Borgia hair "as other acquaintances commence over a bottle."

<u>Exercise</u>: Meaningful Variation, page 156

Aside from minor variations from metrical norm (such as the substitution of a trochee for an iamb), the most meaningful departures in these passages seem to occur in these words or phrases:

1. Dryden: <u>deviates</u>. (Now there's a meaningful deviation!)
2. Pope: the spondees <u>snake</u>, <u>drags</u> and <u>slow length</u>.
3. King: <u>like a soft drum</u>.
4. Longfellow: <u>autumnal</u>, and the last line, which I would scan, "The CAT·a·ract of DEATH FAR THUN·der·ing from the HEIGHTS." Wonderful arrangement of unstressed syllables in that line! Its rhythm is like that of an avalanche bumbling around for a while before rumbling down.
5. Stevens: <u>spontaneous</u>, <u>casual</u>, <u>ambiguous</u>.

<u>Exercise</u>: Recognizing Rhythms, page 156

GEORGE GORDON, LORD BYRON, The Destruction of Sennacherib, page 157

EDNA ST. VINCENT MILLAY, Counting-out Rhyme, page 157

A. E. HOUSMAN, When I was one-and-twenty, page 158

WILLIAM CARLOS WILLIAMS, The Descent of Winter (section 10/30), page 158

RUTH PITTER, But for Lust, page 159

WALT WHITMAN, Beat! Beat! Drums!, page 159

Probably it is more important that students be able to recognize a metrical poem than that they name its meter. The Byron, Millay, Housman, and Pitter poems are thoroughly metrical; Williams and Whitman are not, but include metrical lines when the poets are describing or imitating the sound of something with a regular rhythm: the clank of freight car wheels, the whistle's <u>wha</u>, <u>wha</u>, the beating of drums. In Whitman's poem, besides the <u>refrain</u> (lines 1, 8, and 15) there are the primarily iambic lines that end each stanza.

Byron's anapests have been compared to those of galloping horses, but some readers (and I am one of them) find the meter too rollicking for an account of wholesale destruction. To discuss: is the rhythm of the poem meaningful for it?

Pitter's poem is cast in a seven-syllable line--iambic or trochaic, depending on how you slice its feet. Containing four beats, the line's effect is powerful. What is Pitter saying? Presumably a woman speaks to a man, wishing for another world where lust didn't interfere with friendship and sympathy. The play on words in lines 11-12 (on <u>passion</u> and <u>compassion</u>) seems wonderful. In line 14, the <u>awful living dead</u> suggests vampires. Is she saying that, set upon by a lustful man, she feels like a vampire's victim? Carolyn Kizer once introduced me to this poem, which she greatly admires. Pitter's <u>Collected Poems</u> (New York: Macmillan, 1969) contains mostly competent, formal work; but her finest poems have not yet had the hearing they deserve.

10

CLOSED FORM, OPEN FORM

Beginning students of poetry often have a hard time appreci-
ating either a sonnet or a poem in open verse because they have yet
to distinguish one variety of poetry from the other. On first
meeting an unfamiliar poem, the <u>experienced</u> reader probably recognizes it as metrical or nonmetrical from its opening lines--perhaps
even can tell at first glance from its looks on the page (compact
sonnet or spaced-out open verse). Such a reader then settles down
to read with appropriate expectations, aware of the rules of the
poem, looking forward to seeing how well the poet can play by them.
But the inexperienced reader reads mainly for plain prose sense, unaware of the rhythms of a Whitmanic long line or the rewards of a
sonnet artfully fulfilling its fourteenth line. Asked to write
about poetry, the novice reader may even blame the sonnet for being
"too rigid," or blame William Carlos Williams for "lacking music"
(that is, lacking a rime scheme), or for "running wild." Such
readers may have a right to their preferences, but they say nothing
about a poem, nor about the poet's accomplishment.
     That is why this chapter seems essential. To put across to
students the differences between the two formal varieties, it isn't
necessary to deal with every last fixed form, either. One can do
much by comparing two poems (closed and open) on the theme of sorrow
--Elizabeth Barrett Browning's fine sonnet "Grief" (page 170) and
Stephen Crane's astonishing "The Heart" (page 183); possibly the
two brief elegies on page 181, Robert Herrick's "Upon a Child
That Died" and Saint Geraud's "Poem." Before taking up closed
form, I like to teach some song lyrics--those in Chapter 7, or a
couple of traditional folk ballads. That way the student isn't
likely to regard fixed forms as arbitrary constructions invented by
English teachers. A stanza, I try to show, is the form that words
naturally take when sung to a tune. That is how stanzas began.
Sing a second round of a song, and you find yourself repeating the
pattern of it.

CLOSED FORM: BLANK VERSE, STANZA, SONNET

JOHN KEATS, This living hand, now warm and capable, page 163

     After Keats's death, these grim lines were discovered in the
margin of one of his manuscripts. Robert Gittings has pointed out
that the burden of the poem is much like that of two letters Keats

wrote late in life to Fanny Brawne, charging her conscience with his approaching death and blaming her for enjoying good health. "This," says Gittings, "marks the lowest depths of his disease-ridden repudiation of both love and poetry." (John Keats [Boston: Atlantic/ Little, Brown, 1968], p. 403.) To discuss: can a repudiation of poetry nevertheless be a good poem?

JOHN DONNE, Song (Go and catch a falling star), page 165

Maybe it is worth pointing out that, in bringing together short stanzas to make one longer one, Donne hasn't simply joined quatrain, couplet, and tercet like a man making up a freight train by coupling boxcars. In sense and syntax, each long stanza is all one; its units would be incomplete if they were separated.

RONALD GROSS, Yield, page 167

Fitting together drab and prosaic materials, Gross leaves them practically unaltered. What he lends them are patterns that seem meaningful. By combining traffic-sign messages in "Yield," he implies that the signs insistently pressure us with their yips and barks. "Yield" states its theme implicity: we are continually being ordered to conform, to give in, to go along with laws laid down for us. We must heed the signs in order to drive a car, but perhaps it is chilling to find their commands so starkly abstracted. Students might wish to discuss whether it is reading too much into the poem to suspect that this theme applies to other areas of our lives, not only to driving.

A discussion of Gross's work may be one of those rare sessions that end with the student's realization that to remove speech from its workaday contexts and to place it into lines is, after all, what most poets do. Many poems, not only found poems, reveal meanings by arranging familiar things into fresh orders.

MICHAEL DRAYTON, Since there's no help, come let us kiss and part, page 169

Nay, yea, wouldst, and mightst are the only words that couldn't equally well come out of the mouth of a lover in the twentieth century.

There seems to be an allegorical drama taking place, as Lawrence Perrine has pointed out in "A Drayton Sonnet," CEA Critic 25 (June 1963), p. 8. Love is also called Passion; and apparently his death is being urged along by the woman's infernal Innocence.

ELIZABETH BARRETT BROWNING, Grief, page 170

The octave may be forgettable, but the sestet is perhaps one of the eight or ten high moments in English sonnetry. "Grief" antedates the more famous Sonnets from the Portuguese (mostly composed in 1845 and 1846). In 1842, when working on "Grief" and some sonnet exercises, Mrs. Browning wrote to her friend Mary Mitford, "The Sonnet structure is a very fine one, however imperious, and I never would believe that our language is unqualified for the very strictest Italian form." But as Alethea Hayter has noticed, "Grief" isn't at all in the strictest Italian form; the shift in its argument comes in the middle of line 8. In her early sonnets, says Hayter, the poet seems to be "arranging roses now in a tall vase, now in a flat bowl, but always in something either just too tall or just too shallow." (Mrs. Browning [New York: Barnes & Noble, 1963].) Still, in gratitude for the sestet of "Grief," this reader can accept many awkward roses.

ARCHIBALD MacLEISH, The End of the World, page 171

What is the tone of this sonnet? Not at all grim, though the poet speaks of the most horrific event imaginable. Our pleasure in the poem comes from many other elements besides its subject: its sounds (including rimes), its rhythm (metrical lines of even length), its portrait of a circus frozen in a split second, and its colossal pun in the top blew off (top meaning the "big top" or circus tent, perhaps also the lid of the enormous pot of all Creation). Whose are the "black wings"? Nothingness's.

The octave, with its casual description of routine merriment, stands in contrast to the sestet, which strikes a note of awe. Perhaps the pale faces and dazed eyes of the circus spectators reflect the attitude of stunned wonder that the poet feels--or would have us feel. Obviously, to rearrange MacLeish's lines would be to weaken his poem. For one thing, the closing rimed couplet in the original throws great emphasis on the final nothing at all. In both sound and sense, a black pall / Of nothing, nothing, nothing-- nothing at all seems more powerful than canceled skies / Of nothing . . . In this sonnet, as in Shakespeare's sonnets, the concluding couplet firmly concludes.

ALEXANDER POPE, MARTIAL, SIR JOHN HARRINGTON, WILLIAM BLAKE, E. E. CUMMINGS, J. V. CUNNINGHAM, JOHN FREDERICK NIMS, KEITH WALDROP, a selection of epigrams, pages 172-173

Not all epigrams come in rimed couplets, as Keith Waldrop's epigram will show. Brevity is the essence of an epigram, whether closed or open in form, as is an arch tone and a final stroke of nastiness. (For more epigrams in open form see Ezra Pound's Personae.)

Besides writing what has been called the best epigram in English, Sir John Harrington has another claim to immortality: he invented the watercloset.

Cunningham, our living master of the verse epigram, has had few rivals lately; and instructors who wish further examples of this fixed form will find many to quote in his Collected Poems and Epigrams (Chicago: Swallow, 1971).

Closest rival to Cunningham, Nims has published a collection of his epigrams, Of Flesh and Bone (New Brunswick, N.J.: Rutgers, 1967), from which "Contemplation" is taken. When originally published in The New Yorker, it was called "A Thought for Tristram"--suggesting that you means Isolde, betrothed of King Mark, with whom Tristan/Tristram (in Gottfried von Strassbourg's medieval poem) shares a love potion.

It is a temptation to assign a class to write a few epigrams because, like haiku, epigrams are brief. Resist this temptation. Even from a bright class, the results are likely to be disappointing, unless students already possess some skill in metrical writing. A creative writing class might want to try epigrams after having written poems in some of the less demanding traditional forms: ballads, say, or sestinas. Besides mastering metrical skill, the successful epigram writer has to master that final rapier-thrust of nastiness.

DYLAN THOMAS, Do not go gentle into that good night, page 175

No mere trivial exercise (as a villanelle tends to be), Thomas's poem voices his distress at the decline and approaching death of his father. At the time, the elder Thomas was a semi-invalid, going blind, suffering from the effects of a tongue cancer. As a teacher of English at Swansea Grammar School, the poet's father had ruled his classroom with authority; but those who knew him only in his last years knew a different, humbled man. (See Constantine FitzGibbon, The Life of Dylan Thomas [Boston: Atlantic/Little, Brown, 1965], pp. 294-295.)

Like many other Thomas poems, this one contains serious puns: good night, grave. "Another assumption in this poem," says Amy Mulvahill (in a student paper written at Tufts), "may be Thomas's own self-destructive drive that led him to drink himself to death. It's possible that he preferred to taunt death with his boisterous life--to go down unrepentant and brawling."

Repetitious as a villanelle is, the form suits this poem, making its refrains sound like prayers said over and over. If you have any student poets, they might be challenged to write villanelles of their own. The hard part is to make the repeated lines occur naturally, to make them happen in places where there is something to be said. But the repetitious form is helpful. Write the two refrain-lines and already your labors are eight-nineteenths over.

For another instance of Thomas's fondness for demanding, arbitrary forms, see the poem "Prologue," at the beginning of Daniel Jones's edition of The Poems of Dylan Thomas (New York: New

Directions, 1971). A poem of 102 lines, its first and last lines
rime with each other, as do lines 2 and 101, 3 and 100, 4 and 99,
and so on, until two riming lines collide in the poem's exact
center. Except for that inmost pair of lines, no reader is likely
to notice the elaborate rime scheme since rimes so far apart can't
be heard; but apparently it supplied the poet with obstacles to
overcome and with a gamelike pleasure.

OPEN FORM

WALT WHITMAN, Coffin that passes through lanes and streets, page 178

     In this quotation from "When Lilacs Last in the Dooryard
Bloom'd," the device of the word repeated at the beginning of each
line is echoed by Allen Ginsberg in Howl. "I depended," Ginsberg
has said, "on the word 'who' to keep the beat, a base to keep
measure, return to and take off from again onto another streak of
invention." (The New American Poetry, edited by Donald M. Allen
[New York: Grove Press, 1960], p. 415.) Such a repetition is a
kind of meter.
     For further use of this device, see Psalms 29:3-9 and 109 in
the Bible, King James Version.
     Roger Mitchell has discussed the stress pattern of this passage
in "A Prosody for Whitman?" (PMLA, 84 [October 1969], pp. 1606-1612.)
     Late in life, Whitman made a revealing comment to W. R. Thayer:
"Of course my poetry isn't formless. Nobody could write in my way
unless he had the melody singing in his ears. I don't often contrive to catch the best musical combination nowadays; but in the
older pieces I always had a tune before I began to write." ("Personal Recollections of Walt Whitman," Scribner's 65 [June 1919],
p. 682.)

E. E. CUMMINGS, Buffalo Bill's, page 180

     Cleanth Brooks and Robert Penn Warren have taken this poem to
be an admiring tribute to William Cody (Understanding Poetry, 3rd
ed. [New York: Holt, Rinehart and Winston, 1960]). But Louis J.
Budd, in an interesting dissent, thinks Cummings is satirizing the
theatricality of the old sideshow straight-shooter and finds Mister
Death "a cosmic corporal gathering up defunct tin-gods and stuffed
effigies." (The Explicator, 11 [June 1953], no. 8, item 55.)

EMILY DICKINSON, Victory comes late, page 181

     Of all Emily Dickinson's poems, this is the most formally open;
and as a result it sounds almost contemporary. Clearly the poet is
in charge of her open form, for each line-break comes after a word
that (being essential to meaning) easily stands for the special
emphasis. We could imagine a few other possible locations for line-

breaks. (After <u>Love</u> in the last line?--or would that make the poem
seem to end in a riming couplet?) But no doubt the poet knew her
own mind.

Dickinson's outsized hyphens (or delicate minidashes) usually
seem to indicate pauses, little hesitations, as if to give a word
or phrase (whether following the dash or preceding it) special
emphasis.

If there is time to work further with this splendid poem, both
language and meaning deserve a deeper look. Note the pun in line 3:
<u>rapt</u> for "wrapped." In the next-to-last line, <u>keep</u> seems a sub-
junctive verb: the statement may be a prayer. What sort of "Victory" does the poet mean? Thomas H. Johnson thought she refers to
a Civil War battle, but I think this is one of her several poems
concerned with reputation and fame. Perhaps the sparrows are minor
poets, like Dickinson, unprinted and unacclaimed. Perhaps the
Eagle is a famous bard glutted with renown: Ralph Waldo Emerson,
maybe. The conclusion seems a bitter acceptance, as if to say:
"God is wise not to feed me too generously." (Compare Kafka's
story "The Hunger Artist"--certainly an analogy.) Ironically, the
poem today seems literally true: Dickinson's victory has indeed
come, although she cannot taste it.

ROBERT HERRICK, Upon a Child That Died, page 181

SAINT GERAUD (BILL KNOTT), Poem "The only response," page 181

Knott's poem seems one in which freedom from artifice helps
what is said: a direct, seemingly casual (and yet playful) statement of grief. Herrick's metrically regular lines make his poem
a kind of small, carefully crafted funeral urn of words. Its steady
rhythms almost have the effect of a posthumous lullaby for the
child.

WILLIAM CARLOS WILLIAMS, The Dance, page 182

Scanned, the poem is seen to abound in pairs of unstressed
syllables. The result is a bouncing rhythm--anapestic or dactylic,
depending on where one wishes to slice the lines into feet. This
rhythm seems appropriate to a description of frolicking dancers and
helps establish the tone of the poem, which is light, however serious.

Williams severs his units of sense again and again in midphrase:
placing his line-breaks after <u>and</u>, <u>the</u>, <u>about</u>, <u>thick-</u>, <u>those</u>, <u>such</u>.
In this poem run-on lines predominate, and this is not only a tech-
nical device but a way of underlining the poem's meaning. Williams
conveys a sense of continuous movement in a syntax that keeps over-
flowing line units.

By repeating its opening line, the poem, like Breughel's dancers, comes round in a circle to where it began. Another metaphor
is possible: like a painting enclosed in a frame, the poem encloses
its central scene in a frame of words.

183-185 (text pages)

STEPHEN CRANE, The Heart, page 183

WALT WHITMAN, Cavalry Crossing a Ford, page 183

Two nineteenth-century American poems, the pair seem comparable mainly in brevity and use of narration. The assonance and internal alliteration in Whitman's phrase silvery river are echoed in the poem's very opening line: the assonance of the i-sound in line, wind, islands; the internal alliteration of the r in array, where, green. But any line of this short poem will repay such inspection. Crane's "The Heart" is obviously less heavy on verbal music, although line 4 (Held his heart in his hands) is heavily alliterative; and the second stanza favors the letter b. There is rime, too: it / bitter, bitter / heart.

Whitman seems to lambaste his poem with sound-effects in his enthusiasm for his grand military spectacle. Crane cares for music, too, and yet his is a subtler, harsher one. Although longer in words, Whitman's "Cavalry" contains fewer pauses than "The Heart" (fifteen compared to Crane's eighteen, if every comma and line-end counts as a pause). The result is, in Crane's poem, a much more hesitant, start-and-stop movement--appropriate, perhaps, to a study of self-immolation. Whitman apparently wants an expansive, continuous progress in his syntax, as in his cavalry.

GARY GILDNER, First Practice, page 184

Some possible answers to the questions:

1. Hill is a sadist. He is determined to render defenseless boys as bitter as he is.
2. The speaker doesn't want to identify himself with such a world view; apparently, he wishes to remove it from himself by thrusting the hideous Hill away off in the third person.
3. The broken line indicates a pause--while the boy athletes suck in their breaths and don't dare answer.
4. Closure.
5. The rewrite would make Gildner's appalling poem seem neat, swingy, and jingly.
6. Poems don't have to traffic in moonlight and roses. Nothing in human experience need be alien to them--not even Hill.

LEONARD COHEN, All There Is To Know about Adolph Eichmann, page 185

Like a "found poem," Cohen's list of the mass murderer's characteristics seems to take a preexisting structure (in this case, an application blank or a police blotter form); the poet has gone on to complete it. Read aloud, the lines ending in Medium and Ten sound as though rimed; and None / Ten is an off-rime. One way to state Cohen's theme: even a mass murderer is human, like you, like me. He does not walk around with a sign on him, like a movie vampire.

And by implication, perhaps, there is an element of evil in every
human being. Let us not wax smug, or dismiss genocide as the invention of Hollywood.

BRUCE GUERNSEY, Louis B. Russell, page 186

   Like a sonnet, a formally open poem may have a clear-cut structure, as "Louis B. Russell" demonstrates. Each stanza is a sentence
in itself, closely similar in length. In the first two, Russell
recalls his past; in the third, he takes in the present moment and
looks forward to the day to come. In the second stanza, besides, he
identifies himself with the seventeen-year-old whose heart he has received. Guernsey, incidentally, professed surprise when it was
pointed out that his poem falls into three parts! But a poet does
not need to select a structure consciously in order to fulfill it.
   Having a new heart makes Russell feel like a young sprinter.
In the metaphor-laden last stanza, heartbeat is juxtaposed with the
clock's ticking and (more startlingly) with the beat of tightly
held hammers. The tone of this poem is richly complicated. What
does the central character feel? An elation mingled with wistful
loneliness and perhaps, in the middle stanza, a certain guilty
dread.
   In question 3, the opinion seems too literal-minded and too
rigidly bound by rules. The movement of this poem seems already
strong; a regular heartbeat would seem unlikely to improve it.
   "Louis B. Russell" is from the manuscript of Guernsey's forth-
coming collection January Thaw (University of Pittsburgh Press,
1982).

FOR REVIEW AND FURTHER STUDY

LEIGH HUNT, Rondeau, page 187

   Jenny (so the story goes) was Jane (Mrs. Thomas) Carlyle, who
gave Hunt a buss when he brought word that one of Carlyle's books
had been accepted by a publisher.
   A true French rondeau has fifteen lines, and follows rules
more ingenious than those Hunt set for himself. For specifications,
see Lewis Turco, A Book of Forms (New York: Dutton, 1968).

STEVIE SMITH, I Remember, page 187

   This poem keeps pulling rugs out from under us. From its
opening, we might expect some rollicking, roughly metrical ballad
or song, but then the short fourth line draws us up with a jolt.
Any reader still hoping for a conventional ballad might say line 4
rimes at least. However, the passage introducing the bombers
(lines 5-8) shatters any such anticipation. Far from songlike,

these prosaic lines sprawl, end in far-out feminine rimes (overhead and Hampstead, perversely and Germany), and bring to mind the artful outrages of Ogden Nash. With the bride's question, the poem un-expectedly returns to medium–length lines, and the rime that clicks it shut (collide, bride) is masculine and exact once more. Though full of surprises, this poem has less anarchy than order in it.

As its playful form indicates, "I Remember" is supposed to be fun, yet at the same time it seems awful and ominous. John Simon has made some provocative remarks about it in "The Poems of Stevie Smith," Canto 1 (Spring 1977), pp. 197-198:

> This, you might well say, is poetry of low intensity or, simply, minor poetry. And yet, and yet! Why should a young girl marry an old man of 73? Because she is dying of consumption, and because it is wartime. The younger men are off to war, and may never come back. Even the old bridegroom and the tubercular bride may not live out their short remaining terms: the bombs may kill them first. The two of them may even desire such an ending; they have re-fused the relative safety of an air-raid shelter. . . . Are there perversely preposterous collisions in the sky? Can there be between our own so unalike selves so unlikely a collision, explosion, orgasm? . . . "I do not think it has ever happened," he said. Still, he must have hoped that it might.

Stevie Smith's quiet, semireclusive life with her elderly aunt in Palmers Green, North London, is the subject of a fine, sensitive (but uneventful) film, Stevie, with Glenda Jackson playing the poet, generally released in the U.S. in 1981. The Collected Poems of Stevie Smith (New York: Oxford, 1976) is the best edition. Many of the poems are illustrated with Stevie Smith's sophisticatedly crude, somewhat macabre cartoons.

THOMAS HARDY, At a Hasty Wedding, page 188

A question to help students in summing up Hardy's theme: does the poet really think that hours are years, that eastern stars never wheel westward, that ashes don't follow after fire? (Of course not.)

GEOFFREY CHAUCER, Your ÿen two wol slee me sodenly, page 189

It can be great fun for students to learn (well, more or less) how to pronounce Chaucer's English, provided one has the time and strength to help them make the attempt. One does much better by Chaucer's lines if one puts on an Irish brogue. (A couple of Guinness' stouts before class usually help.)

Some scholars doubt that Chaucer himself wrote this poem; but if he did not, someone who thoroughly knew Chaucer's work probably did.

"Since I escaped from love, I've grown so fat . . ." is, of course, a crude modernization of another poem from the "Merciles Beaute" series. Carlos Baker offers another modern American version of it in his book of poems, A Year and a Day (Nashville: Vanderbilt University Press, 1963).

Any student who successfully completes a roundel beginning with the suggested lines, "Your eyes present a pin to my balloon . . ." is invited to send it to XJK. An appropriate prize will be sent by return mail. Address: 4 Fern Way, Bedford, MA 01730.

WALLACE STEVENS, Thirteen Ways of Looking at a Blackbird, page 189

Suggestive as blackbirds may be, the theme of the poem is, "Pay attention to physical reality." Stevens chides the thin, ascetic men of Haddam who would ignore good blackbirds and actual women for golden phantasms. He also chides that asinine aristocrat who rides about Connecticut (of all places) in a class coach as if thinking himself Prince Charming. The poem ends in a section whose tone is matter-of-fact flatness, rather as though Stevens were saying, "Well, here's the way the world is; if you don't like it, go read newspapers." Taken as a series of notes for an argument for literalism, this much-discussed poem seems to have unity and to lead to a definite conclusion. For another (and more complicated) view of it, see Helen Hennessy Vendler, On Extended Wings (Cambridge, Mass.: Harvard University Press, 1969).

Way-of-looking number five recalls Keats's "Grecian Urn": "Heard melodies are sweet. . . ."

Way number ten eludes final paraphrase. Are the "bawds of euphony" supposed to be, perhaps, crass ex-poets who have sold out their Muses, who utter music to please the box office instead of truth? But blackbirds flying in a green light are so strikingly beautiful that even those dull bawds would be moved to exclaim at the sight of them.

Exercise: Seeing the Logic of Open Form Verse, page 191

E. E. CUMMINGS, in Just-, page 192

MYRA COHN LIVINGSTON, Driving, page 192

DONALD FINKEL, Gesture, Page 193

CHARLES OLSON, La Chute, page 193

Cummings's poem is one of his "Chansons Innocentes," little songs for children. In it, however, we meet a poet familiar with the classics and who naturally associates spring with goat-footed Pan. In Greek mythology, the god's pipes heralded the return of Persephone, and caused birds and beasts to start up at his call. In Cummings's view, he seems a kind of Pied Piper who brings children running.

Line-breaks and capital letters in the poem seem designed to emphasize particulars. Just-spring, capitalized, is the name of a holiday: the moment when spring begins. Dividing its name with a line-break gives it more importance, perhaps; and mud- / luscious similarly takes emphasis. Why are the children's names telescoped (eddieandbill, bettyandisbel)? So that these names will be spoken rapidly, pell-mell, the way their owners run and the way children speak about their friends. And when the lame balloonman completes his transformation into Pan, the word goat-footed is framed with white space on a line by itself. Except by putting it in capitals, the poet could hardly have thrown more weight on it.

Both "Driving" and "Gesture" describe motions. Both arrange lines so that the reader's eyes, following along, have to make movements similar to those being described. Myra Cohn Livingston, a California poet, tries to convey the pleasure of driving at top speed over freeways, moving out of a lane, passing, dropping back into a lane again. Students' attention may be directed to her three riming tercets (roadway / speedway / freeway; gray car / red car / blue car; one lane / two lane / three lane). If the path of the imaginary car (seen from overhead) were drawn on a map, it might look roughly like the poem on the page, whose second tercet (8-10) veers left as if to overtake and pass. The long straight final line conveys, I think, the continuing pleasure of driving on and on. Donald Finkel's poem centers on a playful metaphor: poet presenting poem to reader is like someone cracking a whip. Indentations in lines 6-9 roughly depict the whip's path in uncoiling. Then the eye-arresting block of type--

    snaps
    softly

--brings the reader's eyes to a momentary halt, suggesting the sudden crack of the whip. There is a small pause before whip straightens and poem goes on to end. Livingston and Finkel both contrive poems that need to be seen in print to be fully appreciated.

Charles Olson's "La Chute," like "in Just-," can be effective even if merely heard aloud. So many times repeated, the words drum and lute acquire impressive emphasis; and by repeating phrases and hesitating (who / will bring it up, my lute / who will bring it up where it fell), Olson makes his poem sound unrehearsed and conversational. White space seems used somewhat cryptically and arbitrarily, but it does throw great weight on my lute (line 7) and They (line 10), essential words that can take the emphasis. What is the poem saying? I take it to be (like "Gesture") a poem about poetry, with lute and drum representing the poet's talents. Well aware that he was the forefather of a poetic school (the Black Mountain poets), Olson may have foreseen his death and wondered who would carry on his work for him.

11

POEMS FOR THE EYE

For more examples of graphic poetry, consult the anthologies
edited by Solt, Klonsky, and Kostelanetz (all cited in footnotes to
this chapter). Other useful anthologies include Emmett Williams's
Anthology of Concrete Poetry (New York: Something Else, 1967),
Eugene Wildman's Chicago Review Anthology of Concretism (Chicago:
Chicago Review, 1967), and Emmett Williams's selection of "Language
Happenings" in Open Poetry: Four Anthologies of Expanded Poems,
edited by Ronald Gross and George Quasha (New York: Simon & Schuster, 1973).

GEORGE HERBERT, Easter Wings, page 194

JOHN HOLLANDER, Swan and shadow, page 196

The tradition of the shaped poem, or Carmen figuratum, seems to
have begun in Renaissance Italy, and the form flourished throughout
Western Europe in the seventeenth century. English practitioners
of the form, besides Herbert, included Robert Herrick (in "The
Pillar of Fame") and George Puttenham.
On "Easter Wings," Joan Bennett has remarked, "The shape of the
wings on the page may have nothing but ingenuity to recommend it,
but the diminuendo and crescendo that bring it about are expressive
both of the rise and fall of the lark's song and flight (Herbert's
image) and also of the fall of man and his resurrection in Christ
(the subject that the image represents)." (Quoted by F. E. Hutchinson in his edition of Herbert's Works [Oxford: Oxford University
Press, 1941].) Visual shape and verbal meaning coincide strikingly
when the second stanza dwindles to Most thin.
Like Herbert, Hollander clearly assumes that a word-shape has
to have a meaningful relation to what is said in it. His reflected
swan is one of twenty-five shaped poems collected in Types of Shape
(New York: Atheneum, 1969). Other graphic poems in the book include a car key, a goblet, a beach umbrella, an Eskimo Pie, and the
outline of New York State. Paul Fussell, Jr., discussing "Easter
Wings" and Hollander's shaped poems, expresses reservations about
this kind of poetry. Most shaped poems, he finds, are directed more
to eyes than ears--"or better, we feel that the two dimensions are
not married: one is simply in command of the other." But the
greatest limitation in the genre is that there are few objects that
shaped poems can effectively represent: "their shapes can reflect

75

196-200 (text pages)

the silhouettes of wings, bottles, hourglasses, and altars, but
where do we go from there?" (Poetic Meter and Poetic Form [New
York: Random House, 1965], pp. 185-187.) Students might be told
of Fussell's view and be asked to comment. A further disadvantage
of most shaped poetry is that it cannot be heard aloud without loss.

E. E. CUMMINGS, r-p-o-p-h-e-s-s-a-g-r, page 197

Cummings's poem is like a jigsaw puzzle to be put together, but
I confess I have trouble doing it without having a few words left
over, or else wishing for a few more words. Students may enjoy dis-
puting one another's unscrambled versions. The center of the syntax,
I think, is the word leaps. Whatever the word order, the sense seems
to be: the grasshopper, now gathering himself for a leap (grown
larger into a PPEGORHRASS, in capital letters), leaps as we look up,
and arrives to become a grasshopper. The lovely coined adverb
rearrangingly suggests how he collects himself together again when
he alights.

WILLIAM BLAKE, A Poison Tree, page 198

Reproduced in approximately the same size as the original,
Blake's engraving first appeared in his Songs of Experience (1794).
According to the poet, he had long sought the best method for presenting his poems. At last it was revealed to him by his dead
brother Robert in a dream. He was to engrave both poem and design
on a copper plate and, when the pages were printed, outlines would
be filled in with watercolors. Each copy would be a bit different
from every other. Many editions of Blake's poems and drawings show
this method. An inexpensive color facsimile of the first edition
of Songs of Innocence has been issued by Dover Publications (New
York, 1971).
"A Poison Tree" seems one of Blake's more fortunate marriages
of visual art with poetry. His illustration for his celebrated
"Tyger" (page 292), also from the Songs of Experience, shows a
beast much less formidable than the one we imagine from the words
alone. A topic for discussion or writing: should poetry be illustrated? or should a poem be left to the eye of the mind?

REINHARD DÖHL, A concrete poem, page 200

Döhl's famous apfel with the wurm at its center shouldn't pose
any problems for the student translator. To decide whether to call
it a poem, however, raises the everlasting question: what is
poetry?
This might well be the moment to turn to Chapter 17 ("What Is
Poetry?"), cite a few definitions of a poem, and invite students to
wrestle with the question for themselves. If a poem is said to be
passionate thought concisely expressed in memorable language usually

(but not always) embodying rhythm, imagery, and metaphor, then
Döhl's apple isn't a poem. It contains neither thought nor passion;
it simply depicts, without metaphor. Perhaps, in a sense, the repetition of apfel apfel apfel extablishes a kind of rhythm to the eye,
but surely the experience of beholding this graphic object is no
more rhythmic than that of seeing a dozen eggs arranged in an open
egg carton. In any case, a perceptible beat or pulsation is not the
sort of rhythm we find in verbal poetry. This apple doesn't contain
an image; it is an image, but not in the same sense as that of an
"image" in poetry. In only one way does it seem to work like a
poem: with a small shock of immediate pleasure, it communicates
something that we recognize.

EDWIN MORGAN, Siesta of a Hungarian Snake, page 201

    While too much can be made of this work, evidently it has
sound values as well as eye appeal. Some brave volunteer might
read it aloud. The initial sz sounds like the word Siesta. Perhaps the artist reverses the letters S and Z to make his line sound
more like a snore (inhale: SZ--exhale: ZS). SZ looks and sounds
like the end of an Eastern European name; perhaps that is why the
snake is Hungarian.
    Why the alternation of large and small letters? To look like
stripes in the middle of the snake at his fattest part.
    If a poem by definition is made of words, it may be questioned
whether this concrete poem may be called a poem.

RICHARD KOSTELANETZ, Disintegration, page 202

    The method of Kostelanetz is apparently to regard a word as a
thing and to have its meaning befall it. Let students suggest a
different word that might be turned into a similar one-word concrete
poem.
    Alternate suggestion: try making a concrete poem (perhaps
drawing it on the blackboard) out of any one of the following words:
explosion, revolution, interruption, repetition, diminution,
exaggeration, conglomeration.

DORTHI CHARLES, Concrete Cat, page 203

    This trifle first appeared in the second edition of An Intro-
duction to Poetry and has been retained out of loyalty to the past.
While hunting for an illustration of the sillier kind of concrete
poem that simply and unfeelingly arranges words like so many Lincoln
logs, I found the very thing in one of William Cole's anthologies
of humorous poetry: "Concrete Poem" by the British wit Anthony
Mundy. Mundy's work repeats miniskirt several times in the form of
a miniskirt, and tacks on a couple of leglegleglegs. No doubt
he was parodying concrete poetry, too. But the cheapskate in me

203 (text page)

rebelled at the thought of paying for permission to reprint such a
simple doodad, so I decided to cut and paste together a homemade
specimen. While constructing the cat, I started having some fun
with it, making the tongue a U, and so on. As far as I know, however, the pun in the cat's middle stripe (tripes) is the only place
where language aspires toward poetry and becomes figurative.

12

SYMBOL

T. S. ELIOT, The Boston Evening Transcript, page 205

To help a class see the humor of Eliot's poem, try reading it
aloud and pronouncing the name of the newspaper slowly and deliberately, in the dullest tones you can muster. This small gem can
serve effectively to introduce an early, longer Eliot poem of
spiritual desolation, "The Love Song of J. Alfred Prufrock" (page
310).

EMILY DICKINSON, The Lightning is a yellow Fork, page 206

Perhaps the poet would have added more punctuation to this poem
had she worked longer on it; a rough penciled draft is its only surviving manuscript. Students may ask, isn't the fork a symbol? No,
it is the other half of a metaphor: what the lightning is like.
The lightning (like most literary symbols) is a physical thing or
event, reportedly seen. The Apparatus of the Dark (neither fork nor
lightning) is whatever dimly glimpsed furniture this cosmic house
may hold. The fork seems too simple an instrument to deserve the
name of Apparatus. The lightning is doing the revealing, not itself being revealed.

THOMAS HARDY, Neutral Tones, page 208

Students usually like to sort out the poem's white, gray,
washed-out and ashy things. Can anyone think of a more awful description of a smile than that in lines 9-10? The God in line 2
seems angry and awe-inspiring, like the one in "Channel Firing"
(page 322). He has chided or reproved the sun, and caused it to
turn pale in fear (like a schoolboy before a stern headmaster).
Line 8 is a stickler. In Hardy's first draft it read, "On
which was more wrecked by our love." Both versions of the line
seem awkward, and the present version is obscure, but probably the
sense of this and the previous line goes: we exchanged a few words
about the question, which one of us had lost (suffered) the more by
our love affair? (That is, after which we should mentally insert
"of the two of us.")
For speculation about the facts behind "Neutral Tones," see
Robert Gittings's fine biography Young Thomas Hardy (Boston:

Little, Brown, 1975), pp. 86-93. Much has been guessed about the possible love affair between young Hardy and his cousin Tryphena Sparks; but if the woman in "Neutral Tones" was indeed real, no one has identified her for sure.

Similar in imagery to "Neutral Tones" is this horrific line from Hardy's novel The Woodlanders, Chapter 4, when a poverty-stricken woman, Marty South, sees her last hopes expire: "The bleared white visage of a sunless winter day emerged like a dead-born child." (Cited by F. B. Pinion in A Commentary on the Poems of Thomas Hardy, New York: Barnes & Noble, 1977.)

GEORGE HERBERT, Redemption, page 210

The old burdensome lease that the speaker longs to cancel is original sin, which Christ, by his sacrifice (lines 12-14) allows mankind to throw off. Who is the speaker? Humanity--or perhaps (like Bunyan's Pilgrim) an individual soul in search of salvation.

What figure of speech is a ragged noise? (It's like the blue uncertain stumbling buzz of the Emily Dickinson poem discussed below.)

SIR PHILIP SIDNEY, You that with allegory's curious frame, page 211

This sonnet seems a classic expression of a poet's resentment toward readers and critics who read needlessly profound meanings into his lines--a valuable warning for students to heed when studying symbolism.

The second line may refer to a traditional folk belief. Like an evil fairy, the hunter after allegory spirits away a natural child and leaves a changeling--an odd, ill-favored, supernatural brat--in its place.

For another poem from Sidney's sonnet sequence "Astrophel and Stella" (1591), see "Now that of absence, the most irksome night" (page 367). Both poems suggest that poets, even while professing love, may be conscious of their art.

EMILY DICKINSON, I heard a fly buzz-when I died, page 211

Plump with suggestions, this celebrated fly well demonstrates a symbol's indefiniteness. The fly appears in the room--on time, like the Angel of Death--and yet it is decidedly ordinary. A final visitor from the natural world, it brings to mind an assortment of suggestions, some offensive (filth, stenches, rotting meat, offal, and so forth). But a natural fly is a minor annoyance; and so is death, if one is certain of Eternity. Unsure and hesitant in its flight, the fly buzzes as though faltering. It is another failing thing, like the light that comes through the windows and through the eyes (which are, as a trite phrase calls them, "the windows of the soul"). For other transferred epithets (like blue uncertain

stumbling buzz), see page 93 of the text, in the chapter on figures
of speech.

Most students will easily identify Eyes around as those of sur-
rounding friends or relatives, and that last Onset as death throes.
Is the King Death or Jesus? It seems more likely that the friends
and relatives will behold death. What is the speaker's assignable
portion? Physical things: keepsakes bequeathed to friends and
relatives; body, to the earth.

Discussion will probably focus on the final line. It may help
students to remember that the speaker is, at the present moment of
the poem, in Eternity. The scene she describes is therefore a vision
within a vision. Perhaps all the last line means is (as John Ciardi
has argued), "And then there was no more of me, and nothing to see
with." But to me the last line suddenly thrusts the speaker to
Heaven. For one terrible moment she finds herself, with immortal
eyes, looking back through her mortal eyes at a blackness where
there used to be light.

PHILIP DOW, Drunk Last Night with Friends, I Go To Work Anyway,
page 212

Dow's bottled snail seems a hintful symbol. Surrounded not
only by its shell but also by dreams (and its wine bottle), this
particular mollusk is well insulated. Lazily vegetating, it reminds
us of the speaker himself: helpless and stationary among the weeds,
relieved of his duties, feeling unreal, and wrapped in his half-
painful, half-comfortable hangover. He too feels small, sleepy,
slimy, and stuck fast. Moreover, snail and bottle seem one. Dis-
carded and empty, the bottle has come to hold something little and
exquisite. That it is old recalls the boss who apparently still
dreams of strange dolls from his hard-drinking past. Some may read
this richly imaged poem by the light of experience: remembering the
sensations of waking up with a throat like the throat of a wine
bottle with a snail in it. In Dow's poem, the snail would appear
to be a vision, an epiphany. Incidentally, the poet has mentioned
snails in a note on himself written for an anthology: "Although I
burn to know how the artist does it, poems remain miraculous to me
as snails, ineluctable as the iron flute. . . . I write to cele-
brate." (Quickly Aging Here, edited by Geof Hewitt [New York:
Anchor Books, 1969].)

"Drunk Last Night with Friends" appears in Dow's extremely
good collection Paying Back the Sea (Pittsburgh: Carnegie-Mellon
University Press, 1979). Born in Santa Fe, the poet now lives in
the Napa Valley of California.

212-213 (text pages)

"Night Crow" and "Anecdote of the Jar" contain central symbols; "Poem" and "A Burnt Ship" are to be taken literally. (Apparently Donne is just delighting in the three paradoxes in his last two lines.)

Students familiar with Stevens sometimes reason, "The jar is a thing of the imagination, that's why it's superior to the wilderness--it makes order out of formless nature, the way Stevens thinks art is supposed to do." But Stevens is constantly warning us of the dangers of mind divorced from the physical world, and I think he means this gray, bare, dominion-taking jar to be ominous. Who could think a wilderness slovenly before it came along? Some critics take the phrase of a port in air to mean a portal, "an evanescent entry . . . to order in a scene of disorder." (Ronald Sukenick, Wallace Stevens: Musing the Obscure [New York: New York University Press, 1967].) I read it differently: portly, imposing, pompous. Although it is true that Stevens frequently raises the same philosophic or aesthetic questions, from poem to poem he keeps supplying very different answers. See the brilliant essay on Stevens by J. Hillis Miller in Poets of Reality (Cambridge, Mass.: Harvard University Press, 1965).

13

MYTH

Besides the poems in this chapter, other poems in the text will readily lend themselves to the study of myth and its pervasiveness in poetry.

As an instance of personal myth, Constance Urdang's "The Miracle-Factory" (page 26) is an especially witty contemporary example. Other personal myths may be found in the poems of Blake; in Hardy's "Convergence of the Twain" (page 323); and in certain poems of Yeats outside this chapter, such as "Leda and the Swan" (page 133) and "Sailing to Byzantium" (page 260).

Poems containing central references to familiar classical myths are Cummings's "in Just-" (page 192), with its reincarnation of the Great God Pan; Mark Alexander Boyd's "Cupid and Venus" (page 293); and Allen Ginsberg's "A Supermarket in California" (page 320). The Christian mythos is of course inseparable from the devotional poems of Donne and Herbert; from Hopkins's poems and G. K. Chesterton's "The Donkey" (page 298); from Eliot's "Journey of the Magi" (page 309) and Yeats's "The Magi" (page 396); from Paul Zimmer's "The Day Zimmer Lost Religion" (page 19); from Milton's sonnets; from the hymns of Toplady and Cowper; and from many more.

In this chapter, Thomas Hardy (in "The Oxen") and William Wordsworth (in "The World Is Too Much with Us") sadly contemplate myths in decline--a theme found also in Philip Larkin's "Vers de Société" (page 338) and William Stafford's "At the Klamath Berry Festival" (page 372).

D. H. LAWRENCE, Bavarian Gentians, page 216

Written in 1929 when Lawrence was ill and nearing death, this splendid poem has been read as a kind of testament. As Keith Sagar has paraphrased it, "the poet's soul has been invited to the nuptials and accepts with joy." Dissolution offers not mere oblivion but the promise of renewed life, the cyclical rebirth of both the gentians and Persephone. (The Art of D. H. Lawrence [Cambridge, Eng.: Cambridge University Press, 1966], pp. 244-245.) Another famous poem of Lawrence's last months, "The Ship of Death," may be read as a companion to this.

Why is "Bavarian Gentians" a better title for the poem than Lawrence's first thought, "Glory of Darkness"?

217-219 (text pages)

THOMAS HARDY, The Oxen, page 217

The legend that farm animals kneel on Christmas Eve is widespread in Western Europe. Hardy takes it to suggest the entire Christian mythos, which "in these years" (since Darwin) few embrace as did the "flock" of children and old people remembered in the opening stanza. The gloom in line 15 may resemble the gloom of the unbeliever, and its doleful sound is enforced by its riming with coomb—like barton, a word from older rural speech.

The tone of "The Oxen" is not hostility toward faith, but wistfulness. Not exactly the village atheist Chesterton said he was, Hardy in late life kept going to church and hoping for a reconciliation between the Church of England and science-minded rationalists.

WILLIAM WORDSWORTH, The World Is Too Much with Us, page 218

As its sense and its iambic meter indicate, the opening line calls for a full stress on the with.

Wordsworth isn't arguing, of course, for a return to pagan nature-worship. Rather like Gerard Manley Hopkins blasting trade in "God's Grandeur" (page 134), he is dismayed that Christians, given to business and banking, have lost sight of sea and vernal woods. They should pay less heed to the world, more to the earth. What "powers" have they laid waste? The ability to open themselves to nature's benevolent inspirations. Modestly, the poet includes himself in the us who deserve reproof. The impatient outburst ("Great God!") is startlingly unbookish and locates the break in sense between octave and sestet in an unconventional place.

Compare Wordsworth's "Composed upon Westminster Bridge" (page 390) for a somewhat similar theme. For another comment on the decline of certain traditional myths, see William Stafford's "At the Klamath Berry Festival" (page 372).

WILLIAM BUTLER YEATS, The Second Coming, page 219

The brief discussion in the book leaves several points untouched. Students may be asked to explain Yeats's opening image of the falcon and the falconer; to discuss the meaning of the blood-dimmed tide and the ceremony of innocence; to explain how the rocking cradle at Bethlehem can be said to "vex" twenty centuries to nightmare; and to recall what they know about the sphinx.

In A Vision, Yeats sets forth his notion of the two eras of history (old and new) as two intertwined conelike gyres, revolving inside each other in opposing directions. He put it succinctly in a note for a limited edition of his poem Michael Robartes and the Dancer (1921):

> The end of an age, which always receives the revelation
> of the character of the next age, is represented by the coming
> of one gyre to its place of greatest expansion and of the

84

other to that of its greatest contraction. At the present
moment the life gyre is sweeping outward, unlike that before
the birth of Christ which was narrowing, and has almost
reached it greatest expansion. The revelation which approaches will however take its character from the contrary
movement of the interior gyre.

Students can be asked to apply this explanation to "The Second
Coming." (In fact, this might be a writing assignment.)
    For other evidence of Yeats's personal mythology, direct stu-
dents to "Leda and the Swan" (page 133) and "Sailing to Byzantium"
(page 260). For alternative versions of "The Second Coming," see
Yeats's worksheets for the poem as transcribed by Jon Stallworthy
in Between the Lines: Yeats's Poetry in the Making (Oxford: Oxford
University Press, 1963).

BARRY SPACKS, Teaching the Penguins to Fly, page 220

    Spacks's mythmaking originates in a charming detail, his
daughter's early (and unrelinquished) desire to teach penguins to
fly. The mythseeking eye in the poem is surely the poet's. He
imagines the penguins as a fallen race, descended from legendary
ancestors who could fly, and his daughter as their potential libera-
tor who will accomplish the impossible, teach them to fly once again,
and rise to mythic heights in penguin history.
    Mentions of the Beatles, Aquarius, and the Movement all point
to a parallel between the daughter's ambition (a bit grandiose,
after all) and the shining ideals of the sixties and early seventies, the Age of Aquarius, when the young were the teachers and
everything good seemed possible of attainment. Seen in retrospect,
the poet hints, the noble efforts of the sixties radicals were from
the start as futile as those of his daughter in respect to the penguins. Yet, like the now aging radicals, the daughter can't quite
give up her old affection for so grand a mission. The Movement was
crazy, the poem seems to say, but how glorious if it had all succeeded. It would have been the stuff of myth.

JOHN KEATS, La Belle Dame sans Merci, page 223

    Popular legends of men who foolishly kiss strange, alluring
ladies only to fall under baleful spells have been told since the
Middle Ages, if not before. In Scotland, the story of the poet
Thomas of Erceldoune, whisked away to Elfland by the sinister Fairy
Queen, became the Child ballad "Thomas the Rimer," which Keats may
have known.
    Keats's ballad has often been read as an allegory in which the
merciless lady is Poetry, but if she is Keats's Muse, she seems un-
characteristically grim and misleading. The luckless Knight receives only escape for his reward and his sad awakening finds him
older, like Rip Van Winkle. Robert Giddings has argued that the

poem marks a crucial turning in the poet's attitude toward love.
In earlier work, Keats had seen love and death as opposites; in the
figure of La Belle Dame they become one. See <u>John Keats</u> (Boston:
Atlantic/Little, Brown, 1968), pp. 300-302.

Among other <u>dames sans merci</u>, perhaps the most rewarding to
compare is another lady of ballad fame, "Bonny Barbara Allan"
(page 110). The latter, of course, is a mere mortal, but she is a
death-dealer. A contention impossible to demonstrate but perhaps
worth tossing about in class: rooted in dread of women, such
stories are man-made.

Besides noting the element of myth, a discussion of Keats's
poem might focus on its imagery--on the contrast between things that
suggest decay or decline (<u>glimpses of autumn</u>, <u>haggard Knight</u>,
<u>withered sedge</u>, <u>fading rose</u>, <u>pale warriors</u>, <u>starved lips</u>) and those
in lines 17-28 that suggest youth and bliss. What is a theme in
the poem? Innocence yields to experience.

Most critics have thought that Keats's later revision of lines
29-32 (given on page 233) is weaker. Apparently, Keats had second
thoughts about the specific <u>kisses four</u>, which he joked about in
his letter to his brother George and sister-in-law Georgiana, en-
closing the poem:

> Why four kisses--you will say--why four because I wish
> to restrain the headlong impetuosity of my Muse--she would
> have fain said 'score' without hurting the rhyme--but we
> must temper the Imagination as the critics say with Judg-
> ment. I was obliged to choose an even number that both
> eyes might have fair play: and to speak truly I think two
> apiece quite sufficient.

JOHN MILTON, Lycidas, page 225

"Lycidas" for many students is formidable, and before teaching
the poem, at least a half hour of class time will probably be needed
for preparation. Marlowe's "Passionate Shepherd" can be read first,
to introduce a few pastoral conventions. At least a smattering of
information on the time and place of Milton's elegy is helpful, if
students are to see that their own lives (and friendships) and Milton's life at Cambridge are not completely remote from each other.
A book useful for background is Lois Potter's <u>A Preface to Milton</u>
(New York: Scribner's, 1971), especially pp. 122-125. Many students are intrigued by mythology and find that to read up on a flock
of classical myths reveals much to them, besides making them able to
follow Milton's allusions. I try to allow two class hours to the
poem itself, enough time to deal with only a few passages. Milton's
powerful condemnation of the false shepherds (lines 119-131) is
usually a high point of the poem for students and me, and students
generally end with at least some respect for Milton as a mythmaker.

For the instructor who wishes further aid in reading the poem,
the amount of available criticism is, of course, vast. Modern
studies I have found valuable include Rosemond Tuve's "Theme,

Pattern, and Imagery in <u>Lycidas</u>," in <u>Images and Themes in Five Poems of Milton</u> (Cambridge, Mass.: Harvard University Press, 1957); Jon S. Lawry's "'Eager Thought': Dialectic in <u>Lycidas</u>," in <u>Milton: Modern Essays in Criticism</u>, ed. Arthur E. Barker (Oxford: Oxford University Press, 1965); and Michael Fixler's discussion in <u>Milton and the Kingdoms of God</u> (Evanston, Ill.: Northwestern University Press, 1964), pp. 56-60.

14

ALTERNATIVES

THE POET'S REVISIONS

WILLIAM BUTLER YEATS, The Old Pensioner, page 232

WILLIAM BUTLER YEATS, The Lamentation of the Old Pensioner, page 232

The first pensioner is a lackluster old coot; the later one, strong-willed and defiant. In the "Lamentation" the speaker sees his own ruin clearly and coldly: in line 14, he himself becomes the broken tree. In context, transfigured is a splendid word; it helps to transfigure the original feeble refrain, and in the new refrain Time becomes a flesh-and-blood enemy. The 1890 version is full of end-stopped lines; in the final poem, syntax tends to be seamless: stanzas are whole sentences. About all that Yeats kept from the 1890 version is the chair by the fire and one tree, the dominant rime-sound and the stanza pattern. Perhaps by aging (and by learning more of love and politics), Yeats came to know at first hand how an old man feels.
Another early poem Yeats completely recast is "The Sorrow of Love." See The Variorum Edition of the Poems of W. B. Yeats (New York: Macmillan, 1957).

WALT WHITMAN, A Noiseless Patient Spider, page 234

WALT WHITMAN, The Soul, reaching, throwing out for love, page 235

In revising "The Soul, reaching," Whitman scrapped all but the first two lines; then extended their metaphor into a whole poem. In doing so, he slightly changed his original conception and in its finished form, "A Noiseless Patient Spider" isn't a poem about human beings reaching out in love to other human beings, but about the soul trying to form contact with higher reality.
"A Noiseless Patient Spider" may be used effectively in discussing symbolism in poetry, as well as figures of speech. Whitman's poem is open in form, and yet certain lines fall into traditional measures (almost into rime, too), as would be indicated by rearranging them:

Till the bridge you will need be form'd,
Till the ductile anchor hold,
Till the gossamer thread you fling
Catch somewhere, O my soul.

DONALD HALL, My Son, My Executioner, page 235

Hall's decision to excise his fourth stanza seems wise self-
editing. The stanza mainly repeats in abstract terms what the first
three stanzas have already said. As curtailed, the poem has a
stronger last line. The paradox--that the executioner makes the
victim immortal--invites students to paraphrase it, probably along
these lines: to have a child signifies that the parent is closer
to his own death; but also that some part of the parent will survive. Hall made one other improvement when he revised the poem:
its original title was "Epigenethlion: First Child."
       Between Hall's poem and Sylvia Plath's "Morning Song," page
351, the differences are probably larger than the similarities; but
students may profitably compare the two poems in theme and situation.

TRANSLATIONS

FEDERICO GARCÍA LORCA, La guitarra (Guitar), page 236

       The translator's liberty with Lorca's lines 23-24 seems well
taken: on the branch would be weaker as a line by itself than and
the first dead bird on the branch.
       Lorca's poem comes from his Poema del cante jondo (1921), an
early sequence of brief lyrics based on traditional folk music.
The cante jondo ("deep song") was an Andalusian form related to
flamenco; and in 1922 Lorca and composer Manuel de Falla organized
a festival of the cante jondo, offering prizes for new songs in the
old tradition.
       Carl W. Cobb has suggested that the Heart heavily wounded / by
five sharp swords is the guitar itself, struck by the player's five
fingers. (Federico García Lorca [New York: Twayne, 1967].)

Exercise: Comparing Translations, page 237

HORACE, Odes I (38), page 238

WILLIAM COWPER, Simplicity, page 238

HARTLEY COLERIDGE, Fie on Eastern Luxury!, page 238

EUGENE FIELD, The Preference Declared, page 238

       Cowper's neoclassical translation seems fair both to the tone
of Horace's poem and to its sense. Cowper rearranges ideas to make

his rimes come out right (ringing in <u>Thus outstretched beneath my vine</u> rather early) and to emphasize the boy rather than the drinker. He does not adorn, however, and he preserves the simplicity of style of the original.

The work of Hartley Coleridge (the son of Samuel Taylor Coleridge) had moments of felicity, but this translation is not one of them. He expands the original eight lines to twelve, falls into awkward syntax in the entire second stanza, and chooses a diction that exhibits the "studious pomp" Horace would avoid (<u>toilsome pain, mis-seems</u>).

Vigorous and direct, Field's irreverent version is a small masterpiece of speaking colloquially inside tight metrical verse. Obviously, however, Field shatters the tone of the original. That the author of such sentimental mawkishness as the famous "Little Boy Blue" often could write this well is also evident in Field's other translations from Horace, published with his brother Roswell Martin Field in <u>Echoes from the Sabine Farm</u> (New York: Scribners, 1896). (I offer some gratitude for this neglected book in <u>The Carleton Miscellany</u>, Fall 1963.)

Interesting translations of this famous ode are plentiful: the <u>Poems of Gerard Manley Hopkins</u> contains a bookish one (<u>Ah child, no Persian--perfect art!</u> / <u>Crowns composite and braided bast</u> . . .). Cowper made another version of the poem, apparently, like Campion's "Rose-cheeked Laura," an attempt to write English Sapphics (the Greek measures that Horace was imitating):

> Boy! I detest all Persian fopperies,
> Fillet-bound garlands are to me disgusting,
> Task not thyself with any search, I charge thee,
>   Where latest roses linger;
> Bring me along (for thou wilt find that readily)
> Plain myrtle. Myrtle neither will disparage
> Thee occupied to serve me, or me drinking
>   Beneath my vine's cool shelter.

> (from Cowper's <u>Poems</u> of 1815, ed. John Johnson)

CHARLES BAUDELAIRE, Recueillement (Meditation), page 239

LORD ALFRED DOUGLAS, Peace, be at peace, O thou my heaviness, page 239

ROBERT BLY, Inward Conversation, page 239

ROBERT LOWELL, Meditation, page 240

The three translations from Baudelaire exhibit divergent fashions. Douglas keeps the music while high-handedly changing the sequence of ideas; his version has a most Swinburnean fin-de-siècle tinge (<u>To pluck the fruits of sick remorse and fear</u>). Personally, I like Douglas's version the best of the three--considered

as English poetry. The opening line does not say what Baudelaire
says, but it is splendid in music and sense. The ending, too, seems
an inspired distortion, worthy of Edward FitzGerald.

Bly's translation is a combination of invention and fidelity.
The opening line seems wordy, gauche, and inaccurate. Bly's rotten
herds are far cruder than Baudelaire's multitude vile, and I confess
myself unable to understand what a lyncher without touch is. Bly's
version improves as it goes along, both as a translation and as an
English poem. The sense of loss in line 11 is a fine way to render
Regret, and the last three lines, lovely in English, strike me as
coming closer to the tone of Baudelaire's original than either Douglas or Lowell does. On general principle, Bly refuses to translate
rimed metrical verse into rimed metrical verse. At the end he is
able to keep the sense of Baudelaire's poem though the music is
drastically altered.

Lowell's version is from his collection of Imitations, where it
is offered not as a faithful translation but as a free adaptation.
It is very close in sense, however, to its original. Here and there,
Lowell adds a characteristic stroke of his own: the addition of the
metaphor in coffined (line 3), the blunt rendering of robes
surannées as old clothes (line 10). Though a close cognate of
marche, the last word, march, with its military connotations, seems
an unfortunate choice. But Lowell's translation occupies the middle
ground between fidelity and free improvisation and manages to convey
some sense of the music of the original.

PARODY

Ezra Pound, in his ABC of Reading, urges students of poetry to
write parodies of any poems they find ridiculous, then submit their
parodies to other students to be judged. "The gauging pupil should
be asked to recognize what author is parodied. And whether the joke
is on the parodied or the parodist. Whether the parody exposes a
real defect, or merely makes use of an author's mechanism to expose
a more trivial content."

T. E. BROWN, My Garden, page 241

J. A. LINDON, My Garden, page 241

With a few thrusts of his rake, Lindon punctures T. E. Brown's
hifalutin language (wot and grot are the most flagrantly "poetic"),
his overwrought reliance on exclamation points, and the shaky logic
he uses to prove the existence of God. Of the two, the parody is
unquestionably the better poem.

241-245 (text pages)

HUGH KINGSMILL, What, still alive at twenty-two, page 241

Kingsmill's insistence on dying young suggests "To an Athlete
Dying Young," but the parodist grossly exaggerates Housman's hint
of nihilism. Like bacon, Kingsmill's lad will be "cured"--of the
disease of life. (And how often Housman himself says lad, by the
way.) In his tetrameter couplets, Kingsmill echoes "Terence, this
is stupid stuff." His metaphysical conceit of ink and blotting pad
coarsens Housman's usual view of night and day. (Some comparable
Housman lines, from "Reveille": Wake: the silver dusk returning /
Up the beach of darkness brims, / And the ship of sunrise burning /
Strands upon the eastern rims.)

KENNETH KOCH, Mending Sump, page 242

Perhaps it would be well to read Frost's "Mending Wall" (page
314) before rather than after reading Koch's hatchet job. To appreciate Koch's allusions to Frost, students also might hear a little
of "The Death of a Hired Man." It is often included in high school
textbooks but may not be familiar to all students.

Exercise: Spotting the Originals, page 243

DESMOND SKIRROW, Ode on a Grecian Urn summarized, page 243

JOHN CIARDI, By a Bush in Half Twilight, page 243

GEORGE STARBUCK, Margaret Are You Drug, page 243

Skirrow's condensed version of Keats's ode (which appears on
page 335) provokes a laugh merely by falling so short of approximating its original. Even your weakest student, on an off day,
should be able to give a better summary of the conclusion of Keats's
"Ode" than "Nice, though."
John Ciardi perfectly echoes the sententiousness of a Robert
Frost poem, such as "Mending Wall," with its observations of farm
life that pretend to (and perhaps attain) a larger significance.
The quatrain captures a typical Frost sentence-sound besides, with
its idiomatic array of one-syllable words. I recently asked Ciardi
whether this was intended as a parody on Frost or as a poem in its
own right. He wouldn't say.
"Margaret Are You Drug" is a deliberately crass, lowbrow,
American version of Hopkins's "Spring and Fall" (page 328). See
the note in this manual on page 136.

E. B. WHITE, A Classic Waits for Me, page 244

It was probably Whitman's phrase Me imperturbe that Henry
James had in mind when he said of the Camden bard, "one cannot help

deploring his too extensive acquaintance with foreign languages."
And White knows all the other traits of Whitman's style--long,
rolling lines, and lists, and the pronoun I, and sonorities. Much
of our fun comes from the deliberately bathetic falls from lofty
heights to commonplaces: I, in perfect health except for a slight
cold, and Turbulent, fleshy, sensible, and Bearded, sunburnt, gray-
neck'd, astigmatic.
     Although White finds a few plant-lice on the Leaves, his
satire has another object. As William Watt and Robert Bradford
have noticed, White's attitude in this parody is the same as in his
essays: "suspicion of the institutionalism that inhibits the free
thought and choice of the individual." (An E. B. White Reader [New
York: Harper & Row, 1966].)

15

TELLING GOOD FROM BAD

Ezra Pound long argued for the value of bad poetry in pedagogy. In his ABC of Reading, Pound declared that literary education needs to concentrate on revealing what is sham, so that the student may be led to discover what is valid. It is a healthy gesture to let the student see that we don't believe everything contained in a textbook to be admirable. Begin with a poem or two so outrageously awful that the least sophisticated student hardly can take it seriously--some sentimental claptrap such as "The Old Arm-Chair" (page 256). From these, you can proceed to subtler examples. It is a mistake to be too snide or too self-righteous toward bad poems, and it is well to quickly turn to some excellent poetry if the classroom starts smelling like a mortuary. There is a certain sadness inherent in much bad poetry; one can readily choke on it. As Allen Tate has said, the best attack upon the bad is the loving understanding of the good. The aim in teaching bad poetry has to be the admiration of good poetry, not the diffusion of mockery.

One further suggestion on bad poetry: a program of really execrable verse orated with straight faces by a few students and members of the faculty can be, with any luck, a fine occasion. For bad poems to work on besides those offered in this chapter, see the dustier stacks in a library or the following anthologies: Heart Throbs and More Heart Throbs, ed. Joe Mitchell Chapple (New York: Grosset & Dunlap, 1905 and 1911 respectively; many later editions); The Stuffed Owl: An Anthology of Bad Verse, eds. D. B. Wyndham Lewis and Charles Lee (London: Dent, 1930; reprinted in the United States by Capricorn paperbacks); Nematodes in My Garden of Verse, ed. Richard Walser (Winston-Salem: John F. Blair, 1959); Worst English Poets, ed. Christopher Adams (London: Allan Wingate, 1958); and Pegasus Descending: A Book of the Best Bad Verse, eds. James Camp, X. J. Kennedy, and Keith Waldrop (New York: Macmillan, 1971).

ANONYMOUS, O Moon, when I gaze on thy beautiful face, page 250

Glorious behind seems inexact, and so does boundaries for "boundlessness."

GRACE TREASONE, Life, page 250

WILLIAM ERNEST HENLEY, Madam Life's a piece in bloom, page 250

Henley's tough-talking, serio-comic poem is consistent in developing its allegory. Life is the prostitute who takes the man up to her room, Death is her partner preparing to roll him. Treasone's poem also develops a central metaphor, but its language is wildly imprecise. Is the tooth that <u>cuts into your heart</u> one's own or somebody else's? (It is probable that the poet means not tooth but "toothache.") Anatomically, the image seems on a par with the "heart's leg" of the tradesman poet quoted by Coleridge (page 252). Through the murk of her expression, however, the poet makes clear her theme: the familiar and sentimental notion that life is really all right if you see it through (or have a competent dentist). Henley says life is a confidence game and you're its victim. His poem might seem more grimly sardonic if the personification of Death as a throttler in cahoots with a prostitute were not difficult to imagine with utter seriousness.

Treasone's item first adorned a Dover, New Jersey newspaper column of local poets called "This Way To Parnassus."

Henley's best known poem was "Invictus" (<u>Out of the night that covers me,</u> / <u>Black as the pit from pole to pole</u>), but personally I prefer "Madame Life." In W. H. Auden's anthology <u>Nineteenth-Century Minor Poets</u> (London: Faber, 1966), Henley is praised for breaking away from Victorian genteel conventions and so becoming "a significant forerunner of . . . modern poetry." (Incidentally, Henley has another claim to fame: in <u>Treasure Island</u>, Robert Louis Stevenson took him as the model for Long John Silver!)

STEPHEN TROPP, My Wife Is My Shirt, page 251

To give this item the benefit of doubt, its metaphor is elaborated consistently; but is hard to see anatomically. To compare the shirtsleeves to the wife's armpits and the shirt's neck to her mouth, rather than to other parts of her, seems arbitrary. In a personification an inanimate object is seen as human. In "My Wife Is My Shirt" a person is seen as an inanimate object.

If this paraphrase of his idea is a fair one, Tropp does not get it across at all. The buttoning of the blood--a thoughty and ingenious figure--seems merely horrible. Tenderness is lost.

This poem appears in <u>Beat Coast East: An Anthology of Rebellion</u> (New York: Excelsior Press, 1960) and may be a relic of a kind of work once fashionable, in which the poet tries to turn off his feelings and to "play it cool." Whatever the poet's intentions, the result is bathetic. All we know about Stephen Tropp comes from a note in a poetry magazine that said he lived in New York City and had a little boy named Tree.

251-253 (text pages)

EMILY DICKINSON, A Dying Tiger-moaned for Drink, page 251

   This is not, by any stretch of critical imagination, a good
poem. Besides the poet's innocent lack of perception that His
Mighty Balls can suggest not eyeballs but testicles, the concluding
statement (that the fact that the tiger was dead is to blame) seems
an unDickinsonian failure of invention. Perhaps the poet intended
a religious allegory (Christ the Tiger). Her capitalization of He
in the last line doesn't seem sufficient proof of such intent, for
her habits of capitalization cannot be trusted for consistency.
   The failures of splendid poets are fascinating. As in this
case, they often seem to result from some tremendous leap that sails
over and beyond its object, causing the poet to crash to earth on
the other side.

Exercise: Seeing What Went Wrong, page 252

   1. "I'm Glad" takes a crassly mechanistic view of the universe:
sky and earth are slapped with coats of paint, air is a sandwich.
Trite, padded diction: nice fresh air.
   2. Mills forces his rime, shaving the s from always.
   3. The image of a heart with a leg is ludicrous.
   4. Apparently the poet says dashes only because it rimes with
ashes, even though it completely disrupts the tone of a stately
elegy.
   5. Meynell's second line is redundant: what else besides
sheep would a shepherdess tend?
   6. Dryden's lines suffer from excessive ingenuity, in imitation of the metaphysical poetry of Cleveland and others current in
his youth. The image of the tearful pimple sentimentalizes this
little pustule.
   7. Hardy's germed seems an awkward way to avoid germinated.
Westminster / beautifuller must be one of the most clumsily forced
rimes a major English poet ever came up with.
   8. Sappy, simpleminded sentiment. The rimes seem hairy, except for fan / Diane. This is verse devoid of practically any element of poetry.
   9. Guest falls into a wildly inappropriate hippetty-hop
rhythm, and the unfortunate connotations of scum louse up the lofty
tone of his platitude.
   10. John deliberately gives us a simpleminded, stupid, narrative in a monotonous rhythm. Fond of Latinate diction, he may
have been trying to illustrate the perils of writing in words of
one syllable.
   11. Chivers, a friend and imitator of Poe, weaves a language
so ornate that it often turns incomprehensible. Who can define a
Cydonian sucket? Who has seen a glowing chrysoprase? The rime
suckets / buckets seems unintentionally comic; and the image of the
wild emerald cucumber-tree reduces the poem to nonsense by suggesting the poet's terrible distance from the real world of cucum-
ber vines. The model, of course, is Poe's "Annabel Lee."

12. The rime <u>leave her</u> / <u>Scarlet Fever</u> is unintentionally funny, and the poet repeats with enormous emphasis dull words with dismal connotations.

ROBERT BURNS, John Anderson my jo, John, page 255

Strange to tell, Burns's genuinely touching poem is a polite revision of a bawdy folk song he had found in an old songbook. It goes in part: <u>John Anderson, my jo, John,</u> / <u>When first that ye began</u>, / <u>Ye had as good a tail-tree</u>, / <u>As any ither man</u>. For the whole of the original see Burns's <u>The Merry Muses of Caledonia</u>, eds. James Barke and Sydney Goodsir Smith (New York: Capricorn Books, 1965), pp. 147-148.

<u>Exercise</u>: Fine or Shoddy Tenderness, page 255

HART CRANE, My Grandmother's Love Letters, page 256

ELIZA COOK, The Old Arm-Chair, page 256

D. H. LAWRENCE, Piano, page 257

Crane's poem expresses the poet's feelings persuasively--even though the subject (like a mother's old arm-chair) is one that might invite a flagrantly sentimental treatment. The poet, unlike a sentimentalist, observes these letters specifically: they are <u>brown and soft</u>, / <u>And liable to melt as snow</u>. Sentimentality is avoided, too, by the final image of the rain on the roof: a slightly mocking, gently ironic commentary.

Eliza Cook's "The Old Arm-Chair" seems flagrantly sentimental. Unless one is prone to weep spontaneously at the mere mention of the word "mother," it is hard to take part in this teary bath. The mother is <u>hallowed</u>, <u>sainted</u> (we are told), but we do not see her clearly as a person. Like D. H. Lawrence in "Piano," Cook describes the way a mother looks to a child, but she does so without Lawrence's awareness that a mature mind could find a discrepancy between child's and adult's point of view. Though Cook evidently realizes that others may find her devotion to the arm-chair foolish, she is not about to give it up: <u>who shall dare</u> / <u>To chide me?</u> she asks, with chip on shoulder. Far from communicating a sense of reality, she employs distracting hyperboles: <u>'Tis bound by a thousand bands to my heart</u>; tears are <u>a lava tide</u>. Sentimental poets like Cook tend to care more about their own grief than about what inspired it. Here, the poet glorifies her own sighs that <u>embalmed</u> the chair (surely a word chosen with little awareness of its connotations of undertaking).

Who was Eliza Cook? An English poet (1818-1889) once popular. "The Old Arm-Chair" won such high acclaim in its time that the poet followed it with "The Old Farm-Gate," "I Miss Thee, My Mother," and others of the ilk. Lewis and Lee have an irreverent account of her

and her work in their anthology of bad verse, The Stuffed Owl
(London: Dent, 1930).

"Piano" is not a flawless poem. Lawrence was seldom at ease
in rime, and the strained rime clamor / glamor indicates his dis-
comfort. (However, glamor is in its context an accurate word: it
implies that the mature man knows that the child's eyes cast an
illusory beauty upon the past, as does memory.) In general, the
superiority of Lawrence's poem to Cook's may be seen in the speci-
ficity of his descriptions: the boom of the tingling strings, the
small, poised feet. Lawrence enters into the child's perspective.
Moreover, the speaker is resisting his urge to cry--as the connotations of his words indicate (the song is insidious; it betrays).
But at last, he is unable to prevent his tears and, sensibly, yields
to them. Cook's speaker coaxes them forth and goes wading in them.

ROD McKUEN, Thoughts on Capital Punishment, page 257

WILLIAM STAFFORD, Traveling Through the Dark, page 258

McKuen is still popular among many students, and any dogmatic
attempt to blast him may be held against you. There may be value in
such a confrontation, of course; or you can leave evaluation of
these two works up to the class. Just work through McKuen's effu-
sion and Stafford's fine poem, detail by detail, in a noncommital
way, and chances are good that Stafford will win the contest.

It may not be apparent that Stafford's poem is ordered by a
rime scheme from beginning to end: a b c b stanzas and a final
couplet. Stafford avoids obvious rimes in favor of the off-rimes
road / dead and engine / listen and the cutoff rimes killing /
belly, waiting / hesitated, and swerving / river--this last a device
found in some folk ballads. McKuen's poem announces an obvious rime
scheme but fails to complete it. Unlike Stafford, he throws rime
out the window in the end, with the effect that his poem stops with
a painful inconclusiveness.

Stafford contributes a long comment on his poem to Reading
Modern Poetry: A Critical Introduction, eds. Paul Engle and Warren
Carrier (Glenview, Ill.: Scott, Foresman, 1968).

The last thing this edition needed, I thought, was still another
poem about squashed animals in the roadway! However, Gerald Stern's
excellent "Behaving Like a Jew" (page 372) had to go into the poetry
Anthology. For further discussion or for a writing topic: compare
McKuen's "Thoughts" with Stern's poem and evaluate the two. (Stern,
no less impassioned on the subject than McKuen is, discovers new
depths in himself. He comes close to sentimentality, but I think
he escapes.)

16

KNOWING EXCELLENCE

WILLIAM BUTLER YEATS, Sailing to Byzantium, page 260

Have I implied that this poem is a masterpiece so far beyond
reproach that no one in his right mind can find fault with it? That
is, of course, not the truth. If the instructor wishes to provoke
students to argument, he might read them the withering attack on
Yeats's poem by Yvor Winters (Forms of Discovery [Chicago: Swallow,
1967], pp. 215–216). This attack really needs to be read in its
entirety. Winters is wrong, I believe, but no one can begin to
answer his hard-headed objections to the poem without being challenged and illuminated.

Other discussions of the poem, different from mine and also
short, include Richard Ellmann's in Yeats: The Man and the Masks
(New York: Macmillan, 1949) and John Unterecker's in A Reader's
Guide to William Butler Yeats (New York: Noonday Press, 1959).
Those who wish to go deeper still and to read a searching examination (informed by study of Yeats's manuscripts) can be directed to
Curtis Bradford, "Yeats's Byzantium Poems," PMLA, 75 (March 1960),
pp. 110–125. For those interested in alternatives, Jon Stallworthy
reprints nearly all the legible manuscript versions in Between the
Lines: Yeats's Poetry in the Making (Oxford: Clarendon Press,
1963), pp. 87–112.

Exercise: Two Poems to Compare, page 263

ARTHUR GUITERMAN, On the Vanity of Earthly Greatness, page 263

PERCY BYSSHE SHELLEY, Ozymandias, page 263

The title of Guiterman's bagatelle playfully echoes that of a
longer, more ambitious poem: Samuel Johnson's "The Vanity of Human
Wishes." If Guiterman's achievement seems smaller than Shelley's
in "Ozymandias," still, it is flawless. "Ozymandias," although one
of the monuments of English poetry, has a few cracks in it. Many
readers find line 8 incomplete in sense: the hand that fed what,
or fed on what? From its rime scheme, we might think the poem a
would-be Italian sonnet that refused to work out.

Nevertheless, Shelley's vision stretches farther than Guiterman's. Ozymandias and his works are placed at an incredibly distant
remove from us. The structure of the poem helps establish this

remoteness: Ozymandias' words were dictated to the sculptor, then carved in stone, then read by a traveler, then told to the first-person speaker, then relayed to us. Ironies abound, more subtle than Guiterman's. A single work of art has outlasted Ozymandias' whole empire. Does that mean that works of art endure (as in Not marble, nor the gilded monuments)? No, this work of art itself has seen better days, and soon (we infer) the sands will finish covering it. Obviously, the king's proud boast has been deflated, and yet, in another sense, Ozymandias is right. The Mighty (or any travelers) may well despair for themselves and their own works, as they gaze on the wreckage of his one surviving project and realize that, cruel as Ozymandias may have been, time is even more remorseless.

What are the facts behind Shelley's poem? According to the Greek historian Diodorus Siculus, Ozymandias was apparently a grand, poeticized name claimed for himself by the Egyptian pharaoh Rameses II. Diodorus Siculus saw the king's ninety-foot-tall statue of himself, carved by the sculptor Memnon, in the first century B.C. when it was still standing at the Ramesseum in Thebes, a mortuary temple. Shelly and his friend Horatio Smith had read a description of the shattered statue in Richard Pococke's Description of the East (1742). Smith and Shelley wrote sonnets expressing their imagined views of the wreckage, both of which Leigh Hunt printed in his periodical The Examiner in 1818. This is Smith's effort, and students might care to compare it with Shelley's in quality:

> On a Stupendous Leg of Granite, Discovered
> Standing by Itself in the Deserts of Egypt

> In Egypt's sandy silence, all alone,
>> Stands a gigantic leg, which far off throws
>> The only shadow that the desert knows.
> 'I am great Ozymandias,' saith the stone,
>> 'The king of kings: this mighty city shows
> The wonders of my hand.' The city's gone!--
>> Nought but the leg remaining to disclose
> The site of that forgotten Babylon.

> We wonder, and some hunter may express
> Wonder like ours, when through the wilderness,
>> Where London stood, holding the wolf in chace,
> He meets some fragment huge, and stops to guess
>> What powerful but unrecorded race
>> Once dwelt in that annihilated place.

For more background to the poem, see H. M. Richmond, "Ozymandias and the Travelers," Keats-Shelley Journal, 11 (1962), pp. 65-71.

WILLIAM SHAKESPEARE, My mistress' eyes are nothing like the sun, page 264

Have students state positively each simile that Shakespeare states negatively, and they will make a fair catalogue of trite Petrarchan imagery. Poking fun at such excessive flattery is a source of humor even today, as in an old wheeze still current: "Your teeth are like the stars--they come out at night."

THOMAS CAMPION, There is a garden in her face, page 265

In tone, Campion's lyric is admiring and tender, and yet there are ironies in it. The street vendor's cry, as Walter R. Davis has pointed out, "undercuts, with its earthy commercialism, the high Petrarchan style of the rest of the song." In Campion's society, a girl of marriageable age was, in a sense, on sale to the highest bidder.

For Campion's music to his song--incorporating the set melody of the street cry Cherry ripe, ripe, ripe!--see Davis's edition of Campion's Works (New York: Doubleday, 1967). Campion has been called (by W. H. Auden) "the only man in English cultural history who was both a poet and a composer."

Some students, taking the figures of speech literally, may find the last stanza absurd or meaningless. They can be led to see that Campion's angels with bended bows enact his theme that the young girl's beauties are defended. Who defends them? She herself, by her nay-saying frowns and by her immaturity. Throughout the poem run hints of Eden. The garden, that heavenly paradise, holds sacred cherries--forbidden fruit--and so the guardian angels seem traditional. John Hollander thinks the Petrarchan cliché of bowlike eyebrows "redeemed" by its new associations. "The courtly compliment now turns out to be a central moral vision: . . . Earthly Paradise is to be found in beautiful sexual attainment, in the plucking of cherries that are no forbidden apples, and just for that reason, such attainment isn't always easy." (Introduction to Selected Songs of Thomas Campion [Boston: David R. Godine, 1973].)

WALT WHITMAN, O Captain! My Captain!, page 266

This formerly overrated poem is uncharacteristic of Whitman in its neatly shaped riming stanzas and in its monotonously swinging observation of iambic meter, so inappropriate to a somber elegy. To my mind, the one indication that an excellent poet wrote it is the sudden shift of rhythm in the short lines that end each stanza-- particularly in line 5, with the unexpected turning-on of heavy stresses: O heart! heart! heart!

267-271 (text pages)

MATTHEW ARNOLD, Below the surface-stream, shallow and light, page 267

First printed in Arnold's essay "St. Paul and Protestantism," this poem appears without indication that it is the author's own. Arnold introduces the lines to enforce his point that St. Paul saw the inner meaning of doctrine; but the poem seems equally appropriate to a poet's deepest feelings. Compare the remarks on sincerity by a contemporary poet, W. D. Snodgrass, quoted in the appendix "Writing a Poem," on page 454.

THOMAS GRAY, Elegy Written in a Country Churchyard, page 267

Students, like other critics, may disagree widely in their statements of Gray's theme. Roger Lonsdale (cited below) sees the main preoccupation of the poem to be "the desire to be remembered after death, a concern which draws together both rich and poor, making the splendid monuments and the 'frail memorials' equally pathetic." Concern with being remembered after death informs the Epitaph as well, making it seem intrinsic to the poem (despite Landor's objections). But Gray also seems to suggest that there is positive virtue in remaining little known.

About question 10: most students will readily see that Gray, Shelley, and Guiterman all state (however variously) a common theme --the paths of glory lead but to the grave. In ranking the three poems in order of excellence, however, they risk getting into a futile debate unless they can agree that (1) Guiterman's excellent comic poem need not be damned for not trying to be an elegy; and (2) Gray's poem is more deep-going, moving, musical, and ultimately more interesting in what it says than Guiterman's.

Of three stanzas found in the earliest surviving version of the poem (the Eton manuscript) and deleted from the published version of 1753, one has been much admired. It followed line 116, coming right before the Epitaph:

There scatter'd oft, the earliest of the year,
By hands unseen, are showers of violets found:
The Red-breast loves to build, and warble there,
and little footsteps lightly print the ground.

Topic for discussion: should Gray have kept the stanza?
Topic for a paper of moderate (600- to 1,000-word) length: "Two Views of Anonymity: Gray's 'Elegy' and Auden's 'Unknown Citizen.'"

Twentieth Century Interpretations of Gray's Elegy, ed. H. W. Starr (Englewood Cliffs, N.J.: Prentice-Hall, 1968), is a convenient gathering of modern criticism. A good deal of earlier criticism is summarized by Roger Lonsdale in his edition of The Poems of Gray, Collins, and Goldsmith (New York: Norton, 1969), which provides extensive notes on texts and sources. For a recent poem at least partly inspired by the "Elegy," see Richard Wilbur's

"In a Churchyard" in <u>Walking to Sleep</u> (New York: Harcourt Brace
Jovanovich, 1969). Among the countless parodies, there is an anonymous "Allergy in a Country Churchyard" that begins, <u>The kerchoo
tolls, Nell's 'kerchief swats away</u>.

DAVID BOTTOMS, Smoking in an Open Grave, page 272

Some tentative answers to the questions:

1. There is an irony (also a paradox) in the opening line.
The past, which the speaker and his fellow smokers cheerfully dese-
crate, is hinted at by the old spirituals, by dead soldiers interred
in Confederate Row. Getting high is a form of departure, like
taking a journey. The language of the poem suggests that this trip
is somehow mechanized--the trainlike industrial river that <u>whispers
on its track</u>; the smokers are <u>geared</u>.
2. This critical opinion seems a pompous bit of cant. What
does it say that isn't obvious?
3. Gray's "Elegy" is a difficult act for any contemporary poet
to follow, but whether or not Bottoms's graveyard poem invites comparison, it is, I'd argue, a good poem. In brief compass Bottoms
draws his scene of this half-gloomy pot party with great exactness,
even to the location of the bag and the fact that the brick is <u>half-
fallen</u>. The poem ends in a powerful mixture of feelings: strangeness, joy, nostalgia, and dread. Perhaps this poem pretends to
greater significance than it actually contains. But it captures
something hard to forget, and students are probably going to respond
to it.

"Smoking in an Empty Grave" is reprinted from Bottoms's first
collection, <u>Shooting Rats at the Bibb County Dump</u> (New York:
William Morrow, 1980), which received the Walt Whitman Award of the
Academy of American Poets. At this writing, Bottoms teaches at
Florida State University in Tallahassee. As his poem suggests, he
is a fan of folk and country music; in fact, he has played guitar
and banjo in several bluegrass and country-western bands.

17

WHAT IS POETRY?

ARCHIBALD MacLEISH, Ars Poetica, page 273

MacLeish plays upon a number of verbal paradoxes, which students sometimes like to point out. He says a poem ought to be mute, dumb, and wordless; and yet obviously he is writing a poem in speakable, audible words.

The poem contains a larger paradox, a possible topic for class argument. A poem should not mean / But be, declares the poet. But is his poem pure being? Is it not heavy on meaning--a tendency that an ars poetica, a poem that tells us how poetry should be written, can hardly be expected to avoid?

ANTHOLOGY: POETRY

ANONYMOUS, Edward, page 280

ANONYMOUS, Sir Patrick Spence, page 281

Two Scottish ballads of men sent to death or exile at another's bidding, both "Edward" and "Sir Patrick Spence" are told with a wonderful economy. "Edward," with its surprise ending in the last line, is so neatly built that it is sometimes accused of not being a popular ballad at all, but the work of a sophisticated poet, perhaps working from a popular story. Students might be asked to read the information about ballads in Chapter Seven, "Song," either before or after reading these ballads.

Questions for discussion:

1. In "Edward," why is the first line so effective as an opening? What expectations does it set up in the hearer's mind? How does the last line also display the skill of a master storyteller?

2. Reading a ballad such as "Edward" on the printed page, we notice that its refrains take up much room. Do you find this repetitiousness a hindrance to you enjoying the poem? Is there anything to be said in favor of the repetitiousness?

3. What is the value to the poem of the question-and-answer method of storytelling? ("Edward" proceeds like a courtroom cross-examination in which the mother, by pointed questioning, breaks down her son's story. Dramatically, the method is powerful; and it holds off until the very end the grimmest revelation.)

4. What else could the author of "Edward" conceivably have told us about this unhappy family? Do you find it troublesome that Edward and his mother behave without our quite knowing why? Might the story have suffered if told by a storyteller who more deeply explored the characters' motivations?

5. What do the dramatic situations of "Edward" and "Sir Patrick Spence" have in common? What is similar in the image of the blood-dripping sword in "Edward" and, in "Sir Patrick Spence," the image of the blude-reid wine? (Both images are introduced early in their ballads and foreshadow grim events or revelations.)

6. Does Sir Patrick emerge as a fully understandable character? What do you make of his abrupt transition from laughter to tears?

281-284 (text pages)

7. Coleridge and other critics have greatly admired the stanza in "Spence" about the new moon and the old (lines 25-28). Why is it memorable?

8. Is the author of "Sir Patrick Spence" making (or hinting at) any adverse comment on lords and ladies who lead a comfortable life at court?

For instructors who like to begin with narrative poetry, here are a few suggestions. Other traditional English and Scottish ballads in the book, which might be taken together with these two, are "Bonny Barbara Allan," "The Cruel Mother," and (immediately following "Sir Patrick Spence") "The Three Ravens" and "The Twa Corbies." There is also the anonymous American popular ballad "Scottsboro." These can be supplemented by the narrative songs of known songwriters: the Beatles' "Eleanor Rigby" and Woody Guthrie's "Plane Wreck at Los Gatos." For literary ballads, there are Keats's "La Belle Dame sans Merci" and Dudley Randall's "Ballad of Birmingham." "Richard Cory" resembles a ballad, too, in both its Edwin Arlington Robinson and its Paul Simon versions.

ANONYMOUS, The Three Ravens, page 282

ANONYMOUS, The Twa Corbies, page 283

Questions for discussion:

1. In "The Three Ravens," what is suggestive in the ravens and their conversation? How are the ravens opposed in the poem by the hawks and hounds? (The ravens are selfish eaters of carrion, but the hawks and hounds are loyally standing guard over their dead master's body. Their faithfulness also suggests that of the fallow doe.)

2. Are you persuaded by Friedman's suggestion (quoted in the note under "The Three Ravens") that the doe is a woman who is under some enchantment? What other familiar fairy tales or stories of lovers transformed into animals do you recall?

3. Do you agree that "The Twa Corbies" is "a cynical variation of 'The Three Ravens,'" as it has been called? Compare the two poems in their comments on love and faithfulness.

4. For all the fantasy of "The Three Ravens," what details in the ballad seem realistic reflections of the natural world?

ANONYMOUS, Sumer is icumen in, page 284

If you are not an expert in Middle English pronunciation, ask a colleague who is one to give you a quick briefing and take a stab at reading "Sumer is icumen in" aloud to the class. Even the experts are only guessing (educatedly) how thirteenth-century Englishmen sounded, and your reading need do no more than suggest that the language has not always stood still.

This slight, exquisite, earthy song may be compared with
Shakespeare's "When daisies pied" (page 365), in which the song of
the cuckoo suggests cuckoldry (as it doesn't in this innocent,
humorless lyric).

For a parody, see Ezra Pound's "Ancient Music," beginning
"Winter is icummen in," in his collection Personae (New York: New
Directions, 1949), and in Selected Poems (from the same publisher,
1957).

ANONYMOUS, I sing of a maiden, page 284

How could Christ be conceived and Mary remain a virgin? This
medieval lyric appears to reply to the question: as easily and
naturally as the dew falls.

The cesura in each line shows that English poetry, as late as
the fifteenth century, had not quite broken away from the Old
English two-part line. See the mention of this pattern on page 143
and "The Seafarer" (page 352), Pound's modern version of an Old
English poem.

"I sing of a maiden" can be used to remind students of the
value to poetry of figures of speech. In line 1, makeless (meaning
both "matchless" and "without a mate") is a serious pun. Each of
the poem's three middle couplets contains a simile.

ANONYMOUS, Western Wind, page 285

Originally a song for tenor voices, "Western Wind" probably
was the work of some courtier in the reign of Henry VIII. Untouched
by modernization, it reads (in its one surviving manuscript):

Westron wynde when wyll thow blow
the smalle rayne douune can rayne
Chryst yf my love wer in my armys
and I yn my bed agayne

Questions for discussion:

1. In reading the poem, how does it help to know that the
moist, warm west wind of England brings rain and is a sign of spring?

2. What do the first pair of lines and the last pair have to
do with each other?

3. Do you agree with a critic who suggested that the speaker
is invoking Christ, asking for help in obtaining sex? "By a blas-
phemous implication Christ is in effect assigned the role of a
fertility spirit." (F. W. Bateson, English Poetry: A Critical
Introduction [London: Longmans, 1966].)

4. Consider another critic's view: the unhappy speaker is
stressing his (or her) longing to go to bed with his (or her) loved
one, and so the word Christ is an exclamation. (I prefer this view,
myself. It is that of Arthur O. Lewis, Jr., writing in The Explicator 15 [February 1957], item 28.)

285-287 (text pages)

JAMES AGEE, Sunday: Outskirts of Knoxville, Tennessee, page 285

Agee's poem briefly recites the story of some typical lives and, in doing so, invites comparison with Cummings's "anyone lived in a pretty how town" (page 53). But Agee's view of the usual course of life seems more grim: We that are human cannot hope.

Question for discussion: what does the poet mean by the horror, in the next-to-last line? In answering, students might explain line 16, Our tenderest joys oblige us most; and might also compare Agee's chronicle of how love ends (lines 18-30) with Auden's observation, In headaches and in worry / Vaguely life leaks away ("As I Walked Out One Evening," page 287).

Perhaps, however, my view of the poem is too bleak. Victor A. Kramer thinks the poem demonstrates that, in most lives, fair and foul are inextricably joined. In the closing lines, says Kramer, "Agee's catalogue of suffering dissolves into an image of innocent children at play." (James Agee [Boston: Twayne, 1975], pp. 66-68.) To me, in the last line, the poet is swept by sympathy for time's victims and feels uncertain what to pray for. Should God show the grandchildren the future course of their lives--or mercifully keep them blind to it?

This evocation of Agee's native Knoxville was written at about the same time as the prose sketch "Knoxville: Summer, 1915." The sketch appears as a preface to Agee's posthumous novel, A Death in the Family (New York: McDowell, Obolensky, 1957).

MATTHEW ARNOLD, Dover Beach, page 286

Arnold and his family did such an efficient job of expunging the facts of his early romances that the genesis of "Dover Beach" is hard to know. Arnold may (or may not) have been in love with a French girl whom he called Marguerite, whose egoistic gaiety made her difficult. See Lionel Trilling's discussion of the poem and of Arnold's Marguerite poems in his biography Matthew Arnold (New York: Columbia University Press, 1949). Marguerite, Trilling suspects, viewed the world as much more various, beautiful, and new than young Arnold did.

A sympathetic reading of "Dover Beach" might include some attention to the music of its assonance and alliterations, especially the s sounds in the description of the tide (lines 12-14). Line 21 introduces the central metaphor, the Sea of Faith. Students will probably be helped by a few minutes of discussion of the historical background of the poem. Why, when the poem appeared in 1867, was religious faith under attack? Darwin, Herbert Spencer, and Victorian industrialism may be worth mention. Ignorant armies (line 37) are still with us. Arnold probably had in mind those involved in the Crimean War of 1853-1856, perhaps also those in the American Civil War. For sources of the poem see C. B. Tinker and H. F. Lowry, The Poetry of Matthew Arnold (New York: Oxford University Press, 1940), pp. 173-178.

A dour view of the poem is taken by Donald Hall in "Ah, Love, Let Us Be True" (American Scholar, Summer 1959). Hall finds "love invoked as a compensation for the losses that history has forced us to sustain," and adds, "I hope there are better reasons for fidelity than disillusion. . . . Like so many Victorian poems, its negation is beautiful and its affirmation repulsive." This comment can be used to provoke discussion. A useful counterfoil to "Dover Beach" is Anthony Hecht's satiric poem "The Dover Bitch," in his collection The Hard Hours (New York: Atheneum, 1960) and in many anthologies. For other critical comment see William E. Cadbury, "Coming to Terms with 'Dover Beach,'" Criticism 8 (Spring 1966), pp. 126-138; James Dickey, Babel to Byzantium (New York: Farrar, Straus and Giroux, 1968), pp. 235-238 (a good concise general essay); and A. Dwight Culler, Imaginative Reason: The Poetry of Matthew Arnold (New Haven, Conn.: Yale University Press, 1966).

Compare Hardy's attitude in "The Oxen" (page 217) with Arnold's wistful view of the sea of faith.

JOHN ASHBERY, City Afternoon, page 287

At first I thought this subtle poem was the poet's contribution to the American bicentennial celebration: If one could seize America. And it was no accident, I guessed, that the collection in which it appears, Self-Portrait in a Convex Mirror, came out in 1975. After further thought, I feel certain only that Ashbery's poem resists attempts to pin a subject on it. Ashbery's recent work (which is his best) seems immune to the accusation that Wallace Stevens once leveled at Robert Frost: "Your trouble, Robert, is that you write poems about--things." Ashbery's strategy, instead, is to relate suggestive things by means of ambiguous words. Sometimes he calls upon rime to join things in relationships: something fine does define, air lifts hair. Although not strictly "about" a city afternoon, neither is the poem an infinite series of reflecting mirrors. After one has read it a few times, one knows what to think and how to feel--at least until the next reading.

In the opening lines (I now believe), the poet regards an old and perhaps yellowed photograph of a city street, whose veil of haze keeps its scene preserved. The haze, because of the age of the photograph or because of the weather on the day of the photograph, suggests the fine forgetfulness of line 6. And it seems that the people in the picture have entered what John Crowe Ransom called "the forgetful kingdom of death." The tone shifts startlingly from the quiet opening words to a sudden outcry of sympathy. The force of the poet's dread of the passage of time is indicated by violent imagery and heavy stresses: "SUCKED SCREAMing through OLD AGE and DEATH."

Fine forgetfulness, then, suggests haze and the absentminded- ness of old people, and the permanently absent minds of the dead. But there is another, more central suggestion. In a sense, art too is forgetful. A work of art (whether a photograph or a poem) re- flects the living, who die and forget; and eventually the work dies and "forgets" in its turn. Poets' collections (our volumes) collect the patina of time until they disintegrate. For all a poet's attempts to capture life in an outline, time flows until the outline blurs and disappears.

Three persons in the photograph wear gray garlands. Is it gray hair, or hair that looks gray because limned and defined by hazy light? We are reminded of a poet's garlands of laurel. And in the delicate final image, one person is seen reflected upside down—like an image of actual life momentarily captured in a work of art. The phrase reflecting pool suggests the camera's lens, or film; and on reflection, may suggest the mind of a poet as well.

Any paraphrase will be crude. Still, "City Afternoon" for me has one or two unmistakable themes. If fine forgetfulness is a quality we expect of art, then Ashbery is wishing that he were able to seize actual life and hold it fast in poetry—at least temporarily. A poem, he affirms, is not useless, despite its stain of common mortality. It does define. It commemorates, that is, it overcomes forgetfulness and awakens memory.

W. H. AUDEN, As I Walked Out One Evening, page 287

This literary ballad, with its stark contrast between the innocent song of the lover and the more knowing song of the clocks, affords opportunities to pay close attention to the poet's choice of words. Auden selects words rich in connotations: the brimming of the river (which suggests also the lover's feelings), the crooked neighbor (with its hint of dishonesty and corruption, as well as the denotation of being warped or bent by Time, like the diver's brilliant bow). Figures of speech abound: the opening metaphor of the crowds like wheat (ripe and ready to be scythed by Time the Reaper), the lover's extended use of hyperbole in lines 9-20, the personifications of Time and Justice, the serious pun on appalling in line 34 (both awe-inspiring and like a pall or shroud, as in Blake's "London," page 61), the final reconciliation in metaphor between the original brimming river and the flow of passing Time. Auden's theme appears to be that as young lovers grow old, their innocent vision is smudged and begrimed by contact with realities— and yet Life remains a blessing after all.

The lover's huge promises in stanzas three and four (I'll love you / Till China and Africa meet . . .) have reminded Richard Wilbur of the hyperbolic boasts of the speaker in Burns's "Oh, my love is like a red, red rose" (page 101). Burns speaks for the romantic lover, wrapped in his own emotions, but Auden's view of romantic love is skeptical. "The poem then proceeds to rebut [the lover's] lines, saying that the human heart is too selfish and perverse to make such promises." (Responses [New York: Harcourt Brace Jovanovich, 1976], p. 144.)

This poem may appear to have too little action in it to resemble folk ballads in more than a few touches. Auden himself, according to Monroe K. Spears, did not call this a ballad but referred to it as "a pastiche of folk-song."

"As I Walked Out One Evening" is one of the "Five Lyrics" included on W. H. Auden Reading (Caedmon recording TC 1019). For
comparison with the poet's own modest delivery, Dylan Thomas Reading,
vol. 4 (Caedmon TC 1061) offers a more dramatic rendition of the
poem.

W. H. AUDEN, Musée des Beaux Arts, page 289

     In Breughel's Landscape with the Fall of Icarus, reproduced on
page 289, students may need to have their attention directed to the
legs disappearing in a splash, one quarter inch below the bow of the
ship. One story (probably apocryphal) is that Breughel's patron had
ordered a painting on a subject from mythology, but the artist had
only this landscape painting completed. To fill the order quickly,
Breughel touched in the little splash, gave the picture a mythologi-
cal name, and sent it on its way. Question: how does that story
(if true) make Breughel seem a shallower man than Auden thinks he
is?
     Besides the Landscape, Auden apparently has in mind two other
paintings of Pieter Breughel the Elder: The Census, also called
The Numbering at Bethlehem (Auden's lines 5-8), and The Massacre
of the Innocents (lines 9-12). If the instructor has access to
reproductions, these works might be worth bringing in; however, the
Landscape seems central to the poem. This painting seems indebted
to Ovid's Metamorphoses, but in Ovid the ploughman, shepherd, and
fisherman looked on the fall of Icarus with amazement. The title
of Auden's poem, incidentally, is close to the name of the Brussels
museum housing the Landscape: the Musées Royaux des Beaux Arts.

AMIRI BARAKA (LeRoi Jones), Preface to a Twenty Volume Suicide Note,
page 290

     Baraka's poem is memorably fresh in its imagery: the menacing
ground, the exact and lifelike snapshot of the child. It touches,
though, on a universal theme: one that appears differently in
Sylvia Plath's "Morning Song" and Donald Hall's "My Son, My Executioner." In "Preface to a Twenty Volume Suicide Note," the poet has
a premonition of his inevitable death, made poignant by the birth
of his daughter. Images of mortality pervade the poem: the ground
that envelopes the speaker, the wind broad-edged like a knife. In
such a context, the child, talking to an invisible playmate, becomes another threat--or at least appears subtly disquieting. But
much is left unsaid in this poem, and this interpretation is open
to argument.
     Is Etheridge Knight, in "For Black Poets Who Think of Suicide"
(page 101), addressing Baraka?

WENDELL BERRY, The Peace of Wild Things, page 290

Like Robert Lowell in "Skunk Hour," Wendell Berry in this poem
finds solace in nature from his anxieties. A belief in nature as
comforter is more forthrightly expressed in "The Peace of Wild
Things" than in Lowell's poem. There is no indirection here, but
instead a simple statement.
It seems ironic that, while conventional wisdom might characterize civilization as orderly and the world of wild things as
savage, wanton, and frightening, it is the civilized world that
scares the poet and the natural world that offers him peace.
Berry's emphasis springs from more than old-fashioned romanticism.
In his work, ecology and the mess humans have made of their world
are persistent themes.
Wendell Berry is both a man of letters and a Kentucky farmer.
He writes poetry, novels, and essays. Well worth reading, though
it does not deal directly with "The Peace of Wild Things," is
David Curry's appreciation of Berry and his work, "Wendell Berry's
Natural Piety," reprinted in A Book of Rereadings in Recent American
Poetry, ed. Greg Kuzma (Lincoln, Neb.: Best Cellar Press, 1979).

ELIZABETH BISHOP, Filling Station, page 291

Questions for discussion:

1. What is the poet's attitude toward the feeble attempts at
beautification detailed in lines 23-33? Sympathy, contempt, or
what? How is the attitude indicated? (The attempts are doomed,
not only by the gas station's being saturated with oil, but by the
limitations of the family, whose only reading appears to be comic
books and whose tastes run to hairy plants and daisy-covered doilies.
In line 20, comfy is their word, not the poet's own. But the tone
of the poem seems to be good-humored amusement. The sons are quick
and saucy--likeable traits. The gas station can't be beautified,
but at least its owners have tried. In a futile gesture toward
neatness, they have even arranged the oil cans in symmetry.)
2. What meanings do you find in the last line? (Somebody has
shown love for all motorists by arranging the oil cans so beautifully that they spell out a soothing croon, such as what one might
say over and over to an agitated child. But the somebody also suggests Somebody Up There, whose love enfolds all human beings--even
this oil-soaked crew.)
3. Do you find any similarity between ESSO--SO--SO--SO in
"Filling Station" and rainbow, rainbow, rainbow! in "The Fish"
(page 73)? (Both lines stand next-to-last in their poems and sound
similar; both express the speaker's glimpse of beauty--or at least,
in "Filling Station," the only beauty the people can muster and the
poet can perceive.)

Helen Vendler, discussing the poem in Part of Nature, Part of
Us (Cambridge, Mass.: Harvard University Press, 1980), takes the

closing statement to mean "God loves us all." But Irvin Ehrenpreis disagrees: "The '--so--so--so' of overlapping labels on stacked cans is supposed to comfort automobiles as if they were high-strung horses, i.e., like a mother, not a god." Doily and begonia indicate that some absent woman has tried to brighten up this gas station for her husband and her sons. (Review of Vendler's book in The New York Review of Books, April 29, 1980.)

Robert Pinsky has also written of "Filling Station" with high esteem. He calls the poem a kind of contest between "the meticulous vigor of the writer" and "the sloppy vigor of the family," both filling a dull moment and scene with "an unexpected, crazy, deceptively off-hand kind of elegance or ornament." He particularly admires the poet's choice of modifiers--including the direct, honest-seeming dirty. "Adjectives," he notes, "according to a sound rule of thumb for writing classes, do not make 'good descriptions.' By writing almost as though she were too plain and straightforward to have heard of such a rule, Bishop loads characterizations of herself and her subject into the comfy dog, the dim doily, the hirsute begonia; the quietest possible virtuoso strokes." (The Situation of Poetry [Princeton, N.J.: Princeton University Press, 1976], pp. 75-77.)

WILLIAM BLAKE, The Sick Rose, page 292

WILLIAM BLAKE, The Tyger, page 292

In "The Sick Rose," why is the worm, whose love is rape, invisible? Not just because it is hidden in the rose, but also because it is some supernatural dweller in night and storm. Perhaps the worm is unseen Time, that familiar destroyer--is the rose then mortal beauty? Those are usual guesses. For an unusual guess, see E. D. Hirsch, Jr., Innocence and Experience (New Haven, Conn.: Yale University Press, 1964). "The rose's sickness, like syphilis, is the internal result of love enjoyed secretly and illicitly instead of purely and openly." In Hirsch's view, the poem is social criticism. Blake is satirizing the repressive order, whose hypocrisy and sham corrupt the woman who accepts it. Still, like all the best symbols, Blake's rose and worm give off hints endlessly, and no one interpretation covers all of them.

"The Tyger," from Songs of Experience, is a companion piece to "The Lamb" in Songs of Innocence. But while "The Lamb" poses a relatively easy question (Little Lamb, who made thee?) and soon answers it, "The Tyger" poses questions that remain unanswerable. Alert students may complain that some of Blake's questions have no verbs--what dread hand and what dread feet did what? While the incompleteness has been explained by some critics as reflecting the agitated tone of the poem, it may have been due to the poet's agitated habits of composition. Drafts of the poem in Blake's notebook show that, after writing the first three stanzas, he began the fourth stanza with the line, Could fetch it from the furnace deep, which would have completed the questions in line 12. But then he

292-294 (text pages)

deleted it, and wrote in stanza four almost as it stands now. (See
Martin K. Nurmi, "Blake's Revisions of 'The Tyger,'" PMLA 71 [1956],
pp. 669-685.) Other useful discussions include that of Hirsch, who
thinks the stars are the rebel angels who threw down their spears
when they surrendered; and John E. Grant, in "The Art and Argument
of 'The Tyger'" in Texas Studies in Literature and Language 2 (1960),
pp. 38-60.

MARK ALEXANDER BOYD, Cupid and Venus, page 293

    Offer a prize to any student who, on a few days' notice, can
read this poem aloud. (All it takes is nerve, and a passable Scottish burr.)
    The allusions in lines 5-8 will need unraveling. Eros, god of
love in Greek mythology (Cupid in Roman), is a youth, the son of
Venus, and the lover of the maiden Psyche. Later tradition reduces
him to a child and renders him blind or blindfolded. That Venus
was born from the sea will be remembered from Botticelli's painting
of the goddess on the half-shell, with which some students are
probably acquainted.
    A Scottish Petrarchan, Boyd shares (belatedly) the tradition
that represents the lover as helpless and obsessed--visible in the
Wyatt and Surrey versions of Petrarch's lines on page 128. Ezra
Pound has called this the most beautiful sonnet in the English
language, and students may be asked what there is to admire in it.

GWENDOLYN BROOKS, The Rites for Cousin Vit, page 293

    Cousin Vit, a vital, life-loving woman (a prostitute?), is
dead. In this contemporary sonnet, the poet depicts her as too
lively a presence to be confined by the casket, the stuff and satin
aiming to enfold her, / The lid's contrition nor the bolts before.
To the poet, Cousin Vit appears to be still energetically moving
about: walking, talking, drinking, dancing as of old. The wonderful Is. that ends the poem emphatically sums up the dead woman's
undying vigor.
    "The Rites for Cousin Vit" naturally lends itself to compari-
son with the poem that follows, Sterling A. Brown's "Effie."

STERLING A. BROWN, Effie, page 294

    Admirers of black poet Sterling A. Brown's critically acclaimed
Southern Road (1932) had to wait until 1980 for The Collected Poems
of Sterling A. Brown, selected by Michael S. Harper (Harper and Row),
and for reassurance that the poet, troubled by his lack of recognition, had not fallen silent after his first book. Never a poet of
fashion, Sterling A. Brown had tried to bring out a second book, No
Hiding Place, only to have it rejected by the publisher. A Williams
College Phi Beta Kappa, for many years a teacher at Howard University

and elsewhere, a raconteur, and a man of learning, he has yet been
called "the folk poet of the new black consciousness."

The poems are as notable for their craft as for their content.
Brown's main sources are to be found in black folk poetry and in
black speech. He was also familiar with the work of Sandburg,
Frost, Masters, and Robinson, among others, in the twenties. Their
influence can perhaps be seen in "Effie," a poem for your students
to consider in conjunction with "The Rites for Cousin Vit" by Gwendolyn Brooks. Both poems, by distinguished black poets, deal with
women easy for any chance lover, now dead. But while the Brooks
poem insists upon the irrepressible vitality that even death cannot
still, Brown comes at his subject from the opposite direction,
focusing instead upon the stern stillness newly fallen on the dead
woman.

Memorable is the phrase fixed of form at length, with its
several suggestions: that she is quiet at last, that she resembles
a sculpture, and that at length can mean both "lying down" and "for
a long time."

ROBERT BROWNING, My Last Duchess, page 294

ROBERT BROWNING, Soliloquy of the Spanish Cloister, page 295

These two dramatic poems, both uttered by speakers we find un-
sympathetic, may be taken together as memorable works of character
drawing. In each poem, Browning places us in the midst of a society
thoroughly undemocratic and remote from our own in time. Of the two,
only "My Last Duchess" is a typical dramatic monologue. "Soliloquy,"
as its title indicates, addresses no listener. "My Last Duchess"
may be familiar to students from high school literature courses;
and if a show of hands indicates that they have met it before, I
would spend less time with it. Whether or not it is familiar, it
makes a useful companion to "Soliloquy."

Students may be asked to define their feelings toward the Duke
and to point to lines in the poem that help define those feelings.
Browning stresses the Duke's arrogance (I choose / Never to stoop;
I gave commands; / Then all smiles stopped together) and engages
our sympathies for the poor Duchess in lines 21-31, despite the
Duke's contempt for her facility to be gladdened. I know one instructor who in teaching this classic takes the tack, "Shouldn't
we feel sorry for the Duke, with all his marital troubles?" Students of both sexes are usually provoked to rise and trounce him.
Another question: to what extent is the Duke's attitude toward
women presumably typical of his society? That the Count, the visitor's master, would offer a daughter to a man who had just disposed
of his wife, suggests that the Duke is not alone in regarding women
as chattels. Still, even for a Renaissance duke he seems cold-
hearted; wives and works of art seem identified as objects to collect. What were the Duke's commands that stopped the Duchess's
smiles? "That she should be put to death, or he might have had her
shut up in a convent," Browning once explaind. But lines 2 (Looking

as if she were alive) and 46-47 (There she stands / As if alive)
seem to hint that she was executed. Hypocrisy is still another
aspect of the Duke's character: compare his protest that he lacks
skill in speech (lines 35-36) with his artful flattery of the Count
(49-53).

Like "My Last Duchess," the "Soliloquy" is another poem especially valuable to combat the notion that poetry can deal only in
love and gladness. Here, the subject is a hatred so intense that
the speaker seems practically demented. In the last stanza, he almost would sell his soul to the Devil in order to blight a flowering
shrub. A little background information of abbeys, their ograniza-
tion, and the strictness of their rules may help some class members.
From internal evidence, it is hard to say whether this is a six-
teenth-century cloister or a nineteenth-century one: Barbary cor-
sairs (line 31) plied their trade from about 1550 until 1816. The
business about drinking in three sips (lines 37-39) may need explaining: evidently it refers to a symbolic observance, like
crossing knife and fork.

It might be stressed that the person in this poem is not the
poet: the tone isn't one of bitterness, but of merriment. Comedy
is evident not only from the speaker's blindness to his own faults,
but from the rollicking rhythm and multisyllable comic rimes (abhorrence / Lawrence; horsehairs / corsair's; Galatians / damnations;
rose-acacia / Plena gratia).

Questions: with what sins does the speaker charge Brother
Lawrence? (Pride, line 23--monogrammed tableware belonging to a
monk!; lust, 25-32; and gluttony, 40.) What sins do we detect in
the speaker himself? (Envy, clearly, and pride--see his holier-
than-thou attitude in stanza five. How persuasive are his claims
to piety when we learn he secretly owns a pornographic novel?)
"Soliloquy" abounds in ironies and class members can spend a lively
few minutes in pointing them out.

For a précis or summing-up of the poem, see page 184 of this
manual.

THOMAS CAREW, Ask me no more where Jove bestows, page 297

Carew's poem is an eloquent tribute to a lady whose complexion
is so beautiful, the poet says, that it must emanate, with divine
assistance, from the very roses. Her hair is made of sunbeams, her
voice is like the nightingale's, and the stars twinkle in her eyes.
Exaggerated? Yes. Still, what woman, even in the unromantic 1980s,
wouldn't relish so lyrical a testimonial to her beauty?

You might want to ask your class to compare "Ask me no more
where Jove bestows" with "My mistress' eyes are nothing like the
sun" (page 264), where Shakespeare twits the Petrarchan conventions
while of course relying as heavily as Carew does upon his readers'
ability to appreciate a well-turned conceit.

Herbert J. C. Grierson, in his anthology Metaphysical Lyrics
and Poems of the Seventeenth Century (Oxford, 1921; paperbound
edition, 1965), waxes poetic over the dividing throat: "One seems

to hear and see Celia executing elaborate trills as Carew sits en-
tranced."

There is a famous anecdote about Carew, which may or may not be
true. One evening he was lighting King Charles I to the queen's
chamber. Entering the room first, the poet saw the queen in the
arms of the Lord St. Albans. Before the king noticed that anything
was amiss, Carew tactfully stumbled, thus extinguishing his candle
long enough for the queen to adjust her position. His quick thinking endeared Carew to the queen from that day forward.

G. K. Chesterton, The Donkey, page 298

Questions for discussion:

1. Who is the speaker--some particular donkey? (No, the
genetic donkey, looking back over the history of his kind.)
2. To what prehistoric era does Chesterton refer in lines 1-3?
(To the original chaos out of which the world was made. The poet
apparently imagines it in bizarre, dreamlike imagery: fish with
wings, walking forests, fig-bearing thorn.) Chesterton was fasci-
nated by the book of Genesis "because of its beginning in chaos,"
comments Gary Wills in his introduction to a reprint edition of
Chesterton's novel of 1908, The Man Who Was Thursday (New York:
Sheed & Ward, 1975). The novel hints at a playful God who enjoys
returning things to chaos now and then. Writing about the world of
dream in a newspaper article in 1904, Chesterton remarked, "A world
in which donkeys come in two is clearly very near to the wild ulti-
mate world where donkeys are made."
3. Whose ancient crooked will is meant? The will of the devil
in perversely designing the donkey, or the donkey's own venerable
stubbornness? (I'm not sure, myself.)
4. What fools does the donkey chide in the last stanza? (Anybody who ever abused a donkey, or who thinks donkeys contemptible.)
5. Explain how the allusion in the last stanza is essential
to the meaning of the poem.
6. What devices of sound contribute to the poem's effective-
ness?

SAMUEL TAYLOR COLERIDGE, Kubla Khan, page 298

The circumstances of this poem's composition are almost as
famous as the poem itself, and for the convenience of instructors
who wish to read to their students Coleridge's prefatory note, I
give it here:

In the summer of the year 1797, the author, then in
ill health, had retired to a lonely farmhouse between Por-
lock and Linton, on the Exmoor confines of Somerset and
Devonshire. In consequence of a slight indisposition, an
anodyne had been prescribed, from the effects of which he

fell asleep in his chair at the moment that he was reading
the following sentence, or words of the same substance, in
Purchas's Pilgrimage: "Here the Khan Kubla commanded a
palace to be built, and a stately garden thereunto. And
thus ten miles of fertile ground were inclosed with a wall."
The author continued for about three hours in a profound
sleep, at least of the external sense, during which time
he had the most vivid confidence that he could not have
composed less than from two to three hundred lines; if that
indeed can be called composition in which all the images
rose up before him as things, with a parallel production
of the correspondent expressions, without any sensation or
consciousness of effort. On awaking he appeared to himself
to have a distinct recollection of the whole, and taking
his pen, ink, and paper, instantly and eagerly wrote down
the lines that are here preserved. At this moment he was
unfortunately called out by a person on business from Por-
lock, and detained by him above an hour, and on his return
to his room, found, to his no small surprise and mortifi-
cation, that though he still retained some vague and dim
recollection of the general purport of the vision, yet,
with the exception of some eight or ten scattered lines
and images, all the rest had passed away like the images
on the surface of a stream into which a stone has been
cast, but, alas! without the after restoration of the
latter!

It is clearly a vulgar error to think the poem a mere pipe
dream, which anyone could have written with the aid of opium. The
profound symbolism of "Kubla Khan" has continued to intrigue critics,
most of whom find that the pleasure dome suggests poetry, the sacred
river, the flow of inspiration, or instinctual life. About the
ancestral voices and the caves of ice there seems less agreement,
and students might be invited to venture their guesses. For a valuable modern reading of the poem, see Humphry House, "Kubla Khan,
Christabel and Dejection" in Coleridge (London: Rupert Hart-Davis,
1953), also reprinted in Romanticism and Consciousness, ed. Harold
Bloom (New York: Norton, 1970).

Some instructors may wish to bring in "The Rime of the Ancient
Mariner" as well--in which case it may be a temptation to go on to
Jung's theory of archetypes and to other dreamlike poems such as
Yeats's "The Second Coming" (page 219). A fine topic for a term
paper might be, after reading John Livingston Lowes's classic
source study The Road to Xanadu (Boston: Houghton Mifflin, 1927),
to argue whether it is worth trying to find out everything that may
have been going on in the back of a poet's mind, and to what extent
such investigations can end in certainty.

WILLIAM COWPER, Praise for the Fountain Opened, page 300

Here is a great eighteenth-century hymn, face-to-face with
Emily Dickinson's best known poem on the right-hand page. Many students are intrigued to discover that Dickinson's favorite stanza may
have been taken from the hymns she heard in church, and here is your
chance to demonstrate this theory persuasively. Dickinson, of
course, is freer in her off-riming (although Cowper permits himself
to rime prepared with reward). The proof of the influence is in the
singing--if you care to lead the class in song! "Praise for the
Fountain Opened" may be sung to the tune of the more familiar "O
God, Our Help in Ages Past," although the music of any other hymn
in common meter will fit. "Because I could not stop for Death" will
go surprisingly well to this tune, too.
Cowper's hymn may be a bit sanguine for contemporary taste,
but it is worth noting that its concerns with death and paradise are
often Dickinson's prime concerns as well. Both hymnists write in
the first person, reporting a spiritual experience as personal.
Dickinson, I think, is clearly the superior dramatist.

EMILY DICKINSON, Because I could not stop for Death, page 301

Questions for discussion:

1. What qualities does Emily Dickinson attribute to Death?
Why is Immortality going along on this carriage ride? (For the
poet, death and immortality go together. Besides, Dickinson is
amplifying her metaphor of Death as a gentleman taking a woman for
a drive: Immortality, as would have been proper in Amherst, is
their chaperone.)
2. Is the poem, as the poet wrote it, in some ways superior
to the version first printed? Is strove perhaps a richer word than
played? What is interesting in the phrase Gazing Grain? How can
grain "gaze"? (It has kernels like eyes at the tips of its stalks.
As the speaker dies, the natural world--like the fly in "I heard a
Fly buzz" on page 211--is watching.) What is memorable in the
rhythm and meaning of the line, The Dews drew quivering and chill?
(At quivering, the rhythm quivers loose from its iambic tetrameter.
The image of cold dampness foreshadows the next stanza, with its
images of the grave.)
3. What is the House? What is the Carriage?
4. Where is the speaker at the present moment of the poem?
Why is time said to pass more quickly where she is now? (Eternity
is timeless.)
5. What is the tone of the poem? (Complicated!--seriousness
enlivened with delicate macabre humor? Surely she kids her own
worldly busyness in the opening line.)

Don't fail to have the class try singing this poem and Cowper's
hymn, on the facing page, to the same tune. Whatever the quality of
your rendition, the result will be a class neither you nor the students will forget!

EMILY DICKINSON, I started Early-Took my Dog, page 302

It would be unfortunate if students were to regard this poem as nothing more than a sexual fantasy. Handled with frankness and tact, it can be an excellent class awakener. The poet expresses feelings for the natural world so intense that, like a mystic choosing erotic imagery to speak of the Beatific Vision, she can report her walk on the beach only in the language of a ravishing. The humor of the poem also is essential: the basement-dwelling mermaids, the poet's self-picture as a mouse.

EMILY DICKINSON, My Life had stood-a Loaded Gun, page 302

This astonishing metaphysical poem (another hymnlike work in common meter) can be an excellent provoker of class debate. Before trying to fathom it, students might well examine its diction. Sovreign Woods ("sovereign" would be the more usual spelling) suggest an estate owned by a king. How do the mountains reply? By echoing the gun's report. Apparently the smile is the flash from the gun's muzzle; and the Vesuvian face, a glimpse of the flaming crater of the volcano. The eider-duck, a sea duck, has particularly soft and silky down which is used in pillows and quilts. The gun's Yellow Eye seems, again, its flash; and the emphatic Thumb is presumably the impact of the bullet that flattens its victim. (Some will say the thumb is a trigger-finger but you don't pull a trigger with your thumb.)

Argument over the meaning of the poem will probably divide the class into two camps. One will see the poem, like "Because I could not stop for Death," as an account of resurrection, with the Owner being God or Christ who carries away the speaker, life and all, to the Happy Hunting Grounds of Paradise. Personally, I incline toward the other camp. In that view the Owner seems a mere mortal, perhaps a lover. The last stanza reveals that he can die. So taken, the last two lines make more sense. Not having the power to die, the speaker feels something lacking in her. She doesn't wish to outlive her huntsman and be a lonely killer. But the poem is tantalizingly ambiguous. You never can predict what a class discussion may reveal.

EMILY DICKINSON, Safe in their Alabaster Chambers, page 303

The middle stanza certainly isn't as fine as the two that surround it. It falls into a distracting hippetty-hop kind of rhythm, hardly appropriate to the stillness of a corpse. Students may need some filling-in on the nature of alabaster: a finely textured mineral, usually white and translucent, which was formerly used for making tombs and funeral urns. (There is another kind of harder alabaster that resembles marble.) Rafter of Satin suggests the satin-lined coffin lid; Roof of Stone, either the tombstone or the stone slab that closes the grave.

The last stanza is beautifully crazy. In relating this motion-
less corpse to the wheeling stars, the poem recalls Wordsworth's
brief poem about Lucy Gray, Rolled round in earth's diurnal course
(see "A Slumber Did My Spirit Seal," page 124). Some students may
feel the need to interpret the disc of snow with soundless dots on
it as a spotted dinnerplate, or an ice floe with igloos on it. The
disc of snow is apparently that cold, still soundlessness that even
doges and diadem-crowned heads of state finally come to; but when
Dickinson says disc of snow, I think she means disc of snow. It is
a strange, dreamlike object, but why belabor it?

JOHN DONNE, The Bait, page 303

Izaak Walton, who included "The Bait" in The Compleat Angler,
declared that Donne wrote the poem in order to prove that he could
write softly and smoothly when he wished.
     Writing answers to Marlowe's shepherd apparently was a popular
Elizabethan parlor game. (There is also Sir Walter Raleigh's "The
Nymph's Reply.") Donne certainly alters and complicates the tone
of Marlowe's gentle Petrarchan pastoral. As a comparison of the
figures of speech in the two poems will show, Donne characteristically relies on paradox (For thou thyself art thine own bait) and
on an extended metaphor: loved one is bait; lover, fish. Donne
renders Marlowe's concept thoughtier and injects notes of grating
realism: freeze, cut their legs, coarse hands wrestling live fish
from slimy nest. Donne's lines 13-14 may need paraphrasing. My
attempt: if you don't wish to be seen skinny-dipping, then just
eclipse the sun and moon with your superior radiance.

JOHN DONNE, Death be not proud, page 304

During the Renaissance, when life was short, a man of the cloth
like John Donne would have surprised no one by being on familiar
terms with death. Still, "Death be not proud," one of Donne's "Holy
Sonnets," is an almost startling put-down of poor death. Staunchly
Christian in its sure expectation of the resurrection, Donne's poem
personifies death as an adversary swollen with false pride and un-
worthy of being called mighty and dreadful. (For another bold personification, see "Batter my heart, three-personed God [page 39],
also one of the "Holy Sonnets," where Donne sees God as ravisher.)
     In "Death be not proud" the poet accuses death of being little
more than a slave bossed around by fate, chance, kings, and desperate men--a craven thing that keeps bad company, such as poison,
war, and sickness. Finally Donne taunts death with a paradox:
death, thou shalt die.
     Of interest, though perhaps of less than immediate usefulness
in the classroom, are the articles on Donne's religious poetry by
Helen Gardner, Louis L. Martz, and Stanldy Archer in John Donne's
Poetry: Authoritative Texts, Criticism, selected and edited by
A. L. Clements in a W. W. Norton paperback edition (New York, 1966).

121

All three explore the extent to which Jesuit methods of meditation
might have influenced the "Holy Sonnets."

It might be instructive for students to compare two personifications of death: Donne's and Emily Dickinson's in "Because I could
not stop for Death" (page 301), where death appears in the guise of
a courtly gentleman who stops by to take the poet for a pleasant
ride.

JOHN DONNE, A Valediction: Forbidding Mourning, page 305

In his Life of Donne, Izaak Walton tells us that Donne wrote
this poem for his wife in 1611, when he was about to depart on a
diplomatic mission to France.

Much of the meaning of the poem depends upon the metaphor of
the compasses in the last three stanzas. There is probably no
better way to make sure students understand it clearly than to bring
in a draftsman's compass--even the Woolworth's variety--and to demonstrate the metaphor with it. There'll always be someone who thinks
Donne means the kind of compass that indicates north.

Some questions for discussion:

1. What is a valediction anyway? (What is a high school
"valedictorian"?)

2. Why does the speaker forbid mourning? Do lines 1-4 mean
that he is dying? Explain this metaphor about the passing away of
virtuous men. (As saints take leave of this world--so sweetly and
calmly that one hardly knows they're gone--let us take leave of
each other.)

3. In lines 7-8, what is suggested by the words with religious
denotations? Profanation (the desecration of a sacred thing), the
laity. What is the idea? (Love seems to the speaker a holy mystery. He and his wife are its priests or ministers.)

4. Explain the reference to astronomy in the third stanza.
(Earthquakes shake, rattle, and roll; Ptolemaic spheres revolve
gently and harmlessly. This takes us to the notion of sublunary
lovers in stanza four. In the medieval cosmos, the heavenly bodies
are fixed and permanent, while everything under the moon is subject
to change.)

5. Paraphrase stanza four. (Unlike common lovers, bound to
their earthly passions, we have less need of those things that serve
sensual love: namely, bodies.)

6. Why is beaten gold an appropriate image in the sixth stanza?
What connotations does gold have? (Refined, precious, durable,
capable of being extended without breaking.)

7. Comment on the word hearkens, line 31. (As a draftsman's
compass will illustrate, the fixed central foot leans forward when
the compass is extended, as if, in Donne's metaphor, eager for the
other mate's return.)

JOHN DRYDEN, To the Memory of Mr. Oldham, page 306

With the aid of Dryden's great short poem (and the selections
in the book from Swift, Pope, and Johnson), one at least can acquaint
students with a little of neoclassical poetry. One can point out,
too, that such poetry is not quite dead in America in our own day,
as may be seen from the poems of Yvor Winters (page 389) and J. V.
Cunningham (pages 43, 47, 173). The directness and plainness of
Dryden's poem are clear from its very opening, and in teaching it
one can question the assumption that neoclassical poetry is written
only in bookish and Latinate words. That the poem is cast in heroic
couplets is meaningful, for the regular pauses demanded by its end-
stopped lines produce a rhythm more appropriate to such a meditation than, say, the rhythm of Robert Lowell's run-on lines in "At
the Altar" (page 146).

In teaching Dryden's poem, one can also mention (and define)
the elegy, and can refer students to other famous elegies in the
text: those of Milton (page 14) and Gray (page 267). If one is
going to teach "Lycidas," Dryden's succinct poem might well serve
as an introduction. It may be readily compared with "Lycidas" in
that it mourns the death of a poet, expresses abhorrence for knaves,
and observes a few classical conventions.

A. E. Housman's "To an Athlete Dying Young" also may be likened
to Dryden's poem in that both poets favor classical conventions:
footraces with laurels as crowns and the dead hero's descent into
the underworld. Both poets find that premature death can confer
benefits. What would Oldham have gained had he survived? More
polish as a poet, yet he would have lost much of his force. In
reading Housman's poem, students can be helped to recognize its
metaphors: the comparison in the first two stanzas of victor's
chair and dead lad's coffin, the comparison in line 5 of all human
life to a footrace, with death at the finish line. Students might
be asked if they know of any living proof of Housman's observation
that sometimes the name dies before the man (a truth often shown by
the wistfulness of old football players at alumni weekends).

ALAN DUGAN, Love Song: I and Thou, page 306

Except in his title, Dugan doesn't refer to I and Thou, the
work by Martin Buber, Jewish philosopher and Zionist. But in its
theme, Dugan's poem shares Buber's view that a meaningful rapport
with others is necessary in order to endure the human condition.

Dugan's cockeyed homemade house is his life, which he will
endure like a prolonged crucifixion. The house-warming in line 14
may be infancy: the thumb that the baby Dugan sucked purple is
like the bruised thumb of the amateur carpenter whose hammer slipped.
The prime whiskey of rage is the baby's first stimulant: primal,
because indulged in from the start. In the last lines, trying to
crucify oneself is a hopeless task (like trying to ply a nail-
scissors with both hands). Some things one can't do for oneself.

306-309 (text pages)

Humorous and self-mocking in tone up until the end, Dugan's "Love Song" ends on a note of grudging tenderness.

BOB DYLAN, Subterranean Homesick Blues, page 307

Dylan has been called a surrealist, but the label seems misleading. In this comic nightmare he proceeds by free association, shifting his point of view at will, not especially trying to tell a complete story or to place events in any chronology. Who these characters are and how they relate to one another is up to the listener to decide. Having an academic and tidying sort of mind, I think of the scene as a city commune-house full of runaways. Johnny supports the place by making drugs. The man in the trenchcoat is a plainclothesman who wants his payoff; the new friend is a dealer whose fixes are high-priced. Maggie, who sounds the Cassandra warning, may be another resident. In the first half of each stanza, the point of view is that of the kid himself, depicting the scene and then (in the last two stanzas) reporting what he hears the voices of society telling him. With the refrain Look out kid, the second half of each stanza also brings in those voices--or perhaps it is still the kid, speaking for them in a resentful parody.

Dylan, who borrowed his stage name from Dylan Thomas, has learned from many bookish poets as well as from Woody Guthrie and other singers. One influence, I suspect, is T. S. Eliot. Compare "Subterranean Homesick Blues" with another poem in which the situation is enlightened only far enough to remain mysterious, "Sweeney Among the Nightingales" (not in the text).

If students can stand to look at this song closely without feeling that they are violating it, they may realize that it is what it is because of art. Such sixteen-line stanzas, neatly divided in the middle, do not happen by themselves, even if they do have a tune to follow. Even on the page, Dylan's song keeps asserting its metrical pattern powerfully: two heavy stresses, pause, another pair of stresses, line break, and then the same again: GET SICK / GET WELL / HANG aROUND an / INK WELL. And its feminine rimes, though playful, carry serious suggestions. That leaders rimes with parking meters hints, perhaps, that both are mechanisms for demanding money. People who wear sandals are associated with scandals and vandals, not just associated in the rime scheme but also in the middle-class Establishment's opinion, which Dylan travesties.

Question for the class: in what ways is this "Blues" similar to an urban folk song such as "Good Mornin', Blues" (page 118), and in what ways is it something else?

Whatever this song is about, Dylan clearly knows how it feels to be one of the juvenile street people. At times he has fictionalized his biography, but perhaps there is truth in his remark, "Hibbing was a good ol' town. I ran away from it when I was 10, 12, 13, 15½, 17, an' 18. I been caught and brought back all but once."

124

T. S. ELIOT, Journey of the Magi, page 309

   The speaker is a very old man (All this was a long time ago
. . .), looking forward to his death. As his mind roves back
over the past, it is mainly the discomforts and frustrations of his
journey that he remembers, and when he comes to the part we have
been waiting for, his account of the Nativity, he seems still
mystified, as though uncertainly trying to figure out what had hap-
pened--There was a Birth, certainly. Apparently the whole experience was so devastating that he prefers to omit all further details.
His plight was to recognize Christ as God and yet to be unable to
accept Christ as his savior. Being a king, he did not renounce his
people but they henceforth seemed alien to him, clutching their dis-
credited gods like useless dolls.
   The passage beginning Then at dawn (lines 21-28) is full of
foreshadowings, both hopeful and sinister. Besides the symbolic
white horse, the vine leaves suggest Christ who said to his disci-
ples, "I am the vine, ye are the branches" (John 15:5). The tavern
customers suggest the Roman soldiers who will drink and cast dice
at the cross.
   Although Eliot's dissatisfied Magus isn't one of the kings
portrayed by Yeats in "The Magi" (page 396)--being dissatisfied for
different reasons--it is curious that Eliot may have taken the
dramatic situation of his poem from one of Yeats's stories. In
"The Adoration of the Magi" in Yeats's prose collection Mythologies
(reprinted in 1925, two years before Eliot first published his poem),
three old men call on the storyteller, and drawing close to his
fire, insist on telling him of a journey they had made when young,
and of a vision of Bethlehem. Like Eliot's speaker, who repeats
set down / This set down / This, they demand that their story be
taken down word for word.
   Among the useful discussions of Eliot's poem are Elizabeth
Drew's in T. S. Eliot: The Design of His Poetry (New York: Scribner's, 1949), pp. 118-122, and Grover Smith's in T. S. Eliot's
Poetry and Plays (Chicago; University of Chicago Press, 1960),
pp. 121-125. More recently, Daniel A. Harris has characterized
the Magus as a primitive Christian with a "baffled consciousness
of mystery." See his article "Language, History, and Text in
Eliot's 'Journey of the Magi,'" PMLA 95 (1980), pp. 838-856. But
Harris's opinions are questioned by William Skaff in a letter in
PMLA 96 (1981), pp. 420-422: "In 'Journey' Eliot adopts the dramatic mask of the Magus in order to express his own struggles with
literal belief, his real 'religious position of 1927.'"

T. S. ELIOT, The Love Song of J. Alfred Prufrock, page 310

   Teaching any basic course in literature, I'd have to be
desperate for time not to devote to "Prufrock" at least a class or
two. Eliot's early masterpiece can open such diverse matters as
theme, tone, irony, persona, imagery, figures of speech, allusion,
symbolism, and the difference between saying and suggesting. Most
students will enjoy it and remember it.

310--313 (text pages)

Questions to raise:

1. Why the epigraph from Dante? What expectations does it arouse? (Perhaps that this "song" will be the private confession of someone who thinks himself trapped and unredeemable, and thinks it of his hearer, too.)

2. What facts about J. Alfred can we be sure of? His age, his manner of dress, his social circles? What does his name suggest? Can you detect any puns in it? (A prude in a frock--a formal coat.)

3. What do you make of the simile in lines 2-3? What does it tell us about this particular evening? ((Etherized suggests fog, also submission, waiting for something grim to happen.) What does it tell you about Prufrock's way of seeing things? ("A little sick," some students may say, and with reason.)

4. What gnaws at Prufrock? (Not just his sense of growing old, not just his inability to act. He suffers from Prufrock's Complaint: dissociation of sensibility. In line 105, unable to join thought and feeling, he sees his own nerves existing at one remove from him, as if thrown on a screen by a projector.)

5. Who are "you and I" in the opening line? Who are "we" at the end? (Some possibilities: Prufrock and the woman he is attending. Prufrock and the reader. Prufrock and Prufrock--he's talking to himself, "you" being the repressive self, "I" being the timid or repressed self. Prufrock and the other eggheads of the Western world--in this view, the poem is Eliot's satire on the intelligentsia.)

6. What symbols do you find and what do they suggest? Notice those that relate to the sea, even oyster-shells (line 7). (I point out blatantly that water has connotations of sexual fulfillment, and quote "Western Wind." Eliot hints that unlike Prufrock, the vulgar types who inhabit cheap hotels and fish shops have a love life.)

7. Try to explain the last three lines.

8. Now summarize the story of the poem. What parts does it fall into? (Part one: Prufrock prepares to try to ask the overwhelming question. Then in lines 84-86 we learn that he has failed to ask it. In 87-110 he tries to justify himself for chickening out. From 111 to the end, he sums up his static present and hollow future.)

That Eliot may have taken the bones of his plot from Henry James's story "Crapy Cornelia" (1909) is Grover Smith's convincing theory. "This is the story of White-Mason, a middle-aged bachelor of nostalgic temperament, who visits a young Mrs. Worthingham to propose marriage but reconsiders owing to the difference in their worlds." (T. S. Eliot's Poetry and Plays [Chicago: University of Chicago Press, 1960], p. 15.)

T. S. Eliot Reading His Poetry (Caedmon recording TC 1045) includes the poet's rendition of "Prufrock."

RALPH WALDO EMERSON, Days, page 314

As F. O. Matthiessen has pointed out, Emerson's "Oriental procession through his Concord garden" is an extended metaphor that becomes a parable. (<u>American Renaissance</u> [New York: Oxford University Press, 1941].) The lesson of the parable, which students may be asked to state, is that we foolishly squander life on trivia, overlooking riches before our eyes.

First printed in <u>The Atlantic Monthly</u> (Vol. 1, No. 1), "Days" has been much celebrated. Emerson thought it his best poem; Matthiessen has agreed; and Emerson's biographer Ralph L. Rusk has called it "a masterpiece in unemotional black and white." Still, it seems not immune to further criticism. Why is <u>bread</u> (line 6) a higher good than herbs and apples? One can almost imagine "Days" among James Thurber's "Famous Poems Illustrated": the Day going off scowling, "Why didn't you take more, you dumb-ox?"

ROBERT FROST, Mending Wall, page 314

This familiar poem is often misread, or loaded with needless symbolism. Some possible notions you might meet:

1. That the poem is an allegory: the wall stands for some political barrier such as high tariffs, immigration quotas, the Berlin Wall, or the Iron Curtain. But can the text of the poem lend such a notion any support? Frost, according to Louis Untermeyer, frowned on all attempts to add to the wall's meaning: "He denies that the poem says anything more than it seems to say." (Note in <u>Robert Frost's Poems</u> [New York: Washington Square Press, 1964].)
2. Frost's theme is that fences should be destroyed. Up with communal land, away with private property! But as Radcliffe Squires points out, none of Frost's other poetry supports such a left-wing view. Neither does "Mending Wall" support it, "for the poet-narrator himself cooperates with the wall-builder, replacing the stones in the spring even as he protests in spirit." (<u>The Major Themes of Robert Frost</u> [Ann Arbor: University of Michigan Press, 1963].)
3. The maxim "Good fences make good neighbors" is just a smug platitude for which the speaker has only contempt. This view would make him out to be a cynic. Yet, by cooperating in the wall-mending, the speaker lends the maxim some truth. Although limited in imagination, the neighbor isn't an idiot. (Frost is portraying, by the way, an actual farmer he liked: the cheerful Napoleon Guay, owner of the farm next door to the Frosts' farm in Derry, New Hampshire. See <u>New Hampshire's Child: The Derry Journals of Leslie Frost</u> [Albany: State University of New York Press, 1969].)

At the center of the poem is a contrast between two ways to regard mending a wall. The speaker's view is announced in the first line; the neighbor's is repeated in the last. "The opposing statements," says Untermeyer, "are uttered by two different types of people--and both are right." Students may be asked to define the very different temperaments of speaker and neighbor. A hard-working farmer to whom spring means walls to mend, the neighbor lacks fancy and frivolity. Spring is all around him, yet he <u>moves in darkness</u>, as though blind. Lines 30-40 compare him to a man of the Stone Age. A conservative from habit, he mends walls mainly because his father did. The speaker, full of mischief and imagination, is presumably a poet who wants to do no more hard labor than he can help. Speaker enjoys having some fun with neighbor, telling him that apple trees won't invade pines. Mending walls is a kind of spring ritual, and the speaker likes to pretend there is magic in it: using a spell to make stones balance, blaming the wear-and-tear of winter upon elves--or more exactly, upon some Something not to be offended.

After studying "Mending Wall" and after hearing some of its blank verse, students might enjoy Kenneth Koch's parody, "Mending Sump" (page 242).

ROBERT FROST, Stopping by Woods on a Snowy Evening, page 315

Students will think they know this poem from their elementary school textbooks in which it is usually illustrated as though it were about a little horse, but they may need to have its darker suggestions underlined for them. Although one can present a powerful case for seeing Frost as a spokesman for the death wish, quoting other Frost poems such as "Come In," "To Earthward," and "Into My Own," I think it best to concentrate on this familiar poem and to draw the class to state what it implies. The last stanza holds the gist of it, and I ask, What would he do if he <u>didn't</u> keep his promises? There is sense, however, in an objection a student once made to me: maybe he wouldn't go into the woods and lie down and freeze, maybe he'd just stay admiring the snow for another fifteen minutes and be late for milking. "People are always trying to find a death wish in that poem," Frost told an audience at the Bread Loaf Writers' Conference in 1960. "But there's a life wish there--he goes on, doesn't he?"

I ask students if they see anything unusual about the rime scheme of the poem (rimes linking the stanzas as in <u>terza rima</u> or as in Shelley's "Ode to the West Wind"), and then ask what problem this rime scheme created for the poet as the poem neared its end. How else would Frost have ended it if he hadn't hit upon that magnificent repetition? In 1950 Frost wrote to a friend, "I might confess the trade secret that I wrote the third line of the last stanza of Stopping by Woods in such a way as to call for another stanza when I didn't want another stanza and didn't have another stanza in me, but with great presence of mind and a sense of what a good boy I was I instantly struck the line out and made my exit with a repeat end." (Quoted by Cleanth Brooks and Robert Penn Warren, <u>Understanding Poetry</u>, 2nd ed. [New York: Holt, Rinehart and Winston, 1950], pp. 603-604.) On another occasion, Frost declared that to

have a line in the last stanza that didn't rime with anything would
have seemed a flaw. "I considered for a moment winding up with a
three line stanza. The repetend was the only logical way to end
such a poem." (Letter of 1923 to Sylvester Baxter, given by R. C.
Townsend, New England Quarterly, 36 [June 1963], p. 243.)

That this famous poem may be sung to the old show tune "Hernan-
do's Hideaway" (from Pajama Game) was discovered by college students
working as waiters at the Bread Loaf Writers' Conference in 1960.
They cornered Frost one evening and sang it to him. He laughed till
he cried.

Paper topic: read Lionel Trilling's speech at Robert Frost's
eighty-fifth birthday dinner in which he maintained, "I think of
Robert Frost as a terrifying poet." ("A Speech on Robert Frost:
A Cultural Episode," Partisan Review, 26 [Summer 1959], pp. 445-452;
also reprinted in Robert Frost: A Collection of Critical Essays,
ed. James M. Cox [Englewood Cliffs, N.J.: Prentice-Hall, 1962].)
Referring to "Stopping by Woods" and other Frost poems, state to
what extent you agree with Trilling's view or disagree with it.

Frost reads the poem on An Album of Modern Poetry (Library of
Congress, PL 20) and on Robert Frost Reading His Own Poems, record
no. 1 (EL LCB 1941, obtainable from the National Council of Teachers
of English, 1111 Kenyon Road, Urbana, Ill. 61801). Both recordings
also include "Fire and Ice."

ROBERT FROST, The Witch of Coös, page 316

There was at least one actual Witch of Coös and Frost's poem
was inspired by a local anecdote about her, according to Laurance
Thompson (Selected Letters of Robert Frost [New York: Holt, Rinehart and Winston, 1964], p. 473).

"Robert Frost," said his friend Sidney Cox, "is always a little
mocking toward witches." While letting the mother and her son do
"all the talking," Frost makes it possible for us to read the whole
yarn as a lie. The mother evidently has a local reputation as a
witch and she wants to maintain it. "Folks" seem disappointed that
she doesn't summon spirits and she tells this tale to show that
spirits can be fearsome, as if to excuse herself for not summoning
them. The son can't hear the walking skeleton now, only the mother
can (line 24). Son reports the convincing detail that the skeleton
carried itself like a pile of dishes, but admits he was a baby at
the time. For husband Toffile, the skeleton was quite invisible;
he couldn't even hear it climb the attic stairs (lines 117-118).
We have only the mother's word for it all, and her only evidence is
a bone in her button-box (which doesn't turn up). As she herself
declares, "Summoning spirits isn't Button, button, / Who's got the
button."

Although Frost offers no psychological explanation for Mother's
fantasies, he gives us reason to do our own explaining. Is the
skeleton just a dream of a lover she had merely longed for? So
Richard Poirier suggests in Robert Frost: The Work of Knowing (New
York: Oxford University Press, 1977). As in Frost's dramatic

monologue "A Servant to Servants," "we have a woman imagining a
figure of insane, frustrated, and obscene sexuality caged in a house
with a married couple. And this married couple, too, is ever so
subtly characterized as possibly sexless, possibly frigid." Poirier
finds a symbol of frustration in the double-locked doors swollen
tight and buried under snow (lines 56-57). Whether or not the instructor wishes to encourage such symbol hunting, lines 37-44 give
a capsule account of a moribund marriage and students can at least
be asked to comment on the quality of Mother and Toffile's life together!

For an interpretation that takes the mother's story at face
value, see Allen Tate's "Robert Frost as Metaphysical Poet" in
Robert Frost: Lectures on the Centennial of His Birth (Washington,
D.C.: Library of Congress, 1975). Judging the "Witch" Frost's
finest longer poem, Tate calls it "a marvelous development of the
common saying that we all have a skeleton in the closet."

Whether we believe the mother or doubt her, this delicious
ghost story surely gains from its matter-of-fact telling. If students think its language flat and prosaic (as did one of my students,
who even complained at my calling it poetry), passages can be read
aloud and their blank verse form paid notice. Ordinary speech in a
Frost poem seems ordinary only if one ignores its meter. To hear
Frost read is to understand this more clearly, and also to understand what he meant by "the sound of sense" (briefly discussed on
page 59 of this manual). Frost's dry, deliberate readings of both
"The Witch of Coös" and "Mending Wall" are (conveniently) the first
two selections on side 2 of Robert Frost Reads His Poetry (Caedmon
TC 1060).

TESS GALLAGHER, Under Stars, page 319

The content of this poem is simple enough. The speaker goes
out in the night to post a letter in her roadside mailbox; she
imagines a millworker and his wife beginning their day before she
herself has gone to bed; and she remembers childhood games played
outside in the dark.

The poem contains many small, exact details--the white envelope,
the rain-heavy bushes, the white slices of bread the millworker's
wife has laid out for him, to name a few. Yet the most important
details are omitted entirely. The poet does not tell us who is to
receive her letter, whose are the starry voices toward which she
walks, or to what she is returned by all she touches on the way.
Maybe she is purposely vague about these points because her intent
is not to tell a story, but to create for the reader the kind of
pensive mood familiar to those who have ever found themselves alone
under the stars.

Biographical facts about Tess Gallagher do not really help us
to find our way deeper into "Under Stars," the title poem from her
third published book where it appears last in a section called "The
Ireland Poems." We do learn from James K. Robinson's entry about
her in Contemporary Poets that she traveled in Ireland in 1976. In

this entry, Tess Gallagher comments, "Only in the language I have made for myself in the poems am I in touch with all the past, present, and future moments of my consciousness and unconsciousness. The poem is the moment of all possibilities where I try to speak in a concert of tenses, to reflect the intersection of the various time-zones of actualities and imaginative transformations. I don't want to disappear into the present tense, the awful NOW. I want to survive it and to take others with me."

ALLEN GINSBERG, A Supermarket in California, page 320

A comparison of this poem with Walt Whitman's "I Saw in Louisiana a Live-Oak Growing" (page 385) and "To a Locomotive in Winter" (page 13) demonstrates the extent to which Ginsberg, in his tribute to Whitman, uses very Walt Whitman-like "enumerations." Ginsberg's long sentences, use of free verse, parentheses, and fulsome phrases (childless, lonely old grubber, lonely old courage-teacher, etc.) are further indications that he is paying tribute to Whitman in part by echoing his style.

There is in "A Supermarket in California" as well a quality of surrealism that is Ginsberg's own. The existence of a neon fruit supermarket, the juxtaposition of past and present, the inclusion of Spanish poet García Lorca (like Ginsberg and Whitman, a homosexual) down by the watermelons, and the references to Charon and to the River Lethe all hover at the edges of dream.

Questions for discussion: what does Ginsberg mean when he speaks of the lost America of love? What does the poem say about loneliness? about death? (Whitman's death, in the poem, is as lonely a journey as Ginsberg imagines his life to have been.)

DONALD HALL, The Town of Hill, page 321

In the poem (I think), the mature poet imagines the sunken town and, as though in a dream, sees himself as a boy walking through it. Like its Hall-like name, flooded Hill seems close to him. Perhaps the sunken town is childhood, now submerged in memory, and in the poet's mind something like an underwater door gently closes it. This beautifully phrased poem is symbolism, however, not allegory. Hall has written about the poem (which is the outcome of fifty or sixty drafts) in Fifty Contemporary Poets: The Creative Process, ed. Alberta T. Turner (New York: David McKay, 1977). After answering all the compiler's questions, he warns, "To read the poem, you must stop paraphrasing, stop 'thinking' in the conventional way, and do some receiving instead."

THOMAS HARDY, Channel Firing, page 322

To whom does your refer in Hardy's opening line? To all of us, the living. Writing a poem from the perspective of a buried corpse

131

(as Hardy does) might lead us to expect something dismal and grim.
Although bitter, the poem is funny, but I have found that some
students need to have its humor underlined. One can center on the
portrait of Parson Thirdly, that poor old skeleton sadly wondering
if his life was one huge mistake. (Compare his nostalgia for pipes
and beer to Housman's remark in "Terence, this is stupid stuff"
(page 329): And malt does more than Milton can. Parson Thirdly of
Weatherbury, incidentally, is a character who flits through Chapter
42 of Hardy's novel Far From the Madding Crowd. Perhaps he gets his
name from his rhetorical method of preaching: "And thirdly . . ."

What is meant by the allusions in the last stanza to Stourton,
Camelot, and Stonehenge? The point may be that all these landmarks
are vestiges of the past, now vanished under the impersonal light of
the stars. Hardy implies that a similar fate may befall our own
civilization. We too may vanish and be succeeded by people no less
bellicose, no less confident of their arms, and no less transient.

Students may be asked what "Channel Firing" has in common with
Richard Eberhart's "The Fury of Aerial Bombardment" (page 55). Both
Hardy and Eberhart address the subject of war. Their theme, as I
see it, is this: man obtains a glimpse of God's attitude toward
him and his sins, and feels shock or horror at the glimpse. Eberhart, apparently speaking in his own person (that of the naval
officer), fears that God may be willing to sit back forever, letting
the beast in man run wild. Hardy's dead men are certain that that
is the case. As usual, Hardy portrays Jehovah as a cruel and in-
scrutable tyrant, toying with man for His amusement. Eberhart has
no such hostility toward the God of tradition; he merely suspects
that God may be indifferent after all.

J. O. Bailey suggests a different interpretation: "God is
compassionate: realizing that men 'rest eternal sorely need,' He
may not 'blow the trumpet' for Judgment after all." (The Poetry of
Thomas Hardy [Chapel Hill: University of North Carolina Press,
1970].) In Hardy's view, does God seem kind?

For a sensitive reading of the poem, see John Crowe Ransom's
introduction to his edition of Hardy's Selected Poems (New York:
Macmillan, 1960). Ransom thinks the lyrical last lines mean that
the guns will not prevail; the ancient shrines will endure. "The
finest technical detail of the poem is in the forced stresses which
the meter places upon the last syllables of the final word: star-
lít Stonehénge."

THOMAS HARDY, The Convergence of the Twain, page 323

The bestselling novel Raise the Titanic may have brought this
famous catastrophe into students' general knowledge. Still, a few
facts may help clarify Hardy's poem. The pride of the British
White Star lines, the Titanic was the world's largest ship, celebrated for luxurious trappings (including Turkish baths and a fully
equipped gymnasium). Many of the unlucky passengers were wealthy
and famous. One reason the Titanic sank with such great cost of
life was that the builders, smugly assuming the ship unsinkable,

had provided lifeboats for fewer than half the 2,200 passengers.
(Only 705 survived.) Hardy wrote the poem for the souvenir program
of a benefit show for the Titanic Disaster Fund (to aid survivors
and the bereaved) given at Covent Garden, May 14, 1912.

Hardy has been seen as an enemy of science and industrialism,
those spoilers of rural England, but Donald Davie argues that "The
Convergence of the Twain" shows no such animosity. The poem cen-
sures vanity and luxury, "but not the technology which built the
great ship and navigated her." (Thomas Hardy and British Poetry
[Oxford: Oxford University Press, 1972].)

Although Hardy personally knew two victims of the disaster, the
"Convergence," as J. O. Bailey points out, is not a personal lament;
indeed, the drowned are hardly mentioned. The poem is a philosophic
argument, with the Immanent Will punishing man for pride: "It acts
like the Greek concept of Fate that rebukes hubris." (The Poetry of
Thomas Hardy [Chapel Hill: University of North Carolina Press,
1970].) Fate, however, seems personified in the poem as the Spinner
of Years, a mere agent of the Will.

Students can concentrate profitably on the poet's choice of
words: those that suggest the exotic unnaturalness of the Titanic's
furnishings (salamandrine, opulent, jewels . . . to ravish the
sensuous mind, gilded). Diction will also point to the metaphor of
the marriage between ship and iceberg: the intimate welding and the
consummation. The late Allen Tate was fond of reading this poem
aloud to his friends, with mingled affection and contempt, and re-
marking (according to Robert Kent) that it held "too many dead
words, dead then as now, and all the more obtuse for having been
long dead in Shelley. 'Stilly,' for example." From Hardy's original printed version of the poem, as given in The Variorum Edition of
the Complete Poems of Thomas Hardy, ed. by James Gibson (New York:
Macmillan, 1979), it appears that he originally cast line 6: The
cold, calm currents strike their rhythmic tidal lyres. Isn't thrid
an improvement, even though it is stiltedly archaic?

SEAMUS HEANEY, Sunlight, page 324

What is a sunlit absence? Absence of motion, perhaps, on a
sunny afternoon in the country. This poem's diction is arresting;
students who pay attention to it, with the aid of a dictionary if
necessary, will be amply rewarded. The poet manages to be both
accurate and surprising in such phrases as helmeted pump, slung
bucket, and plaque of heat. (The dictionary defines "plaque" as
"a flat plate, slab, or disk that is ornamental or engraved for
mounting." Imagine a plaque of heat coming at you and you know
that this was one hot stove!)

The woman in the poem says nothing. How, then, does the poet
bring her alive? Ask your class to notice that her hands scuffled
over the bakeboard and that she has measling (measly? thus "con-
temptibly small, meager"?) shins. Encourage students on the basis
of these and additional details to characterize the woman Heaney
portrays.

133

Why, in this poem, are two clocks better than one? (Two clocks double the impact of the poem's quiet power.)

The simile that ends the poem deserves special notice. What does a tinsmith's scoop in the meal-bin have to do with love? Why is the scoop sunk past its gleam? Like the woman herself, perhaps, the love which underlies the performance of her everyday tasks is plain, quiet, simple, past its gleam--but solidly grounded, like the scoop in the meal-bin.

Richard Murphy, in The New York Review of Books, September 30, 1976, has remarked of "Sunlight":

> Every word in it rings true to the culture, to my memory of Ireland in the past, to its sad beauty. The play of light and shadow in this poem, the spaces filled by sunlight, the woman baking bread, the tick of two clocks work like a revelation as in the art of Vermeer. I'm thinking of the Officer and Laughing Girl at the Frick, where a dark moment of time is suspended forever in a ray of light that pours through an open window, crosses a blank wall under a map of Holland, and is caught up by a girl's ecstatic smile.

ANTHONY HECHT, The Vow, page 325

The fear that too powerful a blend of Jewish and Irish spirits caused the miscarriage is foreshadowed in the opening lines: The mirth of tabrets ceaseth, as does the joy of the Irish minstrel harp. (Ceaseth gives the line an Old Testament ring.) Apparently the poem reflects part of the poet's life: Hecht and his first wife, Patricia Harris, were married in 1954; they had two sons. "The Vow" was first printed in 1957.

Does the speaker accept the dream-child's tragic view that the best of all fates is not to be born? Evidently not, or he wouldn't make the vow. The bone gates (line 13) are not only the classical gates of horn, but literally the mother's pelvic girdle. Stanza 3 seems to me a weak one in an otherwise powerful poem. In rhetoric, diction (Mother, . . .), and imagery, it recalls the earlier Robert Lowell (see for instance "Christmas Eve Under Hooker's Statue" in Lord Weary's Castle).

In the last stanza, the metallurgical metaphor will probably need explaining. Gentile and Jewish parents will be tried (re-fined, perfected) by the flames of their love. Possibly Hecht has in mind amalgamation--the only gold-refining process that uses a furnace--in which mercury and crude gold unite, then separate under high heat to produce pure gold.

Hecht has recorded "The Vow" for The Spoken Arts Treasury of 100 Modern American Poets, vol. 15 (SA 1054).

GEORGE HERBERT, Love, page 326

Herbert's poem is often read as an account of a person's reception into the Church; the eaten meat, as the Eucharist. Herbert's extended conceits or metaphors are also evident in "The Pulley" (page 94) and "Redemption" (page 210).

For discussion: compare "Love" with another seventeenth-century devotional poem, Donne's "Batter my heart," (page 39). What is the tone of each poem? Herbert may seem less intense, almost reticent by comparison. Douglas Bush comments, "Herbert does not attempt the high pitch of Donne's 'Divine Poems.' His great effects are all the greater for rising out of a homely, colloquial quietness of tone; and peace brings quiet endings--'So I did sit and eat.'" (English Literature in the Earlier Seventeenth Century [New York: Oxford University Press, 1945], p. 139.)

George Herbert, by the way, is an Anglican saint--according to Anthony Hecht, the only one who does not also appear in the Roman Catholic calendar.

ROBERT HERRICK, Delight in Disorder, page 327

Herrick's lovely poem is easy to paraphrase badly ("sloppiness is sexy") and students will need to see the meanings of its words. Wantonness does not mean licentiousness; and Herrick is not condemning it (a wrong impression some students may get at first by recalling Robert Graves's "Down, Wanton, Down!"). It means a natural and pleasing wildness, that freedom enjoyed by (in poetic diction) "wanton breezes" or "a wanton brook." Enthralls is a wonderful word: literally, the lace keeps the stomacher in check, keeping it pressed against the bosom; in another sense, the lace charms the garment. (The poet seems to attribute to the clothes his own kindled feelings.)

Delightful disorder is a principle of Herrick's poetry. Great master of metrical verse that he is, he knows that a poem "too precise in every part" (perfectly conforming, say, to an iambic pattern) would seem studied and monotonous. "Delight in Disorder," of course, contains many departures from absolutely regular iambic tetrameter. Herrick states his prosodic principle in a poem about his poetry, "A Request to the Graces":

> Teach it to blush, to curtsie, lisp, and shew
> Demure, but yet, full of temptation too.
> Numbers ne'er tickle, or but lightly please,
> Unless they have some wanton carriages.

ROBERT HERRICK, To the Virgins, to Make Much of Time, page 327

Roses would have suited Herrick's iambic meter--why is rosebuds richer? Rosebuds are flowers not yet mature, and therefore suggest virgins, not matrons. There may be a sexual hint besides:

135

rose-buds more resemble private parts than roses. But in this poem time flies; the rose-buds of line 1 bloom in line 3. Rose-buds is also rhythmically stronger than roses, as Austin Warren has pointed out: it has a secondary stress as well as a primary. Warren has recalled that when he first read the poem in college in 1917, he misread rose-buds as roses, kept misreading it ever after, and only a half-century later realized his mistake and found a new poem in front of him. "In untutored youth, the sentiment and the rhythm suffice: the exactness of the language goes unnoticed. And in later life a remembered favorite escapes exact attention because we think we know it so well." ("Herrick Revisited," Michigan Quarterly Review 15 [Summer 1976], pp. 245-267.)

Question for discussion: what do you think of Herrick's advice? Are there any perils in it?

A. D. HOPE, The Brides, page 328

When asked in 1973 if his poem had been glossed correctly, Mr. Hope replied:

> Bowser-boy: This is an interesting example of the dangers of technical terms. Twenty years ago in Australia, when the poem was written, a bowser was the British name for a pump at a gas-station, so that a bowser boy was the lad who served you gas. In Australia now we call them petrol pumps and "bowser" is an obsolete word. Poppet-heads is also a now obsolete term for the valve-heads. Sorry, but Chaucer gives us the same sort of trouble, I suppose.

Ask students to list the virtues possessed by new cars that, in the context of "The Brides," make them ideal wives. Although present-day women students may not be amused, the tone of the poem is humorous; and its subject matter ought to provoke a lively class discussion. A. D. Hope is clearly well aware that love affairs between young men and their cars are anything but rare, and that cars have long been recognized as classic Freudian symbols.

Question for discussion: to what extent are the poet's satiric thrusts at 1950s values still applicable in the 1980s?

GERARD MANLEY HOPKINS, Spring and Fall, page 328

Hopkins's tightly wrought syntax may need a little unraveling. Students may be asked to reword lines 3-4 in a more usual sequence ("Can you, with your fresh thoughts, care for leaves like the things of man?") and then to put the statement into more usual words. (An attempt: "Do you, young and innocent as you are, feel as sorry for falling leaves as for dying people?") Lines 12-13 may need a similar going-over and rough paraphrase. ("Neither any human mouth nor any human mind has previously formed the truth that

the heart and the spirit have intuited.") Sorrow's springs are the
same--that is, all human sorrows have the same cause: the fact that
all things pass away. A world of constant change is the blight man
was born for: an earth subject to death, having fallen from its
original state of a changeless Eden. The difficulties of a Hopkins
poem result from a swiftly thoughtful mind trying to jam all possible meaning into a brief space (and into words that are musical).

Wanwood is evidently a term the poet coined for pale autumn
woods. W. H. Gardner, editor of Hopkins's poems, finds in it also
the suggestion of "wormwood"--bitter gall, also wood that is worm-
eaten. The term leafmeal reminds him of "piecemeal," and he paraphrases line 8: "One by one the leaves fall, and then rot into
mealy fragments."

Ransom's "Janet Waking" is another poem in which a sophisticated poet contemplates a grieving child. How do the poems differ?
Ransom tries to convey the intensity of Janet's grief over her dead
hen; Hopkins is content to talk to Margaret, like a priest trying
to console her, and to philosophize.

Hopkins's great lyric ought to survive George Starbuck's
brilliant travesty (page 243). The two are worth comparing in case
students assume that what matters in poetry is the message alone,
that particular words have no consequence. It will be a dull student who doesn't notice that Hopkins selects his words with greater
precision and suggestiveness than does Starbuck (who is, of course,
deliberately putting the idea crudely). Starbuck obviously is
having a good time translating "Spring and Fall" into the American
vernacular. His parody may be useful as a way into a number of
crucial matters: the diction of a poem, its levels of usage (formal,
colloquial, vulgate), and the tone of a poem and how language indicates it. Who or what is the butt of Starbuck's ridicule? Is it
Hopkins and his poem; or the speaker himself, his crudeness, his
hard-boiled simplemindedness? (Howard Moss performs a comparable
reduction of a sonnet of Shakespeare's on page 85.)

GERARD MANLEY HOPKINS, The Windhover, page 329

"The best thing I ever wrote," said Hopkins. If your students
have enjoyed "Pied Beauty" (page 78) or "God's Grandeur" (page 134)
without too much difficulty, then why not try "The Windhover," despite its famous ambiguities? Some students may go afield in reading the opening line, and may take I caught to mean that the poet
trapped the bird; but they can be told that Hopkins, a great con-
denser, probably means "I caught a glimpse of."

Dispute over the poem often revolves around whether or not the
windhover is Christ and around the meaning of Buckle! Most commentators seem to agree either that the bird is indeed Christ, or else
that Christ is like the bird. (Yvor Winters, who thought the poem
"minor and imperfect," once complained, "To describe a bird, however beautifully, and to imply that Christ is like him but greater,
is to do very little toward indicating the greatness of Christ.")
Some read Buckle! as a plea to the bird to descend to earth; others,

329-332 (text pages)

as a plea to all the qualities and things mentioned in line 9
(Brute beauty, valor, act) to buckle themselves together into one.
Still others find the statement ending in Buckle! no plea at all,
but just an emphatic observation of what the poet beholds.   If
Christ is the windhover (other arguments run), in what sense can he
be said to buckle? Two of the answers: (1) in buckling on human
nature and becoming man, as a knight buckles on armor; (2) in having
his body broken on the cross. Students can be asked to seek all the
words in the poem with connotations of royalty or chivalry--sugges-
tive, perhaps, of Christ as King and Christ as noble knight or
chevalier. Why the sheer plod? Hopkins reflects (it would seem)
that if men will only buckle down to their lowly duties they will
become more Christ-like, and their spiritual plowshares will shine
instead of collecting rust. Hopkins preached a sermon that expressed a similar idea: "Through poverty, through labor, through
crucifixion His majesty of nature more shines." The embers, I think,
are a metaphor: moist clods thrown by the plow going down the
sillion. Hopkins likes to compare things to hearthfire: for instance, the fresh-firecoal chestnut-falls in "Pied Beauty."

     For detailed criticism, one might start with Paul L. Mariani,
Commentary on the Complete Poems of Gerard Manley Hopkins (Ithaca,
N.Y.: Cornell University Press, 1970); and might then consult the
discussions by Winters (quoted above), Romano Guardini, and Marshall
McLuhan conveniently gathered in Hopkins: A Collection of Critical
Essays, ed. Geoffrey H. Hartman (Englewood Cliffs, N.J.: Prentice-
Hall, 1966).

A. E. HOUSMAN, Terence, this is stupid stuff, page 329

     Questions for discussion:

     1. Terence is the poet, addressed in the opening lines by a
friend. What is the friend's complaint?
     2. For whom does the poet recommend ale instead of poetry?
Lines 21-22 echo Milton's invocation at the beginning of Paradise
Lost, in which Milton calls on the Muse to aid him in writing his
epic poem, that he may justify the ways of God to men. Is it Housman's view that malt does more than Milton can / To justify God's
ways to man, or is this his mocking version of someone else's view?
     3. What defense of his poetry (the stuff I bring for sale)
does the poet offer? How does the story of Mithridates support his
point?

A. E. HOUSMAN, To an Athlete Dying Young, page 331

     For a comment on this poem, see the note on Dryden's "To the
Memory of Mr. Oldham," page 306.

LANGSTON HUGHES, Dream Deferred, page 332

Simile by simile, Hughes shows different attitudes, including violent protest, that blacks might possibly take toward the long deferral of their dream of equality. Students might be asked what meanings they find in each comparison. The sugared crust (line 7) is probably the smiling face obligingly worn by Uncle Toms.

The angry, sardonic tone of the poem is clearly different from the sorrowful tone of the Countee Cullen and Dudley Randall poems suggested for comparison. Hart Crane in "Black Tambourine" does not seem concerned with the dream; rather, with the nightmare the black man endures.

Hughes's poem supplied the title for Lorraine Hansberry's long-running Broadway play A Rasin in the Sun (1958), in which the Youngers, a family descended from five generations of slaves, come to a Chicago ghetto in hopes of fulfilling their dream.

LANGSTON HUGHES, Song for a Dark Girl, page 332

Daniel D. Emmett's well-known "Dixie," written for a minstrel show in 1859 and adopted as the war song of the South in the Civil War, has a lively refrain familiar to most Americans even today:

I wish I was in Dixie, hooray, hooray,
In Dixie land we'll take our stand
To live and die in Dixie.
Away, away, away down South in Dixie,
Away, away, away down South in Dixie.

With bitter irony, Langston Hughes echoes that refrain in "Song for a Dark Girl." The young woman in the poem mourns for her lover, who has evidently died the victim of a lynching. She underscores the gulf between the black's perception of life in the South in the 1920s and the song's conventional view by speaking her grief in stanzas that begin with just enough rousing words from "Dixie" to recall the whole refrain to the reader's mind. Her lover did indeed live and die in Dixie, but nothing in the song even remotely suggests that, for blacks, death in Dixie could and too often did come prematurely, violently, and at the hands of whites.

More irony derives from the poem's Christian allusions. Even though her lover died because he was black, the "dark girl" must pray to a white Jesus for comfort. In a death that distantly echoes Christ's crucifixion, "they" (white Christians?) hung the "dark girl's" lover on a cross road's tree. Her conclusion that in Dixie Love is a naked shadow / On a gnarled and naked tree is in grim contrast to love as preached by "the white Lord Jesus" and in His church.

Worthy of attention is James A. Emanuel's "Christ in Alabama: Religion in the Poetry of Langston Hughes," published in Modern Black Poets, ed. Donald B. Gibson (Englewood Cliffs, N.J.: Prentice-Hall, 1973). One of the poems Emanuel includes in his

essay is "Song for a Dark Girl," which he discusses both as an in-
dictment against hypocritical religion in America and as a strong
poem.

DAVID IGNATOW, Get the Gasworks, page 333

What is the tone of this poem by a Brooklyn-born poet? In his
vigorous glimpses of tough, wisecracking, fast-paced city life
(summed up in the metrical line gaswork smokestack whistle tooting
wisecracks), Ignatow evidently admires the grimy kids who go on
playing ball in the streets, even though one of their number died.
Compare Elizabeth Bishop's affection for the quick and saucy / and
greasy sons in "Filling Station," page 291.
    Students might also be asked how the gasworks are shown to be
a symbol for America. (Even the kids' speech is like gas; and the
gasworks, like American living and thinking, are practical.)
    The poem seems Ignatow's poetic manifesto. He wants a kind of
poetry written in speech (You've got America, boy; He gets it over
the belly, all right), a poetry that will take in actual life, however grimy. The poet depicts that life with humor and affection
and, like Papa flinging his newspaper, favors a passionate response
to it.

RANDALL JARRELL, The Death of the Ball Turret Gunner, page 333

RANDALL JARRELL, The Woman at the Washington Zoo, page 334

    In both poems, the speakers are (in different ways) victims
of the State: two unknown citizens like Auden's (page 23), Jarrell's
laconic war poem is complex in its metaphors. The womb is sleep;
the outside world, waking; and the speaker has passed from one womb
to another--from his mother into the belly of a bomber. His existence inside the ball turret was only a dream, and in truth he has
had no mature life between his childhood and his death. Waking
from the dream, he wakes only to nightmare. In another irony, the
matter-of-fact battle report language of the last line contrasts
horribly with what is said in it. How can the dead gunner address
us? Clearly the poet had written his epitaph for him--and has done
so as Jarrell said he wrote "The Woman at the Washington Zoo,"
"acting as next friend."
    Students will soon see that the "Woman at the Washington Zoo"
is an aging civil servant, but may need some discussion to understand the reasons for her desperation. In what ways does she identify with the zoo animals? They are caged, as she is caged by her
anonymous job and by the bars of her aging body. In some ways the
animals are better off; they at least are wild and people come to
admire them. Not even the Deputy Chief Assistant pays her any
heed. (Jarrell said that he had met a deputy chief assistant who
saw nothing remarkable in the title!) Imagery and figures of speech
make the poem memorable, beginning with the other worldly saris and

the extended comparison of dress and body (lines 3-12). Jarrell
contributed a detailed explication of the poem to Cleanth Brooks's
and Robert Penn Warren's Understanding Poetry, 4th ed. (New York:
Holt, Rinehart and Winston, 1976). He remarks in part, "The series
peck, settling on, and tearing has inside it a sexual metaphor: the
stale flesh that no one would have is taken at last by the turkey-
buzzard with his naked red head and dangling wattles." Suzanne
Ferguson has offered a good paraphrase of the closing lines: "She
wants to be changed to a new form of life through the agency of love.
If she is now 'the white rat that the foxes left,' cannot the buzzard be metamorphosed man, ready to resume his human form, and
change her back to hers?" (The Poetry of Randall Jarrell [Baton
Rouge: Louisiana State University Press, 1971].)
    How successful is Jarrell in seeing through a woman's eyes?
As successful as Lawrence (page 339)?

JOHN KEATS, Ode on a Grecian Urn, page 335

    Why is the symbol of the urn so endlessly suggestive? It may
help students to recall that Grecian urns are vessels for the ashes
of the dead, and that their carved or painted figures (Of deities,
or mortals, or of both) depict a joyous afterlife in the Elysian
fields. The urn being circular, its design appears to continue
endlessly. What greater image for eternity, or for the seamless-
ness of perfected art?
    Most good discussions of the "Urn" confront a few of the poem's
celebrated difficulties. Some questions to help speed the confrontation:

    1. Assuming that the urn is said to be sylvan because it
displays woodland scenes, in what sense is it a historian? What
history or histories does it contain, or represent?
    2. How can unheard melodies be sweeter than heard ones?
    3. Why are youth, lover and loved one, trees, and musicians
so lucky to exist upon the urn? (Lines 15-27.)
    4. What disadvantages do living lovers labor under? (Lines
28-30.)
    5. In stanza four, the procession of thought turns in a new
direction. What additional insight occurs to the poet? (That the
urn, whose world had seemed perfect, is in some ways limited and
desolate. Altar cannot be reached nor sacrifice fulfilled, nor can
the unseen little town ever be returned to.)
    6. Paraphrase the statement that the urn doth tease us out of
thought / As doth Eternity. (The urn lures us out of our habit of
useless cogitation. Eternity also stops us from thinking because,
for us mere mortals, it too is incomprehensible.)
    7. How is the urn a Cold Pastoral? (Literally, it's lifeless
clay; figuratively, it stands aloof from human change and suffering.
Compare Stevens's "Jar," page 213.)
    8. How then can a Cold Pastoral be called a friend to man?
(It provides a resting place for human ashes; it inspires and de-
lights; and, as the last lines attest, it teaches us.)

141

9. If you were to add quotation marks to the last two lines, where would you insert them and what difference to the sense of the lines would your insertions make? Put them around the whole of the last two lines, and you make the urn declare in effect, "Take it from me, this is the lowdown--now stop thinking!" (It teases us out of thought.) Put them around just Beauty is truth, truth beauty, and you make Keats say that the words of the urn are all we need. Another reading consistent with this punctuation is Earl Wasserman's: All ye need to know refers to the entire statement beginning When old age . . . . (The Finer Tone [Baltimore, Md.: Johns Hopkins University Press, 1953].) In this reading, the "all" we need to know is that the message of the urn will be available to future generations.

This may be heresy, but I doubt that the poem will be destroyed if we choose wrong. Wherever quotation marks may fall, the great maxim remains for us, but what does it mean? Neither for my students nor for me has the sense of Beauty is truth, truth beauty ever been obvious. To begin to understand it, we have to see the poem in its entirety. After having shown the urn's enviable changelessness, Keats shows us that its world is in some ways frozen and desolate. His conclusion, it would seem, both praises the urn for its value to mankind (as a sort of Zen koan), and affirms his acceptance of the actual, transitory world. However crudely, I would paraphrase the maxim, "The beauty of art is true, but it is not the only truth. True life is also beautiful, despite suffering, change, and mortality."

For deeper criticism than this, see Stuart A. Ende, Keats and the Sublime (New Haven, Conn.: Yale University Press, 1976). George MacBeth has an outrageous translation of the poem into slang in his Collected Poems 1958-1970 (New York: Atheneum, 1972). Photographs of Grecian urns that may have inspired Keats are conveniently gathered by D. G. Kehl in Poetry and the Visual Arts (Belmont, Calif.: Wadsworth, 1975), but no urn exactly corresponds to Keats's description.

For a short laugh, Keats's great ode may be compared with Desmond Skirrow's gross oversimplification of it on page 243. I'd teach Keats before Skirrow so that students can understand something of the volumes of meaning that the parodist so fliply leaves out.

JOHN KEATS, On First Looking into Chapman's Homer, page 336

Questions for discussion:

1. What are the realms of gold? Can the phrase have anything to do with the fact that early Spanish explorers were looking for El Dorado, a legendary city of treasure in South America?
2. Does Keats's boner about Cortez mar the poem?
3. Did you ever read anything that made you feel like a stout Cortez? If so, what?

JOHN KEATS, To Autumn, page 337

More obviously (and more sumptuously) than the "Urn," this later poem also celebrates change and mortality.

Although "To Autumn" was to prove the last of the poet's greatest lyrics, we have no evidence that Keats (full of plans and projects at the time) was consciously taking leave of the world. On September 21, 1819, three days after writing the poem, Keats in a letter to his friend John Hamilton Reynolds spoke of his delight in the season: "I never lik'd stubble fields so much as now--Aye better than the chilly green of the Spring. Somehow a stubble plain looks warm--in the same way that some pictures look warm-- this struck me so much in my Sunday's walk that I composed upon it."

Questions for discussion:

1. In the opening stanza, what aspects of autumn receive most emphasis? To what senses do the images appeal?

2. In the first two stanzas, autumn is several times personified (lines 2-3, 12-15, 16-18, 19-20, 21-22). Who are its different persons? (Conspiring crony, careless landowner, reaper, gleaner, cider presser.)

3. In the third stanza, how does tone change? Has there been any progression in scene or in idea throughout the poem? (Tone: calm serenity. In the first stanza, autumn is being prepared for; in the second, busily enjoyed; in the third, calmly and serenely contemplated. There is another stanza-by-stanza progression: from morning to noon to oncoming night. Like the soft-dying day, the light wind sometimes dies. The gnats in wailful choir also have funereal, mourning suggestions, but the stanza as a whole cannot be called gloomy.)

4. What words in stanza 3 convey sounds? (Songs, music, wailful choir, mourn, loud bleat, sing, treble, whistles, twitter. What an abundance of verbs! The lines convey a sense of active music making.)

5. Do you see any case for reading the poem as a statement of the poet's acceptance of the facts that beauty on earth is transitory and that death is inevitable? (Surely such themes are present; the poem does not have to be taken to mean that the poet knows he himself will soon perish.)

For a recent (and unusually grim) reading of the poem, see Annabel M. Patterson, "'How to load . . . and bend': Syntax and Interpretation in Keats's To Autumn," PMLA 94 (1979), 449-458. Finding that the poem "undermines" our traditional notion of Autumn, Patterson argues that Keats subversively portrays the goddess as deceptive, careless, and demanding. Her preferred ripeness leads only to stubble-plains and last oozings--dead ends not to be desired. In the poet's view (as she interprets it), "Nature is amoral and not to be depended upon." Try this argument on the class. Do students agree? Whether or not they side with Patterson, they will have to examine the poem closely in order to comment.

338-340 (text pages)

MAXINE KUMIN, Woodchucks, page 338

Questions for discussion:

1. In brief, what is the speaker's <u>case</u> against the woodchucks? To what is her <u>case</u> compared that is also <u>airtight</u>?
2. What <u>Darwinian pieties</u> does the speaker invoke to justify
her killing the woodchucks? (Survival of the fittest, and she's
the more fit.)
3. Is there a moment in the poem at which her attitude toward
the woodchucks appears to change? In what details does the poet
reveal her sympathy for them? (She regards them as neighborly
fellow poison-consumers in lines 7-9; but is really hurled over to
their side on seeing <u>the littlest woodchuck's face</u>. The first baby
lies dead among the roses like someone mourned.)
4. What names does she call herself? What self-discovery does
she wish she had not made? (That something in her enjoys the feud.
Her final realization--that she envies the Nazis their quiet, hidden
gas ovens--is all the more horrific for the poet's being a Jew.)
5. Work out the rime scheme of the poem. (From stanza to
stanza it varies, but each stanza is like the sestet of an Italian
sonnet.) Were you aware of the closed form while first reading the
poem? (I wasn't and I take that to be a sign of the poet's skill.)
How naturally does the strict form accommodate what is said in it?

PHILIP LARKIN, Vers de Société, page 338

Questions for discussion:

1. What is suggestive in the name Warlock-Williams? (The
invitation evidently comes from a male witch trying to lure the
recipient under his spell. In line 11, is <u>Which</u> a pun?)
2. Why, according to Larkin, is solitude considered selfish
nowadays?
3. Explain the line <u>Only the young can be alone freely</u>. Do
you agree?
4. How has the imagery of the poem (<u>swaying trees</u>, <u>uneasy
wind</u>, <u>moon like a sharpened knife</u>) prepared for the conclusion
that disturbing things lurk beyond the speaker's lamplight? Why
is he tempted to accept the invitation after all?

D. H. LAWRENCE, A Youth Mowing, page 339

Students enjoy figuring out the dramatic situation: the young
mower apparently doesn't yet know that the speaker is pregnant by
him. Why is she sorry for him? The lad is like a handsome wild
animal; now he'll have to be tamed and become responsible. Imagery
of scythe strokes and sharp breaths (lines 2-3) suggests lovemaking.
What is the speaker, whose language is that of a Nottingham-
shire peasant, doing beside the Isar? Lawrence is evidently trying

to render German peasant speech into English, like Ezra Pound making a Chinese farmer say, "Yaller bird, let my crawps alone." Is the attempt effective in Lawrence's poem? Like the gamekeeper in Lady Chatterley's Lover, the young woman who carries the dinner pail falls into dialect when most affectionate.

The poem dates from the time when Lawrence and Frieda von Richthofen Weekley had eloped to the continent.

IRVING LAYTON, The Bull Calf, page 340

Sentimental poets frequently shed tears over concrete objects, while (in their imagery and diction) failing to open their eyes to the physical world. Such is not the case in Irving Layton's "The Bull Calf," in which the Canadian poet tells us that he weeps only after having portrayed the dead calf in exact detail (one foreleg over the other).

Layton's poem develops a series of contrasts. In the first section, the calf's look of nobility (the promise of sovereignty, Richard II) is set against his immaturity. The fierce sunlight, in an implied metaphor, is compared to the calf's mother: taking in maize, licking her baby. In line 14, the empty sky, suggestive of the calf's coming death, seems the turning point of the poem. In the remainder, the calf, which had been portrayed at first as full of life and pride, becomes an inanimate object, a block of wood, a numb mass that emits ugly sounds when handled (a sepulchral gurgle). But in the closing lines, introducing still another contrast, Layton seems to show the calf as a living sleeper, or perhaps a statue or finished work of art.

Probably the best-known living poet in Canada, Layton was born in Rumania and came to Montreal early in life. Standing outside both British and French communities, Layton's perspective often has been that of an outsider, a Jew, a satirist, and a revolutionary. The Selected Poems of Irving Layton, with an introduction by Hugh Kenner (New York: New Directions, 1977), is a recent attempt to widen his audience south of the border.

DENISE LEVERTOV, Sunday Afternoon, page 341

The daughters wear veils and colorless dresses momentarily bleached white to go to church, and vital, bloodred velvet when they return to their usual boisterousness. The word burned matters in that it parallels the girls' own flaming. Not an anticlerical comment, this brief poem is simply a study in two moods. It appears to be set in Mexico, where the poet's mother lived for many years.

Compare these white dresses with the connotative white nightgowns in Stevens's "Disillusionment of Ten O'Clock," page 63.

PHILIP LEVINE, To a Child Trapped in a Barber Shop, page 341

Levine's ironies may need underscoring. He is not, of course, berating the scared child (he is advising him to let the fearful cops rescue him), nor does the poet really think that drinking a little hair tonic would be a terrible crime against property and the state, however bad it might be for the child's digestion. The poem is actually addressed to the reader--one of the "we" who have lived through similar terrors. The ironic statements stop with the fourth stanza, and in the last three stanzas we can take what the poet tells us at face value. Most children fear barbers (or hairdressers) at first, and yet their fears prove groundless. Everyone growing up has to go through an ordeal, the poet seems to be saying, and life isn't so terrible as it looks through a child's eyes.

The poem has a subtle form besides its look of symmetry. It is roughly in syllabic verse, with a rime scheme (including some off-rimes).

ROBERT LOWELL, Skunk Hour, page 342

Students should have no trouble in coming up with the usual connotations of skunk, but they may need help in seeing that the title is a concise expression of Lowell's theme. This is an evil-smelling hour in the speaker's life; and yet, paradoxically, it is the skunks themselves who affirm that life ought to go on. After the procession of dying and decadent people and objects in the first four stanzas, the mother skunk and her kittens form a triumph: bold, fecund, hungry, impossible to scare. Although they too are outcasts (surrounded by their aroma as the poet is surrounded by his madness and isolation?), they stick up for their right to survival.

The poem is rich in visual imagery. In the mind's eye, there are resemblances between the things contained in stanza 5 (the Ford car and the hill's skull), also the objects set in fixed rows (love-cars, tombstones, beached hulls). Water and the sea (by their de-cline or absence) are to this poem what they are to Eliot's Waste Land. Even the Church is chalk-dry; its spire has become a spar like that of a stranded vessel.

This poem is intensively analyzed in The Contemporary Poet as Artist and Critic: Eight Symposia, ed. Anthony Ostroff (Boston: Little, Brown, 1964). Richard Wilbur, John Frederick Nims, and John Berryman comment on the poem, after which Lowell comments on their comments. Lowell calls the opening of the poem "a dawdling more or less amiable picture of a declining Maine sea town . . . Sterility howls through the scenery, but I try to give a tone of tolerance, humor, and randomness to the sad prospect." He sees the skunk hour itself as a sort of dark night of the soul and refers readers to the poem by Saint John of the Cross. Lowell's night, however, is "secular, puritan, and agnostical." Lowell notes that the phrase red fox stain was intended only to describe the color of vegetation in the fall on Blue Hill, a mountain in Maine.

Less regular in form than Lowell's earlier "At the Altar" (page 146), "Skunk Hour" nevertheless is carefully controlled by its rime scheme and its stanzaic symmetry.

CHRISTOPHER MARLOWE, The Passionate Shepherd to His Love, page 343

How do you teach a poem that seems so remote from the twentieth century? You might begin by asking whether it is so remote after all. What do contemporary swains promise their loved ones? Things, clothes, good times, a lovely neighborhood. Certainly remote from most contemporary love songs, however, is the tone of Marlowe's poem: a rare and appealing innocence. In demonstrating this quality to your students, try comparing this famous love lyric to one more complex and ironic: Marvell's "To His Coy Mistress" (page 8) or Donne's deliberate variation on "The Passionate Shepherd," "The Bait" (page 303). Either one will make Marlowe's poem an excellent foil. (For a note comparing "Bait" and "Passionate Shepherd," see page 121 of this manual.)

GEORGE MEREDITH, Lucifer in Starlight, page 344

The name Lucifer (Latin for "light-bringing") comes from Isaiah 14:12: "How art thou fallen from heaven, O Lucifer, son of the morning!" Early interpreters of Scripture thought this line meant the fallen archangel; later translators changed Lucifer to day star. Students may not be aware that Lucifer is a name both for the devil and for the planet Venus as the morning star. (Venus is sometimes the evening star, too, but only as the morning star is it called Lucifer.)

Meredith, however, seems well aware of the name's duality. Although his sonnet can be read first as an account of the Miltonic fiend's taking a new flight (and meeting chagrin), it is also satisfying to read the poem as a description of Venus as planet. We are told that Lucifer uprose and sank. Amid the stars, his huge bulk—a black planet—crosses Africa and shadows the Arctic, arriving at a middle height in the sky. The last two lines are puzzling, but seem to refer both to God's law and to the orderly path each star and planet follows as it circles the sun.

An Italian sonnet, "Lucifer in Starlight" illustrates a clear division in meaning between octave and sestet. In lines 1–8, the fiend appears triumphant and domineering: this is his night to howl. In lines 9–14, however, he crumples in defeat once more; or, if Lucifer is also the morning star, he rises in the octave and sets in the sestet.

JAMES MERRILL, Laboratory Poem, page 345

If you have any students who assume that poetry deals only with the pleasant and the beautiful (and how widespread this assumption is!) then you may find Merrill's clinical love poem a useful thing to surprise them with. Try paying attention to its language in particular: the outrageous pun taking heart in the opening line, the kymograph (a device with a revolving drum that records pulsations such as muscle contractions or heartbeats), her solutions tonic or malign (stimulants or sedatives, preservatives or poisons?). Merrill's language is exact in the extreme, a love poem written with loving care. (After all, why should love be banned from a laboratory?)

Discussion will probably focus on the last stanza. Of the exquisite disciplines, at least one of them is Naomi's research. The turtle's heart, violently removed, becomes a fact in a theorem. Like turtles, Charles realizes, some people give their lives for some abstract perfection, whether science, art, or any knowledge in whose service one may die. There is lovely irony in the contrast between Naomi's coldly clinical dissections (she has to take heart, build up her nerve to perform them) and the human situation (easy in the presence of her lover).

W. S. MERWIN, For the Anniversary of My Death, page 345

Unlike Emily Dickinson, who sometimes addresses us from Eternity, the poet who speaks to us in this poem is still (as some students may not see at first) very much alive. We mark our birthdays, he assumes--well, why don't we mark the anniversaries of our deaths, ahead of time? Even now, his death approaches like some phenomenon he cannot perceive, like the beam of a lightless star. In the final line, the poet bows to whatever will happen in some future year, on this very day, whether it be his death or some other event worth commemorating. What is Merwin's theme? Not merely that death is to be anticipated, but that life is to be cherished.

JOHN MILTON, When I consider how my light is spent, page 346

While usually taken to refer to the poet's lost eyesight, this famous sonnet is not about blindness at all. The familiar title "On His Blindness" was not given the poem by Milton, but by a printer a century later.

Questions for discussion:

1. If the poem is not about blindness, what might it be about? (Possible suggestions: Milton's declining powers of poetry; Milton's fame as a Puritan apologist.)

2. Is talent a pun referring to Milton's talent for writing poetry? What other meanings of the word seem appropriate in this poem? In the New Testament parable (Matthew 25:14-30), the hidden talent is money that should have been earning interest. That Milton is thinking primarily of work and business can be plausibly argued; other words in the poem convey such connotations--spent, true account, day-labor, and perhaps useless, which suggests the Medieval Latin word for interest, usuria.

The theme of frustration in life (and reconciliation to one's lot) is dealt with differently in Shakespeare's "When in disgrace with Fortune and men's eyes" (page 365).

MARIANNE MOORE, The Mind is an Enchanting Thing, page 346

About this poem the poet has written, "One of the winters between 1930 and 1940, Gieseking gave at the Brooklyn Academy a program of Handel, Bach, and Scarlatti, the moral of this poem being that there is something more important than outward rightness. One doesn't get through with the fact that Herod beheaded John the Baptist, 'for his oath's sake'; as one doesn't, I feel, get through with the injustice of the deaths died in the war, and in the first world war." (Note on the poem in Kimon Friar and John Malcolm Brinnin's anthology Modern Poetry [New York: Appleton-Century-Crofts, 1951].)

These remarks, and the poem's appearance in 1944, have led critics to call "The Mind is an Enchanting Thing" a war poem. What to make of the poet's statement? To put it baldly, perhaps she means that nobody but a bigoted Herod would condemn a superb German musician for being German and for playing splendid German and Italian music, even in the 1930s. The drift of the poem is that it takes the mind to recognize beauty and to do so, the mind must pierce through the heart's illusions (and prejudices?). In her tribute to the mind's conscientious inconsistency, perhaps Marianne Moore recalls Emerson's adage, "A foolish consistency is the hobgoblin of little minds." Still, one needn't speculate about the poem's wartime relevance in order to see it as a restatement of the poet's favorite poet's theme, "Beauty is truth, truth beauty." Only the mind can apprehend things truly; like Gieseking's violin and like the apteryx's beak, it is a precision instrument.

Class discussions of this poem tend to be slow, but good and ruminative. Many students greatly admire the poem and I have received outstanding papers written about it.

What form is the poem written in? Syllabics, with lines arranged in a repeated stanza pattern—like Dylan Thomas's "Fern Hill" (page 379), which students may be invited to compare. Once, in an interview with Marianne Moore, Donald Hall asked her, "Do you ever experiment with shapes before you write, by drawing lines on a page?" "Never, I never 'plan' a stanza," she replied. "Words cluster like chromosomes, determining the procedure. I may influence an arrangement or thin it, then try to have successive stanzas identical with the first." Asked "How does a poem start for you?" she answered, "A felicitous phrase springs to mind—a word or two, say—. . . 'katydid-wing subdivided by sun / till the nettings are legion.' I like light rhymes, inconspicuous rhymes. . . ." (Interview in The Paris Review [Winter 1961], reprinted in A Marianne Moore Reader [New York: Viking, 1961].)

Hall discusses the poem helpfully, too, in his study Marianne Moore (New York: Pegasus, 1970). He admires the poet's ability to weave a single word through the length of the poem, subtly changing its meaning: "The word <u>eye</u>, for example, is first the eye of the mind, then the eye of the memory, then the eye of the heart, suggesting three ways of 'seeing' that do not involve sight, but insight."

HOWARD NEMEROV, Storm Windows, page 347

"Storm Windows," written in the 1950s before combination windows were as common as they are today, may call for a little classroom reminiscing on the instructor's part about the spring and fall rituals of exchanging storm windows for screens and vice versa. As those who have lifted such windows up and down well know, this was a fairly strenuous outdoor job that needed doing when season and weather were right. Many older houses still have such windows.

Storm windows, of course, herald the onset of winter, a fact significant in establishing the bleak tone of this poem. Who is the "you" in "Storm Windows"? It seems to be someone with whom the poet is communicating imperfectly, perhaps someone from whom he is painfully parted. The tone of the poem is wistful, infused with a parched yearning unrelieved by the heavy, wintry rain. The blurred windows stand in the way, barriers between the dry grass underneath them and the rain above.

The storm windows, minutely observed objects in the real world, are richly symbolic. Lying on the ground and preventing the rain from wetting the grass beneath them, they are aptly expressive of <u>missed desires</u>. In addition, because the windows are <u>Brimful of bouncing water</u>, their <u>swaying clarity</u> beautifully conveys how memories, clear and inexact at the same time, waver to the surface of the speaker's mind. The windows can also be regarded, perhaps, as barriers to perfect communication in a relationship that has been interrupted, even as the task of hanging windows has been interrupted by a storm.

JOHN FREDERICK NIMS, Love Poem, page 348

This beautiful, witty poem was a feature of <u>An Introduction to Poetry</u> in the book's earlier editions and is now restored thanks to popular demand--well, three instructors asked for it. Who says the contemporary love poem is defunct?

For a lively comparison, teach this with Alan Dugan's "Love Song: I and Thou" (page 306). Both love poems proceed through comedy. Nims is kidding his loved one affectionately, of course, and the mingled tone of his tribute, both tender and chiding, also recalls Swift's wonderful "On Stella's Birthday" (page 30). Another subject common to Nims and Dugan is incompetence, although Nims's lady is good with <u>words and people and love</u>. In Dugan's poem the incompetent is the speaker himself.

SYLVIA PLATH, Daddy, page 348

There are worse ways to begin teaching this astonishing poem than to ask students to recall what they know of Dachau, Auschwitz, Belsen (line 33) and other Nazi atrocities. Every woman adores a Fascist--what does Plath mean? Is she sympathizing with the machismo ideal of the domineering male, lashing his whip upon subjugated womankind? (No way.) For an exchange of letters about the rightness or wrongness of Plath's identifying with Jewish victims of World War II, see Commentary (issues of July and October 1974). Irving Howe accuses Plath of "a failure in judgment" in using genocide as an emblem of her personal traumas. (How just is Maxine Kumin's allusion to Nazi gas ovens in "The Woodchucks," page 338?)

Incredible as it seems, some students possess an alarming fund of ignorance about Nazis, and some might not even recognize the cloven foot of Satan (line 53); so be prepared, sadly, to supply glosses. They will be familiar with the story of Dracula, however, and probably won't need much help with lines 71-79. Plath may be thinking of Nosferatu, F. W. Murnau's silent screen adaptation of Bram Stoker's novel Dracula, filmed in Germany in 1922. Hitler's propagandists seized on the Nosferatu theme and claimed that the old democratic order was drinking the country's blood. Plath sees Daddy as doing the same to his daughter.

SYLVIA PLATH, Morning Song, page 351

Sylvia Plath's image of the cloud being effaced seems almost a premonition of her own death. But "Morning Song" is rich in humor: the wonderful self-portrait of the cow-heavy mother, the baby's cries coming out in balloons (as in a comic strip?). The title refers to the child's crying (music to wake up by!), as well as to the poem itself.

"Morning Song" may be compared with Donald Hall's "My Son, My Executioner" (page 235). In her third stanza Plath apparently shares Hall's sense of the baby as the parent's killer. This point will probably emerge from class discussion in which students are asked to explain how the two poems are similar in theme. They can be asked, too, to define the point of view of each poem and the person addressed: is the poet really talking to the baby in each case, or thinking out loud, addressing self?

Still another poem for comparison is Amiri Baraka's "Preface to a Twenty Volume Suicide Note." (See the note in this manual on page 111.)

EZRA POUND, The River-Merchant's Wife: A Letter, page 351

After the death of Ernest Fenollosa, a scholar devoted to Chinese language and literature, Pound inherited Fenollosa's manuscripts containing rough prose versions of many Chinese poems. From one such draft, Pound finished his own version of "The River-Merchant's Wife." Fenollosa's wording of the first line went:

351-354 (text pages)

> My hair was at first covering my brows (child's method of
> wearing hair)

Arthur Waley, apparently contemptuous of Pound for ignoring dictionary meanings of some of the words of the poem, made a translation that began:

> Soon after I wore my hair covering my forehead . . .

Pound's version begins:

> While my hair was still cut straight across my forehead . . .

Pound, says the recent critic Wai-lim Yip, has understood Chinese
culture, while Waley has not, even though he understands his dictionary. "The characters for 'hair/first/cover/forehead' conjure
up in the mind of a Chinese reader exactly this picture. All little
Chinese girls normally have their hair cut straight across the fore-
head." Yip goes on to show that Pound, ignorant of Chinese as he
was, comes close in sense and feeling to the Li Po original. (Ezra
Pound's Cathay [Princeton, N.J.: Princeton University Press, 1969],
pp. 88-92.)

What is the tone of the poem? What details make it seem moving
and true, even for a reader who knows nothing of Chinese culture?

EZRA POUND, The Seafarer, page 352

Scholars have pointed out howlers in this translation, but for
contemporary readers who cannot read Old English with ease (and I
am one), Pound's "Seafarer" probably remains the best hope of a
sense of Anglo-Saxon poetry.

Pound's liberties with the original text (both deliberate and
unintentional) have been listed by K. K. Ruthven in A Guide to Ezra
Pound's "Personae" (1926) (Berkeley, Calif.: University of California Press, 1969). Pound made a few boners: in line 66, for
instance, he translated laene as loan, though the word means "transitory." In other lines, the poet high-handedly took Old English words
and phrases and settled for sound equivalents in Modern English.
And so stearn ("tern," the bird) became stern in line 23; tweon ("to
doubt") became twain in line 69. Still, Pound captures both the
sense and the flavor of the original in his literal renderings of
the kennings, or fixed figures of speech: breastlock (line 58),
whale-path (63), sword-hate (70), and (best of all) flesh-cover
(94)--that last a translation of flaeschoma, "body."

Students might be asked to discern the form of the poem.
(Alliterations on either side of a cesura in the middle of each
line--which form can only suggest, not reproduce). They can also
be invited to forget that this brilliant translation is a tour de
force and to read it as a sailor's lament for his hard life.

For an appreciation of Pound's poem, see Hugh Kenner, The
Pound Era (Berkeley: University of California Press, 1971), pages

92 and 349-354. Not the least of Pound's feats, in Kenner's view, was to put self's song's truth into his opening line, "compelling us to hear them, craggy monosyllables, one at a time."

DUDLEY RANDALL, Ballad of Birmingham, page 354

Randall's poem is an authentic broadside ballad: it not only deals with a news event, it was once printed and distributed on a single page. "I had noticed how people would carry tattered clippings of their favorite poems in their billfolds," the poet has explained, "and I thought it would be a good idea to publish them in an attractive form as broadsides." (Interview in Black World, December 1971.) "Ballad of Birmingham" so became the first publication of Randall's Broadside Press, of Detroit, which has since expanded to publish books and issue recordings by many leading black poets, including Gwendolyn Brooks, Don L. Lee, and Nikki Giovanni.

The poem seems remarkably fresh and moving, though it shows the traits of many English and Scottish popular ballads (such as the questions and answers, as in "Edward," and the conventional-sounding epithets in stanza 5). Randall presents without comment the horror of the bombing--in the mother's response and in the terrible evidence--but we are clearly left to draw the lesson that if the daughter had been allowed to join the open protest, she would have been spared.

Four black girls were killed in 1963, when a dynamite blast exploded in Birmingham's Sixteenth Street Baptist Church. In September 1977 a Birmingham grand jury finally indicted a former Ku Klux Klansman, aged 73, on four counts of first degree murder.

JOHN CROWE RANSOM, Janet Waking, page 355

Beautifully moving and yet full of ironies, Ransom's poem builds to its final metaphor of the forgetful kingdom. Janet thinks her parents capable of the Christ-like power to make the dead rise and walk, and cannot understand that the dead forget the living.

Some students accuse this poem of being sentimental, and seem offended by all the kissing in stanza 2 and by Janet's little pink feet. If you get this reaction, you might wish to review the difference between sentiment and true feeling. (Some suggestions for distinguishing the two are offered in Chapter 15.) The poet is not being vague, but entirely specific. Some attention to his diction will identify the point of view as that of a sophisticated ironist, no softminded weeper. The adjective transmogrifying (while accurate) makes the bee that killed the hen seem grand and important, as indeed, to Janet, it was.

A close comparison can be drawn between the dramatic situation in this poem and that of Gerard Manley Hopkins's "Spring and Fall (To a Young Child)" (page 328).

356-357 (text pages)

HENRY REED, Naming of Parts, page 356

This is one of the most teachable poems ever written. There are two voices: the voice of the riflery instructor, droning on with his spiel, and the voice of the reluctant inductee, distracted by the springtime. Two varieties of diction and imagery clash and contrast: technical terms opposed to imagery of blossoming nature. Note the fine pun in line 24, prepared for by the rapist bees in the previous line. Note also the connotations of the ambiguous phrase point of balance (line 27)—a kind of balance lacking from the recruits' lives?

Students need to be shown the dramatic situation of the poem: the poor inductee, sitting through a lecture he doesn't want to hear. One would think that sort of experience would be familiar to students, but a trouble I have met in teaching this poem is a yearning to make out of it a vast comment about Modern Civilization.

The poet himself has recorded the poem for An Album of Modern Poets, 1 (Library of Congress, PL 20). Dylan Thomas reads "Naming of Parts" even more impressively in his Reading, Vol. IV: A Visit to America and Poems (Caedmon TC 1061).

ADRIENNE RICH, Aunt Jennifer's Tigers, page 357

The poet herself has made revealing mention of this poem in a College English essay reprinted in Adrienne Rich's Poetry, eds. Barbara Charlesworth Gelpi and Albert Gelpi (New York: Norton, 1975):

> Looking back at poems I wrote before I was 21, I'm startled because beneath the conscious craft are glimpses of the split I even then experienced between the girl who wrote poems, who defined herself in writing poems, and the girl who was to define herself by her relationships with men. "Aunt Jennifer's Tigers," written while I was a student, looks with deliberate detachment at this split. In writing this poem, composed and apparently cool as it is, I thought I was creating a portrait of an imaginary woman. But this woman suffers from the opposition of her imagination, worked out in tapestry, and her life-style, "ringed with ordeals she was mastered by." It was important to me that Aunt Jennifer was a person as distinct from myself as possible--distanced by the formalism of the poem, by its objective, observant tone-- even by putting the woman in a different generation.

Adrienne Rich's feminism clearly was beginning to emerge, how-ever, as far back as 1951 when this poem was first published. It is apparent in the poem that the poet perceived something wrong with the passive role assigned to women. The pride, confidence, and fearlessness ("masculine" virtues, whatever the sex of the tigers) of Aunt Jennifer's imaginary creations contrast sharply with Aunt

Jennifer herself--a frail lady with fluttering fingers, terrified
hands. Worth comment is the poet's use of the word ringed--sug-
gesting "encircled"--to refer both to the wedding ring that sits
heavily upon Aunt Jennifer's hand and to ordeals she was mastered
by, specifically marriage and being expected to conform. Although
she goes down in defeat, her tigers triumph.

Question for discussion: is Aunt Jennifer's plight that of
the woman artist in our society? (Because of the wedding ring's
weight, she must struggle to ply her instrument, the ivory needle.)

Compare Aunt Jennifer with the dead woman who once embroidered
fantails in Wallace Stevens's "The Emperor of Ice Cream" (page 67).
For another, in some ways comparable, contrast between a dull world
of reality and the colorful life of the imagination, see Wallace
Stevens's "Disillusionment of Ten O'Clock" (page 63), in which

> Only, here and there, an old sailor,
> Drunk and asleep in his boots,
> Catches tigers
> In red weather.

ADRIENNE RICH, Diving into the Wreck, page 357

Although it is always risky to read a poem as a personal statement, perhaps this wreck may be (among other things) the wreck of
the poet's marriage. (The poet's husband, from whom she was
separated, died in 1970.) Like a diver, the speaker came to see the
damage that was done / and the treasures that prevail. The climax
of the poem occurs in line 77: the two spouses (mermaid and merman)
merge identities. Pronouns become confounded in line 87. The object of the dive has been to find the truth: the wreck and not the
story of the wreck / the thing itself and not the myth. The last
stanza is a negative kind of triumph. The speaker returns to the
surface bearing the same workaday equipment she submerged with, and
having successfully avoided lying to herself about the wreck of
their lives. She has made no myth out of it.

This reading of the poem may be overly biographical; others
have seen the poem differently. Wendy Martin, in an essay on Rich's
poetry, thinks the wreck is the wreck of male-dominated civilization.
("From Patriarchy to the Female Principle," in Adrienne Rich's Poetry,
cited above.) Erica Jong (in "Visonary Anger," in the same gathering)
sees the poem's diver as an androgyne, the "mentally bisexual"
artist or new woman whose name now goes unlisted in the book of "the
old myths of patriarchy . . . that split male and female irrecon-
cilably into two warring factions." The wreck is the world, which
needs to be salvaged.

However dissimilar in theme, Hardy's "The Convergence of the
Twain" (page 323) is worth comparing to Rich's poem for its similar
view of a wreck, its undersea creatures, and its backward glance at
history.

360-362 (text pages)

EDWIN ARLINGTON ROBINSON, Mr. Flood's Party, page 360

Eben Flood's name is a pun: what flood is "ebbin'"? It is the stream of his life and his hopes (also his liquor supply).

This poem lends itself well to a discussion of tone. Is Mr. Flood simply a comic drunkard (seeing double moons)? Stanza 3 likens him to Roland and lends him dignity. Robinson's portrait of the old man clearly is tinged with compassion.

"Mr. Flood's Party" may be compared with other poems on themes of solitude: Philip Larkin's "Vers de Société" (page 338) and the Lennon-McCartney song "Eleanor Rigby" (page 115). What general observations on the subject of loneliness do these three poems make?

THEODORE ROETHKE, Elegy for Jane, page 361

By piling up figures of speech from the natural world, Roethke in "Elegy for Jane" portrays his student as a child of nature, quick, thin, and birdlike. A wren, a sparrow, a skittery pigeon, Jane has a pickerel smile and neckcurls limp and damp as tendrils. She waits like a fern, making a spiny shadow. She has the power to make shade trees and (even more surprising) mold burst into song. For her, leaves change their whispers into kisses.

Then she dies. The poet acknowledges that for him there is no consolation in nature, in the sides of wet stones or the moss; his grief is not assuaged. Because he mourns the girl as teacher and friend, no more, he recognizes a faint awkwardness in his grief as he speaks over her grave:

I, with no rights in this matter,
Neither father nor lover.

Roethke, writing about this poem in On the Poet and His Craft (Seattle: University of Washington Press, 1965), pp. 81-83, reminds the reader that it was John Crowe Ransom (to whose "Bells for John Whiteside's Daughter" this poem has often been compared) who first printed "Elegy for Jane." Roethke discusses his use of enumeration, calling it "the favorite device of the more irregular poem." He calls attention to one "of the strategies for the poet writing without the support of a formal pattern," a strategy he uses in "Elegy for Jane": the "lengthening out" of the last three lines in the first stanza, balanced by the progressive shortening of the three lines at the poem's end.

Some readers have interpreted "Elegy for Jane" as the work of a man who never had children of his own; but in fact Roethke as a young man had fathered a daughter for whom he felt great affection. Although "neither father nor lover" of Jane, he at least could well imagine a father's feelings.

THEODORE ROETHKE, The Waking, page 362

As the poet tells us, he thinks we think by feeling; and his
sonorous villanelle is more rewarding (in my experience) if taught
for its rhythms, sound, and form than if taught for its literal
sense, theme, or subject (not that it doesn't have any). Examined
word by word in a sober hunt for its sense, it is likely to bind
students in despair; but if you want to try, a few questions follow
(and I must confess not to be at all sure of the answers). What
waking is the poem about? Does I wake to sleep mean "I wake in
order to sleep," or "I wake up to find I'm still asleep," or what?
Why is the lowly worm climbing the winding stair? (Is it the stair
of evolution that the worm ascends--to become man, the awakened
animal?) What is another thing that Nature will do to us? (Age
us, kill us, or make us fall in love?) What is this shaking?
(Shaking with the rhythms of the dance, or shaking with palsy in
old age?) What does What falls away is always mean? (Attempt at
a paraphrase: whatever chance befalls us, some kind of permanence
will remain.)
    Students may be asked to compare Roethke's villanelle with
Dylan Thomas's "Do not go gentle." Is either poem (like some
villanelles) an elaborate and trivial exercise? (To my mind,
Thomas's poem is a better one than Roethke's. It is unified
thematically and its refrain lines seem to occur more naturally.)

GIBBONS RUARK, Saying goodbye to my daughters, page 362

    Ruark's poem seems clearly contemporary in diction and form--
written in syllabics, each line consisting of twelve syllables.
Yvor Winters's "At the San Francisco Airport" is heavily metrical
and neoclassical in its diction. Yet these two poems seem close in
feeling: expressing the mingled emotions of fathers bidding
daughters goodbye.
    In Ruark's poem, the white bird seems the central symbol, or
perhaps it is no more than a metaphor. Flapping harmlessly, demanding its release, it is like the birdlike young girls who calm
their wings and wait to be set free.
    "Saying goodbye to my daughters" is taken from Ruark's second
collection Reeds (Lubbock, Tex.: Texas Tech Press, 1978).

ANNE SEXTON, For My Lover, Returning to His Wife, page 363

    This poem is notable for its apt figures of speech, which
students might be asked to notice. The point of view is that of
the "other woman" in a love triangle. She describes herself as
the luxury, the bright red sloop in the harbor who knows she cannot
possibly compete in any permanent way with her lover's wife, the
woman who is all harmony, who sees to oars and oarlocks for the
dinghy. The wife is solid. As for me, says the poem's narrator,
I am a watercolor. I wash off. Knowing that her lover's return to

his wife is inevitable, she says, <u>I give you back your heart. I
give you permission—</u>
     How does the poem's narrator feel? Is she crushed? sorrowful?
bitter? resigned? (Resigned, apparently.) What distinguishes this
poem from prose?

WILLIAM SHAKESPEARE, That time of year thou mayst in me behold,
page 364

WILLIAM SHAKESPEARE, When, in disgrace with Fortune and men's eyes,
page 365

     Shakespeare's magnificent metaphors probably will take some
brief explaining. How is a body like boughs, and how are bare
boughs like a ruined choir loft? Students will get the general
import, but can be helped to visualize the images. <u>Consumed with
that which it was nourished by</u> will surely require some discussion.
Youth, that had fed life's fire, now provides only smothering ashes.
The poet's attitude toward age and approaching death stands in contrast to the attitudes of poets (or speakers) in other poems of
similar theme: sweet acceptance of old age in Burns's "John Anderson my jo, John" (page 255); admiration for the exultant sparrows
in William Carlos Williams's "To Waken an Old Lady" (page 389);
defiance in Yeats's "Lamentation of the Old Pensioner" (page 232).
     Figures of speech are central to "That time of year," but
barely enter into "When, in disgrace" until the end, when the
simile of the lark is introduced. The lark's burst of joy suggests
that heaven, called <u>deaf</u> in line 3, has suddenly become keener of
hearing. Critical discussion of both sonnets goes on: recent and
valuable is <u>Shakespeare's Sonnets,</u> edited with analytic commentary
by Stephen Booth (New Haven, Conn.: Yale University Press, 1977).

WILLIAM SHAKESPEARE, When daisies pied and violets blue, page 365

WILLIAM SHAKESPEARE, When icicles hang by the wall, page 366

     Students are usually pleased to add the word <u>cuckold</u> to their
vocabularies. (The origin of the word is uncertain, but it evidently refers to the cuckoo's habit of laying its eggs in other
birds' nests.) Both songs take birdcalls for their refrains. How
is the owl's call evocative of winter? Despite the famous harsh
realism of the winter scene, discussion may show that winter isn't
completely grim, nor is summer totally carefree.
     Bertrand Bronson has a good discussion of these two poems in
<u>Modern Language Notes,</u> 63 (January 1948), pp. 35-38.

KARL SHAPIRO, The Dirty Word, page 366

   Shapiro's theme, which the class may be asked to make explicit,
is that the dirty word one secretly loves in childhood is seen in
maturity to be powerless. Is it a paradox that the word-bird is
said to outlive the man, and yet later the speaker tells us he
murdered it? It would seem, rather, that at these two moments in
his poem Shapiro sees the word from two different points of view.
In one sense, the word will continue to live after the speaker's
death because (figuratively) it is freed from the cage of his mind
and also because (literally) words live longer than their speakers
do. In the last paragraph the speaker means that he neutralized the
bird's magic. Simply by growing up, he abolished its power over
him.
   Arranged in paragraphs rather than in conventional lines of
poetry, "The Dirty Word" may lead some students to ask why this is
poetry, not prose. It is a good opportunity to point out that poetry
is a name we can apply to any language we think sufficiently out of
the ordinary and that poetry is not determined merely by arranging
lines in a conventional order on a page. To a much greater extent
than a prose writer usually does, Shapiro expresses himself through
metaphor. Besides the central metaphor of word as bird, there are
the metaphors of mind as cage, brain as bird food, self as house,
skull as room, secret thoughts as closet, vocabulary as zoo, feathers
as language. The poem needs to be heard aloud, for it is full of
unprosaic sounds: rimes (bird . . . word, sweet meat); alliterations
(buried, body, bird; worn, wing; murdered, my, manhood); and internal alliterations (ripping and chopping, walls of the skull).
It is also rich in bizarre and startling imagery.

SIR PHILIP SIDNEY, Now that of absence, the most irksome night,
page 367

   This poem, from Astrophel and Stella, can be studied for its
variations on strict sonnet form, and for the poet's verbal play-
fulness. Every line ends with a night or a day. Lines 5, 6, 9, 10,
11, and 12 contain both. Line 5 probably deserves to be read aloud
several times for what the repetitions of the word long do to the
line's sound and rhythm. Sidney's eloquence in the face of the
stringent verbal limits he has set for himself is remarkable.
Piling exaggerations and paradoxes one upon the other, the poet
almost overdoes the pain of his unrequited love for Penelope Dever-
eaux, the "Stella" of his poems.
   A problem with this sonnet is its syntax, particularly in the
last eight lines. Some students might be called upon to try dia-
gramming the poem's sentences. Do they make grammatical sense, or
has Sidney taken liberties with the requirement that a sentence
contain both subject and verb? (There does seem to be a shortage
of independent clauses in the poem.)

367-370 (text pages)

CHARLES SIMIC, Butcher Shop, page 367

"Butcher Shop" is a constellation of metaphors. Associating
the everyday instruments of a butcher's trade with things we
wouldn't expect--things whose connotations are emotionally power-
ful--Simic works a kind of nighttime transformation. The light recalls a convict struggling to escape. Knives recall church,
cripple, and imbecile. Most pervasive of the metaphors in the poem
is the river of blood (lines 8 and 14). In a sense, we are nourished
by a river of blood when we dine on the flesh of animals. Perhaps
(like convict, cripple, and imbecile) the animals too are sufferers.
Perhaps all of these victims in chorus lift the mysterious voice
that the poet hears in the closing line.

CHRISTOPHER SMART, For I will consider my Cat Jeoffry, page 368

Telling us more about cats than Carl Sandburg (page 79) and
T. S. Eliot (in "Prufrock," lines 15-22, page 310) put together,
Christopher Smart salutes Jeoffry in one of several passages in
Jubilate Agno that fall for a little while into some continuity.
This fascinating poem, and the whole work that contained it, have
come down to us in a jumble of manuscripts retrieved from the
asylum, sorted out brilliantly by W. H. Bond in his edition of
Smart's work (Cambridge, Mass.: Harvard University Press, 1954).
Some of Smart's gorgeous lines seem quite loony, such as the command to Moses concerning cats (line 35) and the patriotic boast
about English cats (line 37). Other statements, as Bond points out,
are not madness but only misinformation: the ichneumon (or
Icneumon, line 63) is not a pernicious rat, but a weasellike, rat-
killing mammal.
Read aloud, Smart's self-contained poem in praise of Jeoffry
can build a powerful effect. In its hypnotic, psalmlike repetition,
it might be compared with the section of Whitman's "When Lilacs Last
in the Dooryard Bloom'd" quoted on page 178.
Talking with Boswell of Smart's confinement, Dr. Johnson observed,

I did not think he ought to be shut up. His infirmi-
ties were not noxious to society. He insisted on people
praying with him; and I'd as lief pray with Kit Smart as
with any one else. Another charge was, that he did not
love clean linen; and I have no passion for it.

A possible paper topic: "Smart's Cat Jeoffry and Blake's
Tyger: How Are These Poems Similar in View?"

WILLIAM JAY SMITH, American Primitive, page 370

We might expect a painter called an American primitive to be
naive, unsophisticated, and childlike in his view. So is the

speaker who draws this verbal scene. Not only do the references
to Daddy seem juvenile, but so does the line the screen-door bangs,
and it sounds so funny. (Smith, incidentally, has written much fine
verse for children in addition to his more serious poetry, and he
understands the way a child thinks and speaks.) There is, of course,
an ironic distance between the speaker's point of view and the poet's.
Irony is enforced, too, by contrast between the grim event and the
bouncy rhythm and use of feminine rimes.

Another possible way of looking at the poem is that Daddy himself is the primitive: the primal dollar-worshiping American. The
capitalization of Dollar (as in the familiar phrase "the Almighty
Dollar") may support this view. We are not told why Daddy died, an
apparent suicide, but it is evident that riches did not buy him
life. Besides inviting comparison with Sylvia Plath's ironic poem
about the death of a terrible "Daddy" (page 348), Smith's mock-
elegy may be set beside Wallace Stevens's "The Emperor of Ice-Cream"
(page 67), with students asked to compare the two in tone and in subject matter.

W. D. SNODGRASS, The Operation, page 370

Awaiting surgery, the speaker feels himself enacting myths and
taking part in rituals. Students will see this if asked to sort out
all the speaker's comparisons of himself to others: a sacrificial
victim being shaved, a child (as if returned to childhood by the
razor), Pierrot, a girl making her first communion, a "blank hero"
(an antihero who will not act, but will be acted upon). While it
is possible to make too much of the poem's myth and symbolism,
Robert Phillips is surely right in suggesting that the poet in the
hospital is undergoing a kind of purification, and metaphorically
is being reborn. The hospital, says Phillips, is a world "in which
one dies to become resurrected, is cut to become whole." (The Confessional Poets [Carbondale, Ill.: Southern Illinois University
Press, 1973].) Phillips also observes that "The Operation" is
probably the great original that launched what Anne Sexton once
called the My-stomach-laced-up-like-a-football school of poetry.

"The Operation" is an excellent poem to read aloud slowly, with
attention to its meaningful sound effects: the old woman arched to
her gnarled stick, the rather menacing and mysterious cargoes under
dark tarpaulins. In the development of its narrative, it is an
interesting poem to set next to Robert Lowell's "Skunk Hour" (page
342). In "The Operation" we have a fearful procession of awful
details, building to the crucial moment when the narrator feels
death (or madness) imminent (shackled and spellbound, declares Snodgrass; my mind's not right, says Lowell). Both poems are resolved
on a note of triumph and repose. In both, the closing image is of
an object out of the world of nature, slightly sullied by contact
with civilization but blooming (or feeding) and going on--as the
poet at last seems able to do.

371-373 (text pages)

GARY SOTO, Daybreak, page 371

Who are <u>you</u> in this poem? We readers, who eat onions with no
awareness of the Chicano field-workers who pick them for us. Soto's
is an insider's view, unlike Woody Guthrie's distant glimpse of
migrant workers in his song "Plane Wreck at Los Gatos" (page 114).
Much of the power in Soto's poem inheres in its action verbs and its
metaphors, especially the rain's <u>broken fingers</u>: punished in
striking the earth, like the blistered hands of the onion pickers.
    <u>The Elements of San Joaquin</u>, from which this poem comes, is the
title sequence of Soto's first collection (Pittsburgh: University
of Pittsburgh Press, 1977).

WILLIAM STAFFORD, At the Klamath Berry Festival, page 372

    Questions for discussion:

    1. What is ironic in the performance of traditional dances,
by a scout troop on an Indian reservation, for an audience including
a sociologist? What does the sociologist signify? What is the significance of the fact that other Indians are gambling outside,
turning their backs on the dances? Sum up the poet's theme.
    2. Why is the war chief <u>bashful</u>? How do you account for his
behavior (<u>listening and listening, he danced after the others</u>
<u>stopped</u>)? (Listening past the noise of the gamblers to the quiet
of mountains and river, he gets caught up in the old dance in spite
of himself, and thoughtfully keeps dancing, forgetful of himself
and of the modern world.)
    3. How would you scan <u>He took two steps</u>? The poet introduces
the statement four times—what is the effect of this repetition?
(It makes for a row of heavy stresses followed by a pause. The
poet is approximating the rhythm of the war chief, who makes heavy
footfalls, pauses, then goes on with his dance.)

GERALD STERN, Behaving Like a Jew, page 372

    "Behaving Like a Jew" is a crying out against

        the spirit of Lindbergh over everything,
    that joy in death, that philosophical
    understanding of carnage, that
    concentration on the species.

Seeing a dead opossum on the road, the poet decides he will <u>behave</u>
<u>like a Jew</u>. He will mourn openly; he will refuse to rationalize
away the grief this one small death causes him to feel. To react
with this <u>animal sorrow</u>, he seems to say, is the only way to remain
fully human.
    Stern's poem is similar in theme to Rod McKuen's bad poem and
William Stafford's excellent one on pages 257-258. See the note in
this manual on page 98.

WALLACE STEVENS, Peter Quince at the Clavier, page 373

Questions for discussion:

1. We know that it is Peter Quince who speaks to us in the opening section; what are we to make of what follows? (We are to laugh when he sits down at the clavier. The story of Susanna is to be a tale told by a clown, not a faithful and serious recital; nor are we to take the clown's anguish [lines 5-15] in total earnest.)
2. Point out all the onomatopoeia you can find in the poem. Why is it appropriate to a poem whose imagery is largely taken from music?
3. Music is feeling, then, not sound (line 4). How is the truth of this statement demonstrated in the rest of the poem? (Each character in the poem has a theme song. Whenever we hear the music of the elders, as in lines 12-15 and 39-40, it is like that of a coarse jazz band, or like show-off violinists excitedly plucking their violins instead of playing them: pizzicati of Hozanna-- praise not of God, but of Susanna. The elders are unimaginative men, coarse sensualists bound to the physical world. All they can hear is Death's ironic scraping, not Susanna's music of immortality. Other theme songs are audible. Susanna, as she lolls in her bath, touches springs of melody--an autoerotic suggestion? The simpering Byzantine maids titter like tambourines. All have their appropriate music.)
4. Beauty is momentary in the mind-- / The fitful tracing of a portal; / But in the flesh it is immortal. Is this statement non-sense? What sense can you make of it? (Stevens weaves a metaphor: the beauty of a woman is like music. Not that bodily beauty lasts forever; instead, it becomes a legend, and so continues to inspire works of art that live on in human memory.)

Harold Bloom has found an affinity between "Peter Quince" and Browning's dramatic monologue "A Toccata of Galuppi's." In Browning's poem, a man apparently playing the music of the Venetian composer on the clavichord finds himself remembering Venetian gallants and ladies, and their long-vanished lust. But in Stevens's opening lines, says Bloom, "it is Stevens who speaks directly of his own desire." This desire "deprecates itself, by an identification with the desire of the elders for Susanna rather than with the more refined and repressed desire of Susanna herself, in section II." (Wallace Stevens, The Poems of Our Climate [Ithaca, N.Y.: Cornell University Press, 1977], p. 36.)
A difficult and demanding comparison: Stevens's notion that Beauty is momentary in the mind and John Ashbery's concept of art as a fine forgetfulness in "City Afternoon" (page 287).

MARK STRAND, Keeping Things Whole, page 375

While most of us tend to regard the world as backdrop, Strand in this deceptively simple poem throws a new and startling light upon our place relative to that backdrop. The poet in "Keeping Things Whole" views himself not as central but rather as an absence of field, an interruption in the air that surrounds him, a cutout in the backdrop. The effect, both witty and eerie, is to render insubstantial both his physical self and the world around him. As we read the poem, we're surely meant to feel the little jolt that accompanies any sudden awareness of our mortality.

MAY SWENSON, Question, page 375

The poem called "Question" is really a series of questions that add up to one big one: what will happen to me once death has over-taken my body? Singular and tentative, the poet's view of life after death cannot be called conventionally Christian; but that she sees the individual human spirit as living on into eternity seems clear.

The poet introduces three metaphors for the body: house, horse, and hound, the three bound together by both consonance (h and s are repeated) and assonance (ou in house and hound). Line 4, when you are fallen, follows from all three metaphors.

In stanzas 2 and 3, Swenson extends each metaphor separately, in the order in which they are first mentioned. Stanza 4 begins by referring again to the house metaphor but veers off in a startling new direction when the poet imagines herself with wind for an eye. How can this be? The effect of the phrase is to emphasize dramati-cally the disembodied state the poet envisions.

The element of surprise continues in the last two lines and introduces a paradox:

    With cloud for shift
    how will I hide?

The lines suggest that, though having become pure spirit, the poet with cloud for shift will be as visible as when she inhabited her body.

JONATHAN SWIFT, A Description of Morning, page 376

This slice of eighteenth-century London life seems replete with human failings: Betty (a conventional name for a servant) sleeping with her master and trying to hide the evidence, prisoners released from jail in order to steal. Swift's couplets describe not the highborn but the common people, for whom a hackney coach heralded dawn in place of mythology's grander chariot driven across the sky by Phoebus Apollo. Although Swift crams his lines with images of city dirt and human corruption, the humor of his poem implies con-siderable affection for London's streets and sinners. If students see no humor in his view, let them compare this poem with another poem about eighteenth-century streets, Blake's angry "London" (page 61), or a rhapsodic, Romantic description of a London morning, Wordsworth's "Composed upon Westminster Bridge" (page 390).

ALFRED, LORD TENNYSON, Dark house, by which once more I stand,
page 377

In Memoriam, section VII. "This is great poetry," wrote T. S.
Eliot, "economical of words, a universal emotion related to a particular place; and it gives me the shudder that I fail to get from
anything in Maud." (Introduction to Poems of Tennyson [London:
Nelson, 1936].) The dark house was indeed a particular place--
"67, Wimpole Street," as Tennyson noted--the house of Henry Hallam.
The poem contains at least two allusions, whether or not we are
expected to pick them up: "And then it started, like a guilty
thing" (Horatio describing the ghost in Hamlet, I, i, 148); and
"He is not here, but is risen" (Luke 24:6). In line 11 of one
manuscript version, Tennyson wrote dripping instead of drizzling.
Why is drizzling superior? The highest moment in the poem occurs
in the last line in the two spondees, at least equal in their
effect to Yeats's "And the white breast of the dim sea" ("Who Goes
with Fergus?," page 123).
    For some of these notes I am indebted to Christopher Ricks's
matchless edition of The Poems of Tennyson (London: Longmans, and
New York: Norton, 1969).

ALFRED, LORD TENNYSON, Ulysses, page 377

    The following inadequate précis, meant to make lovers of
Tennyson's poem irate, might be quoted to students to see whether
they agree with it: a hardy old futzer can't stand life in the old
folks' home, and calls on his cronies to join him in an escape,
even though the whole lot of them are going to break their necks.
    For criticism, see Paull F. Baum, Tennyson Sixty Years After
(Chapel Hill, N.C.: University of North Carolina Press, 1948),
pp. 92-94; and John Pettigrew, "Tennyson's 'Ulysses': A Reconciliation of Opposites," Victorian Poetry I (January 1963), pp. 27-
45. For another possible extended metaphor of a westward journey,
compare Wordsworth's "Stepping Westward" (page 390).

DYLAN THOMAS, Fern Hill, page 379

    Fern Hill is the farm of Thomas's aunt, Ann Jones, with whom
he spent boyhood holidays. In line 2 the poet cites a favorite
saying of his father's, "Happy as the grass is green." The saying
is echoed again in line 38. As students may notice, Thomas likes
to play upon familiar phrases and transform them, as in line 7,
"once below [not upon] a time."
    It came as a great shock when I first realized that this poem,
which I had thought a quite spontaneous burst of lyric energy, is
shaped into a silhouette, and that the poet contrived its form by
counting syllables. Such laborious working methods were customary
for Thomas. John Malcolm Brinnin has recalled seeing more than two
hundred separate and distinct versions of "Fern Hill"--a fact worth
conveying to students who think poets simply overflow.

I take the closing line to express Thomas's view of his own poetry, lyrical and rule-bound at the same time: a song uttered in chains. Of course, the last line also means that the boy in the poem was held in chains by Time, the villain, who informs the whole poem (except for stanzas 3 and 4, which see childhood as Eden). Students may be asked to trace all the mentions of Time throughout the poem, then to sum up the poet's theme. William York Tindall, who offers a line-by-line commentary, makes a fine distinction: "Not how it feels to be young, the theme of 'Fern Hill' is how it feels to have been young." (A Reader's Guide to Dylan Thomas [New York: Noonday, 1962].) And I'd add, "how it would have felt to grow old, if the boy had realized he wouldn't live forever."

According to Tindall (in a lecture), Thomas used to grow huffy whenever asked if he were an admirer of Gerard Manley Hopkins. Still, to hear aloud both "Fern Hill" and Hopkins's "Pied Beauty" is to notice much similarity of sound and imagery. Hopkins studied Welsh for a time, while Thomas never did learn the language; but both at least knew of ancient Welsh poetry and its ingeniously woven sound patterns.

Thomas's magnificent (or, some would say, magnificently hammy) reading of this poem can be heard on Caedmon recording TC 1002 (cassette 51002).

DYLAN THOMAS, Twenty-four years, page 380

Thomas write this poem a few days before his twenty-fourth birthday--October 27, 1938. To his friend Vernon Watkins he noted that its last line had been the first line of an old poem he had scrapped, "and at last--I think--I've found the inevitable place for it." (Quoted by Daniel Jones in his edition of The Poems of Dylan Thomas [New York: New Directions, 1971].) "As womb put Thomas in mind of tomb, so his birthday put him in mind of the day of his death," remarks Tindall. (A Reader's Guide to Dylan Thomas [New York: Noonday, 1962].) "By lucky accident his springing forth concided with the year's autumnal decline."

Like other early Thomas poems, "Twenty-four years" wears the strangeness of surrealism, but makes sense. The second line gives readers the most difficulty (and according to Tindall, the poet wasn't satisfied with it). The natural doorway is the door leading out of the womb. Preparing for the journey of life, the unborn child (as if sewing a shroud) prepares his caul. To begin to live is to begin to die. The meat-eating sun is no unnatural monster, but the literal sun whose risings and settings eventually lay waste our flesh. With my red veins full of money expresses a happy, spendthrift feeling, and (even though veins are blue) has logic: under a microscope, red corpuscles look like coins. What is the elementary town? The graveyard? Still, the final line radiates faith and hope.

DAVID WAGONER, Staying Alive, page 380

Relevant to this poem is the fact that David Wagoner has lived since 1954 in the Pacific Northwest. Those students knowledgeable about wilderness survival may be asked whether Wagoner's advice in "Staying Alive" is practical enough to benefit anyone actually lost in the woods.

Because several lines in the poem seem to hint at another, deeper level of meaning, a second question is worth posing: to what extent is the poet in "Staying Alive" providing a guide not only through the wilderness but through life? In line 10, for instance, he says, Spit out all bitterness. Line 14 goes on to advise, It may be best to learn what you have to learn without a gun. In line 26 we are told, The bottom of your mind knows all about zero . . . . Invite students to examine these and other insights in the poem for their possible application to survival, not only in the wilderness, but anywhere.

DEREK WALCOTT, Sea Canes, page 382

Derek Walcott, a West Indian black poet and playwright, deals frequently in his work with the theme of personal isolation. All the same, Half my friends are dead seems a startling opener for a poem first published when the poet was only forty-six. The friends of his youth seem to have had an appallingly high rate of mortality.

Discussion might focus on the central symbol of the sea canes. How are they seraph lances of faith? Flashing (because wet with sea water?) in the moonlight, they have something to do with aspiration, with one's hopes for one's friends—now at an end. Though the canes divide the speaker from his friends like a wall, the wind overcomes them, bringing the friends back, as they were—at least in memory.

"Sea Canes," incidentally, is another illustration of an elegy (defined in the text on page 270).

EDMUND WALLER, Go, Lovely Rose, page 383

In some ways quieter than Marvell's "To His Coy Mistress" or Herrick's "To the Virgins, to Make Much of Time," this poem has the same theme: carpe diem. "Go, Lovely Rose" merits admiration for its seemingly effortless grace and for the sudden, gently shocking focus on our mortality in the poem's final stanza.

Students may enjoy reading Ezra Pound's imitative tribute to Waller: the "Envoi" to Hugh Selwyn Mauberley, beginning "Go, dumb-born book . . . ," in Personae, Pound's collected shorter poems (New York: New Directions, 1949).

383-386 (text pages)

ROBERT PENN WARREN, Brotherhood in Pain, page 383

What is Warren saying? Words don't convey reality; things
have their own reality before we give them names. Indeed, iso-
lating a thing for the purpose of naming it causes it suffering:
The matrix from which it is torn / Bleeds profusely. People and
things share a brotherhood in pain. Both suffer from a species of
loneliness.

It was probably Frost in his "Directive" who showed the way for
poets to write directive poems like this, instructing readers to perform acts beyond their understanding. David Wagoner's "Staying
Alive" (page 380) is another such directive.

TOM WAYMAN, Wayman in Love, page 384

By a younger Canadian poet, "Wayman in Love" is included mainly
to provide a note of comic relief to any class in need of emergency
leavening. Students may enjoy offering what they know about Marx
and Freud in accounting for the obsessive concerns of these two unexpected bedfellows.

Is the poet himself the person Wayman in this poem? Impossible
to tell, but this Wayman seems almost a cartoon character in an
absurd universe. Compare Paul Zimmer's use of himself as a character in "The Day Zimmer Lost Religion" (page 19). The young Zimmer,
defying Jesus but still fearing him, seems a character more psycho-
logically real than Wayman in love. (But then, in this poem, the
poet Wayman obviously isn't trying for profundity.)

For more of Wayman's work, see Introducing Tom Wayman:
Selected Poems 1973-1980 (Princeton, N.J.: Ontario Review Press,
1980).

WALT WHITMAN, I Saw in Louisiana a Live-Oak Growing, page 385

WALT WHITMAN, When I Heard the Learn'd Astronomer, page 385

Whitman often regards some other living thing and sees himself reflected in it. In "Live-Oak" (one of the Calamus poems),
the tree becomes his mirror in line 4; and one might expect the
poem, like "A Noiseless Patient Spider," to extend the comparison.
But the poem takes a surprising twist: Whitman himself cannot
abide the live-oak's solitude. (This poem has not been shown to
refer to any particular friends or events in the poet's life.)

The "Learn'd Astronomer" is a good illustration of Whitman's
psalmlike repetitions (also illustrated and discussed in the text
on pages 178-179). Alliteration (both initial and internal) in the
phrase mystical moist night-air throws terrific emphasis on it.
The rhythmic structure of the poem is thoroughly discussed by
Sylvan Barnet, Morton Berman, and William Burto in An Introduction
to Literature, 6th ed. (Boston: Little, Brown, 1977), pp. 458-459;
and more briefly by Paul Fussell in "Free Verse," an article in

Antaeus, no. 30/31 (Spring 1978), pp. 296-308. The poet, says
Fussell, "devotes seven lines to establishing a loose 'sincere'
quasi-prosaic grid as a field against which the remarkably regular
final line of iambic pentameter emerges with special emphasis re-
inforcing the irony." The last line comes as a shock, "registering
a different and more valid way of perceiving: 'Look'd up in perfect silence at the stars.'"

Pablo Neruda's tribute to Whitman may well be applied to both
these poems:

> There are many kinds of greatness, but let me say
> (though I be a poet of the Spanish tongue) that Walt Whit-
> man has taught me more than Spain's Cervantes: in Walt
> Whitman's work one never finds the ignorant being humbled,
> nor is the human condition ever found offended.

(Quoted by Gay Wilson Allen in Poetry Pilot, newsletter of the
Academy of American Poets, November 1976.)

RICHARD WILBUR, Playboy, page 386

Wilbur's poem is rich in irony, beginning with its title.
As great a distance yawns between stockboy and Hefnerian playboy
as between the curves that Archimedes contemplated and those that
the boy studies in his copy of Playboy while he munches his sandwich. There is additional irony in his being likened to a sage.
Worth particular notice, too, is the poem's visual imagery.
The exploding rose / Fired from a long-necked crystal vase underscores the half-comic, half-deplorable intensity of the stockboy's
erotic reverie. Students may be asked why they think Wilbur
describes the nude model's skin as strangely like a uniform.
(Perhaps because, in Playboy's scheme of things, she is merely a
stylized body like all in the undressed regiment.)
Though its language resembles ordinary speech, "Playboy" is a
traditionally formal poem, beautifully crafted. Wilbur's choice of
the word cunning, whose multiple meanings all fit line 25, illustrates his usual concern for le mot juste—a concern that students
might well be encouraged to emulate.

OSCAR WILDE, The Harlot's House, page 387

Diction and imagery in this richly musical poem stress that
the customers and inhabitants of this brothel are mechanical. Like
robots, they seem wire-pulled automatons. One is a clockwork puppet;
another, a horrible marionette, not truly alive. These details enforce the figures' seemingly macabre unreality, as do the descriptions of them as ghostly dancers, silhouetted skeletons who cast
fantastic arabesques for shadows. Wilde's marvelous ear makes
this tightly rimed, assonance-filled poem well worth reading aloud.

387-388 (text pages)

Compare "The Harlot's House" to Richard Wilbur's "Playboy" in theme. Wilbur examines a young man spellbound in imagined lust; Wilde's point seems to be that actual lust can appear imaginary (and that the corruption of innocence is terrible). For a different view of prostitution, see Hardy's "The Ruined Maid" (page 52).

Brothels seem to have inspired Wilde with horror, and I have never taught this poem without repeating the anecdote told by Yeats in The Trembling of the Veil, reprinted in The Autobiography of William Butler Yeats (New York: Macmillan, 1953). In exile and disgrace after his release from prison, Wilde met the dissipated poet Ernest Dowson in Dieppe, France. Dowson urged Wilde to visit a brothel and acquire "a more wholesome taste."

> Meanwhile the news had spread, and they set out accompanied by a cheering crowd. Arrived at their destination, Dowson and the crowd remained outside, and presently Wilde returned. He said in a low voice to Dowson, "The first these ten years, and it will be the last. It was like cold mutton"--always, as Henley had said, "a scholar and a gentleman" he now remembered that the Elizabethan dramatists used the words "Cold mutton"--and then aloud so that the crowd might hear him, "But tell it in England, for it will entirely restore my character."

WILLIAM CARLOS WILLIAMS, Spring and All, page 388

Questions for discussion:

1. Why cannot Williams's attitude toward spring be called "poetic" and "conventional"? What is his attitude toward the approaching season? By what means is it indicated? Consider especially lines 14-15 and 24-25, and the suggestions of contagious in the opening line. (Spring is stealing over the land as a contagious disease infects a victim. But spring is not a disease: it has a stark dignity.)

2. An opinion: "This poem clearly draws from the poet's experience as a pediatrician who had attended hundreds of newborns, and whose work was often to describe with clinical exactness the symptoms of his patients." Discuss. (Lines 16-18 especially seem to contain a metaphor of newborn infants. The adjectives mottled, dried, sluggish could occur in a physician's report. In lines 9-13 also, the description of bushes, trees, and vines seems painstakingly exact in its detail.)

WILLIAM CARLOS WILLIAMS, To Waken an Old Lady, page 389

Questions for discussion:

1. By which words or phrases does Williams suggest the physical ravages of old age? What very different connotations do the
phrases broken seedhusks and shrill piping carry, as well as the
suggestions of feeble and broken senility? (Broken husks suggest
a feast, piping suggests merriment.)
2. What is the dark wind? Can a wind be literally dark?
(No, it can't, Williams means dark in the sense of sinister or
menacing. This wind is like the passage of time that buffets or
punishes.)
3. What is the dictionary definition of tempered? What does
the word mean in this poem?

YVOR WINTERS, At the San Francisco Airport, page 389

Students might be asked to compare the language of this poem
with that of a neoclassical poem such as Dryden's "To the Memory of
Mr. Oldham" (page 306). Both poems demonstrate that it is possible
for a poet to write of a subject of personal concern and yet to
select a diction relatively devoid of imagery, tending to be general
and abstract. (For the result to be good poetry, the abstract words
have to be accurate, as in these illustrations.)
Of all the terms in Winters's poem, the most tangible things
named are light, metal, planes, and air. It is not to Winters's
purpose here to number the streaks on any tulip; his concerns take
in knowledge and passion, being and intelligence. At the outset
Winters indicates that to see perfectly with one's physical eyes
may be, in a sense, to see falsely and imperfectly. The glittering
metal of the planes is a menacing distraction. He restates this
observation in lines 16-17: The rain of matter upon sense /
Destroys me momently. It is not until the third stanza, when the
poet is able to see beyond the immediate moment, that he achieves
understanding. In the last line we are back to the original paradox, stated another way: to be awake in a merely physical light is
not to be awake at all.
Like Winters's criticism, the poem praises will, reason, and
intelligence. I admit, though, to some reservations about it. In
lines 18-20, the diction becomes so abstract as to seem grandiose.
We might wish to know more about the situation. Why is the girl
leaving? Where is she going? But if we accept the poet's lofty
tone--in which seeing one's daughter off on an airplane becomes an
event as momentous as the launching of Cleopatra's barge--it seems
an impertinence to ask.

390-391 (text pages)

WILLIAM WORDSWORTH, Composed upon Westminster Bridge, page 390

Imaginary conversation:

Instructor: What do you make of the title? Is this a poem
composed upon the subject of a bridge, or a poem composed
while standing on a bridge's sidewalk?
Student: The latter, obviously.
Instructor: How do you know?
Student: His eye is located up on the bridge. Otherwise he
couldn't see with such a wide-angle lens.
Instructor: You smart twit! To the head of the class!

Whose is the __mighty heart__? Wordsworth is describing the city
as a sleeping beauty about to awaken. Of course, the brightness of
the scene is increased by the poet's being out for his stroll before
a hundred thousand chimneys have begun to smoke from coal fires preparing kippers for breakfast. Charles Lamb, in a letter to Wordsworth, had chided the poet that the urban emotions must be unknown
to him, so perhaps this famous sonnet is an answer to the charge.
Compare "The World Is Too Much with Us" (page 218) for a different Wordsworth attitude toward commerce; or compare Wordsworth's
London of 1807 with Blake's "London" of 1794 (page 61)--practically
the same city, but a different perspective. (Wordsworth up on the
bridge at dawn, letting distance lend enchantment; Blake down in the
city streets by night, with the chimney sweep, the teenaged whore,
and the maimed veteran.)

WILLIAM WORDSWORTH, Stepping Westward, page 390

"I cannot describe how affecting this simple expression was in
that remote place, with the western sky in front, yet glowing with
the departed sun." (Dorothy Wordsworth's entry for September 11,
1803, in her __Recollections of a Tour Made in Scotland__.)
Stepping westward possibly means only walking west, but the
title recalls "the westward journey," "to go west," and other
euphemisms for dying; perhaps it also brings to mind the westward
journey of Ulysses in Tennyson's poem (page 377). Bernard Groom
has argued that Wordsworth's poem contains some such metaphor: at
its heart lies "the relationship between home and heaven." In
Groom's reading, the courteous greeting of the two women brings to
the poet's mind the spiritual import of his wanderings. Wordsworth's journey is like that of Bunyan's Pilgrim: the poet wanders
through the world toward the distant brightness of eternity. This
future is the __heavenly destiny__ the poet means. Compare __The Prelude__
VI, 605: "Our destiny is with infinitude." (I have added slightly
to Groom's remarks, set forth in __The Unity of Wordsworth's Poetry__
[New York: St. Martin's, 1966], pp. 64 and 208.) Do students agree
with this interpretation?
What does Wordsworth mean by __human sweetness__ (line 24)? It is,
says Donald Davie, "a recognition that ardent wanderlust is provided

172

for and sanctioned by popular feeling--the folk know that sort of yearning and acknowledge it as human." Wordsworth's perception that traditional sentiment favors wanderers, and thus sweetens wandering, is "the sort of idea that could have occurred only to Wordsworth," a notion quite original, novel, and strange. (Articulate Energy [New York: Harcourt, Brace, 1958], pp. 156-157.)

JAMES WRIGHT, A Blessing, page 391

At first, students are likely to regard "A Blessing" as "a delicate poem about the kinship between men and horses," as Ralph J. Mills sees it. (Contemporary American Poetry [New York: Random House, 1965].) They will be right, of course; but to take them a step further, they can be asked what blessing the poem refers to, and to ponder especially its last three lines. In a sense, the image of stepping over barbed wire into an open pasture (line 7) anticipates the idea of stepping out of one's body into--what? Any paraphrase is going to be clumsy; but Wright hints at nothing less than the loneliness of every creature alive. Although they are together, the two ponies are lonely to an extreme and are apparently overjoyed to see people. By implication, maybe the speaker and his friend are lonely together as well. In lines 15-21 the speaker, to his astonishment, finds himself falling in love with one of the ponies; he sees her beauty as that of a girl. At this point, we might expect him to recoil and cry, "Good grief! what's the matter with me?"--but he persists and becomes enlightened, at least for a moment. Only his physical body, he realizes, keeps him alone and separated. What if he were to shed it? He'd bloom.

A master of open form, Wright knows how to break off a line at a moment when a pause will throw weight upon sense: "Suddenly I realize / That if I stepped out of my body I would break / Into blossom.'

Maybe the best way to teach "A Blessing" is just to read it aloud, and then say nothing at all.

JAMES WRIGHT, Autumn Begins in Martins Ferry, Ohio, page 392

Martins Ferry is the poet's native town. Dreaming of heroes, the speaker sits in the high school stadium, the only place in town where heroes are likely to appear. Certainly the heroes aren't the men portrayed in lines 2-4: beery, gray-faced, ruptured, worn out by their jobs in heavy industry. These are the same proud fathers who, ashamed of their failures (including their failures as lovers to their wives), won't go home but prefer to hang around taverns. Without fathers to supply them with hero figures, their sons set out to become heroes themselves on the football field. The season of their "suicidal" ritual is fittingly the season of the death of the year. Will they become heroes? Most likely they'll just break their necks.

392-393 (text pages)

Perhaps the fathers were once football heroes themselves, as George S. Lensing and Ronald Moran point out in Four Poets and the Emotive Imagination (Baton Rouge, La.: Louisiana State University Press, 1976), a study that discusses nearly the whole of Wright's work. "From this there is the suggestion that the futures of the current community heroes may be as bleak as the present time assuredly is for the fathers."

SIR THOMAS WYATT, They flee from me that sometime did me sekë, page 392

Surely Wyatt knew what he was about. Sounding the final e's helps to fulfill the expectation of iambic pentameter in lines 2, 12, 15, 17, 20, and 21, lines that otherwise would seem to fall short. In other lines, however, Wyatt appears to make the rhythm deliberately swift or hesitant in order to fit the sense. Line 7 (Busily seeking with a continual change) seems busy with extra syllables and has to be read quickly to fit the time allotted it. Such a metrical feat seems worthy of Yeats, as does line 11, in which two spondees (loose gown, did fall) cast great stress upon that suddenly falling garment.

What line in English love poetry, by the way, is more engaging than Dear heart, how like you this? And when have a lover's extended arms ever been more nicely depicted? (This line may be thrown into the teeth of anyone who thinks that, in descriptive writing, adjectives are bad things.)

WILLIAM BUTLER YEATS, Crazy Jane Talks with the Bishop, page 393

Piecing together a history from this Crazy Jane poem and others, John Unterecker has identified the Bishop as a divinity student who had courted Jane in his youth. She rejected him in favor of a wild, disreputable lover: Jack the journeyman. As soon as he got enough authority, the Bishop-to-be had Jack banished, but Jane has remained faithful to her lover (at least, in spirit). (See A Reader's Guide to William Butler Yeats [New York: Noonday, 1959].) In this poem, the Bishop's former interest in Jane has dwindled to a concern for her soul only. Or has it? Perhaps the Bishop, no doubt a handsome figure in his surplice, may be demonstrating Yeats's contention that fair needs foul. Jane is living in lonely squalor. The grave, she says, can affirm the truth that her friends are gone, for it holds many of them; and her own empty bed can affirm that Jack is gone, too. Still, she firmly renounces the Bishop and his advice.

Each word of the poem is exact. Love has pitched his mansion as one would pitch a tent. The next-to-last line ends in two immense puns: sole or whole. The Bishop thinks that soul is all that counts, but Jane knows that both soul and hole are needed. Such puns may be why Yeats declared (in a letter) that he wanted to stop writing the Crazy Jane series: "I want to exorcise that slut, Crazy Jane, whose language has become unendurable."

174

What does Yeats mean by the paradoxical statement in the last
two lines? Perhaps (1) that a woman cannot be fulfilled and remain
a virgin--that, since fair and foul are near of kin, one cannot
know Love, the platonic ideal, without going through the door of
the physical body; and (2) that the universe is by nature a yin/
yang combination of fair and foul (or, as Yeats would have it in
A Vision, a pair of intertwining gyres). Crazy Jane may be crazy,
but in Yeats's view she is a soothsayer.

WILLIAM BUTLER YEATS, For Anne Gregory, page 393

Anne Gregory was the granddaughter of Lady Gregory, the poet's
friend and patron. The poem is cast as a dialogue between her and
another speaker, presumably the poet.
What is the tone of this poem? Tender, loving, gently
teasing--but also deeply serious. Yeats doesn't say that Anne in
herself isn't loveable; his point is that only God, being pure
spirit, is capable of loving soul independent of body. Men, being
mortal, can't help loving the physical attributes of a woman, too.
This poem is one of many written in Yeats's middle or late years in
which the inextricable oneness of body and soul is affirmed.
Another is "Crazy Jane Talks with the Bishop," page 393.
The metaphor of Anne's great honey-colored ramparts is worth
scrutiny. Ramparts, as singers of the national anthem will recall,
are embankments or turrets circling a fort or castle, protecting it
from attack. Perhaps the poet thinks of Anne's wonderful hair in
somewhat the way that Campion regards a young girl's eyebrows as
bended bows defending her innocence, in "There is a garden in her
face," page 265.

WILLIAM BUTLER YEATS, The Lake Isle of Innisfree, page 394

As a young man in London in 1887-1891, Yeats found himself
hating the city and yearning for the west of Ireland. He recalled:
"I was going along the Strand and, passing a shop window where there
was a little ball kept dancing by a jet of water, I remembered
waters about Sligo and was moved to a sudden emotion that shaped
itself into 'The Lake Isle of Innisfree.'" (Memoirs [New York:
Macmillan, 1972], p. 31.) In London (he recalled in his Autobiography), he sometimes imagined himself "living in imitation of
Thoreau on Innisfree, a little island in Lough Gill." The nine
bean rows of the poem were evidently inspired by Thoreau's bean
patch.
Yeats's lines provide rich rows of sound for the student to
hoe: assonance (from I . . . arise in the first line through the
o-sounds in the closing stanza), onomatopoeia (lapping), initial
alliteration, internal alliteration (arise, Innisfree; hear,
heart's core). Sound images of bees, cricket, linnet, and lake
water are predominant. Whatever noises come from roadway or pave-
ment, however, are left unspecified.

394-396 (text pages)

In later years, according to John Unterecker, Yeats was
shocked that "The Lake Isle" had become his most popular poem. He
had taken a dislike for its "Biblical opening lines." But audi-
ences always demanded it of him, and his sonorous reading of the
poem is available on a recording (Spoken Arts 753).

WILLIAM BUTLER YEATS, Lapis Lazuli, page 394

Late in life, Yeats wrote several poems affirming that, even
though the new apocalypse may be at hand, gaiety is still possible.
"The Gyres" and "Two Songs from a Play" are other instances. For
a grimmer vision of the end of the world--or the end of the
Christian era--see Yeats's earlier "The Second Coming" (page 219).
One reason for the poet's gaiety in "Lapis Lazuli" is his assumption that, like the phases of the moon, all will come round again
and history will repeat itself. In his opening lines, Yeats sums
up an attitude that he does not share: the assumption that poets
ought to be solemn just because the world is full of war and strife.
Good poets do not waver from their art, any more than good actors
break up their lines to weep (line 15). Poetry, Yeats felt, has to
be impersonal; "all that is personal soon rots," he said in his
Essays; "it must be packed in ice or salt." This admirable (if
slightly inhuman) detachment is achieved by the merry-eyed Chinese
in the carving described in the closing passage, which is a fairly
literal description of the piece of lapis lazuli.

WILLIAM BUTLER YEATS, The Magi, page 396

After writing a lesser poem than this--"The Dolls," in which
dolls hurl resentment at a noisy and filthy thing, a human baby--
Yeats had a better idea. "I looked up one day into the blue of the
sky, and suddenly imagined, as if lost in the blue of the sky, stiff
figures in procession." (Yeats's note at the back of his Collected
Poems.) Like dolls, the Magi seem frozen, somewhat inhuman (rain-
beaten stones), unfulfilled. They are apparently troubled that
Christ, whose birth was a miracle, died as a man. In hopes of re-
gaining the peace of the Nativity, they pursue a second journey.
Bestial will seem to students an odd word to apply to a stable
floor, unless they catch its literal sense: "belonging to beasts."
But they will also need to see that its connotations of brutality
fit the poem and interact with Calvary's turbulence. Compare "The
Magi" with the rough beast in "The Second Coming" (page 219), a
poem written after Yeats had more fully worked out his notion that
historical events move in a cycle of endless return. ("Leda and
the Swan," page 133, can be brought in, too, if there is time for
it.)
In comparing Yeats's unsatisfied wise men to Eliot's in
"Journey of the Magi," good questions to ask include "Which poet
writes as a Christian?" and "How can you tell?"

ANTHOLOGY: CRITICISM

        This additional anthology is designed not to give you anything
more to teach, but to supplement your teaching resources.   While
there isn't anything you'll _need_ to do about it, this anthology of
criticism offers additional possibilities for paper topics and some
broad, general subjects for discussion.   It provides, moreover,
brief texts of certain famous critical statements that some instructors have said they would like to have available.   These include
Plato's account of Socrates' theory of inspiration and his banish-
ment of poets from the Republic, Aristotle on imitation, Sidney on
nature, Samuel Johnson on the superiority of universal truths to
tulips' streaks, Wordsworth on emotion in tranquillity, Coleridge
on the imagination, Shelley's view of poets as "unacknowledged legislators," Emerson on the relation of thought to form, Poe on long
poems, Frost on the "sound of sense," and Eliot on personality.
All seem part of the permanent baggage of received critical ideas
that the reader who cares deeply for poetry will tote along.
        The Anthology is arranged in chronological order.   Most of the
extracts at the more recent end of the anthology have not yet become permanent, but are (I hope) lively critical notions that may
interest students, cause them to reflect and perhaps to argue.   Here
are a few topics (for either writing assignments or class discussion)
suggested by these selections, including the classic ones.

PLATO, Inspiration, page 399

        1.   According to Socrates, what is the source of poets' in-
spiration?   How is it possible for the worst of poets to sing the
best of songs?
        2.   Can readers be inspired as well?   (Yes, and critics such
as Ion.   This is the point of the metaphor, the magnet that attracts
iron rings and makes magnets of them, too, early in this passage.)

PLATO, Socrates banishes poets from his ideal state, page 400

        1.   What is the tone of this dialogue?   (In banishing poets,
Socrates appears to have a smile on his lips.   As the passage ends,
he is trying to find a way to let them return.)
        2.   What distinction does Socrates draw between admissible
poetry and inadmissible poetry?   What danger to the republic does

he find inherent in epic and lyric verse? (The danger is that feeling and emotion will be encouraged to unseat reason. Therefore, only hymns to the gods and praises of famous men, legitimate and useful expressions of feeling, are to be allowed.)

    3. Compare Socrates' view of poets with Shelley's (page 405).

ARISTOTLE, Two causes of poetry, page 402

    In your own words, sum up what Aristotle appears to mean by imitation. Can it be charged that he reduces poetry to journalism, poems to mere descriptions of the world? (But mere descriptions don't embody harmony and rhythm—two equally essential sources of a poem.)

SIR PHILIP SIDNEY, Nature and the poet, page 403

    Is Sidney of one mind with Aristotle on the subject of imitation? (No, he says, in this particular passage, that poets don't imitate nature, they create something better than nature has ever conceived!)

SAMUEL JOHNSON, 'The business of a poet,' page 403

    1. Do poets, in Johnson's view, appear to be Muse-inspired utterers of surprising statements not their own? (Look back once more on Socrates' remarks on inspiration.)

    2. What, then, is a poet's task as Johnson sees it?

    3. Write a one-paragraph review of a book of Imagist poetry (including, say, Pound's "In a Station of the Metro," H. D.'s "Heat," and Elizabeth Bishop's "The Fish"—this last a later poem, but owing much to Imagism) as Dr. Johnson might have written it. Would he condemn such poets for numbering the streaks of the tulip instead of articulating universal ideas?

WILLIAM WORDSWORTH, 'Emotion recollected in tranquillity,' page 404

    1. In Wordsworth's description of the poetic process, how does a poet usually go about writing a poem?

    2. Take another look at Wordsworth's poem "I Wandered Lonely as a Cloud" (page 18). What light does this statement cast upon it? What lines in the poem seem to describe the same process of poetic composition?

SAMUEL TAYLOR COLERIDGE, 'That synthetic and magical power,' page 404

    1. This won't be easy, but try to state in your own words Coleridge's doctrine of the imagination, as you understand it from this passage. What does the mind of a poet <u>do</u> in composing a poem? (Coleridge's doctrine is more fully set forth in the <u>Biographia Literaria</u>, Chapter 13. But this concise description, without special philosophical terms, of the <u>synthesizing</u> power of the imagination will serve, perhaps, to give the beginning student the essence of it.)
    2. Name a poem, by any poet, in which you find what Coleridge might call "the balance or reconcilement of discordant qualities." (Suggestion: "The Love Song of J. Alfred Prufrock," in which Eliot certainly blends unlikely, conflicting matter--visions of loveliness such as the mermaids with ratty and sordid urban imagery.)

SAMUEL TAYLOR COLERIDGE, The 'obscurity' of Milton, page 405

    1. When is 'obscurity' in poetry desirable? When is it bad?
    2. Compare these remarks to Randall Jarrell's (page 410). How applicable to contemporary poetry does Coleridge's insight seem to you?

PERCY BYSSHE SHELLEY, 'Unacknowledged legislators,' page 405

    How is Shelley's view of the value of poetry different from that of Socrates' in the statement about banishing poets from the republic? How does Shelley's thinking resemble that of Socrates' in the remarks on inspiration?

RALPH WALDO EMERSON, 'Meter-making argument,' page 406

    Have you read any poems in this book that appear to be the work of mere music-box heads, like Emerson's acquaintance? (Perhaps the best illustration of a poem that seems all sound, and no sense, is the extract from Thomas Holley Chivers on page 253.)

EDGAR ALLAN POE, 'A long poem does not exist,' page 406

    Do you agree or disagree? If Poe is right, should we discard <u>The Odyssey</u>, <u>The Divine Comedy</u>, and "Lycidas"? If he is wrong, then how do you account for the fact that certain long poems contain patches of deadly dullness?

407-410 (text pages)

ROBERT FROST, 'The sound of sense,' page 407

    1. Experiment: Let someone in the class follow Frost's instructions, go out into the hall, and try speaking these or other sentences in a soft voice through a closed door. What element (if any) can the hearers still recognize?
    2. Point to sentences in Frost's poems that sound as though written according to his ideas. Any Frost poem will do.

WALLACE STEVENS, Proverbs, page 408

    1. Explain any of these remarks that seem cryptic.
    2. Make up a few proverbs (about poetry) of your own.

WILLIAM CARLOS WILLIAMS, 'The rhythm persists,' page 408

    Williams's own poetry is often regarded as an influential model of vers libre, or free-form verse. What isn't free or formless about it? How do Williams's remarks help you perceive what he is doing in his poems?

WILLIAM CARLOS WILLIAMS, The crab and the box, page 409

    What is the point of the poet's blast against sonnets? Would you agree or disagree that a twentieth-century sonnet (such as MacLeish's "The End of the World") can be called a crab in a box?

EZRA POUND, Poetry and music, page 409

    Do you agree? Or are there any poems you know that aren't particularly musical but which are worth reading? Give examples.

T. S. ELIOT, Emotion and personality, page 409

    Why does Eliot think Wordsworth (in his remarks on emotion recollected in tranquillity) is wrong? Compare these two poets' statements.

YVOR WINTERS, 'The fallacy of expressive form,' page 410

    1. Winters is reacting against critics who charge that traditional metrical verse is no good because it doesn't capture the nervous, start-and-stop pace of city traffic; because it doesn't reflect the sprawling formlessness of our rapidly changing society. What is his defense of formal poetry?
    2. How do you suppose Winters would react to Dr. Williams's remarks about the crab in the box?

RANDALL JARRELL, On the charge that modern poetry is obscure, page 410

    1. To the reader who protests that modern poetry is obscure, Jarrell replies, "That's not the reason you don't read it." What does he imply the reason actually to be?
    2. Compare his remarks on obscurity in poetry to Coleridge's. Isn't it possible, for reasons given by Coleridge, that certain contemporary poems may indeed be obscure?

BARBARA HERRNSTEIN SMITH, Closure and Anti-closure, page 411

    1. What does the critic appear to mean by closure and anti-closure in poetry?
    2. What similarity does she find between poetry and other forms of contemporary art?
    3. Compare Professor Smith's remarks to William Carlos Williams's on rhythm in poetry (page 408). What limits do both writers set on "openness" in poetry? According to both, what is to stop a "free verse" poet from freeing a poem all the way?

    Professor Smith's Poetic Closure: A Study of How Poems End (Chicago: University of Chicago Press, 1968), is a provocative, critical book well worth reading in its entirety. In the passage reprinted in the text, one of the author's arguments has been greatly condensed from pages 240-244. Professor Smith kindly read and approved this condensation.

415-428 (text pages)

SUPPLEMENT

WRITING ABOUT LITERATURE

WRITING ABOUT A POEM

These sections in the text are provided for the instructor whose students complain, "I've never written about poetry before-- what am I supposed to do?"

This material need not take up a great amount of time in class; it is here mainly to give students a few illustrations of decent papers and some pointers on method and mechanics. If the instructor likes, it can be assigned for outside reading at the time of the first writing assignment. (Perhaps the more general "Writing about Literature" might be good to assign even sooner.) To make sure that students are at least aware that this material exists, it might be dealt with very briefly in class, with a few minutes devoted to any questions students may have about it and about the expected format of their papers.

Some instructors like to assign few papers and to exact polished prose from their students. Others prefer to keep students scribbling away constantly, on the assumption that the practice is valuable, whether or not the instructor reads all of their output word by word. Some instructors who favor the latter approach tell me that they simply assign poems in the book that have questions after them (this edition has more than 200 such poems), and ask students to answer the questions in writing outside of class. These papers are col- lected and the instructor later skims through them, selecting a few lively points from them to read in class and discuss. (The papers are not returned.)

Once--at the end of a class in which discussion had waxed hot over the question "Is 'Naming of Parts' an antiwar poem or isn't it?"--I made the mistake of telling students to go home and write their own opinions down on paper. The result was to cool future class discussions: students were afraid that if they animatedly talked up, they would be told to write.

Students often come into a poetry course laboring under the suspicion that anybody who thinks and writes about poetry is heart- less or obtuse and is tearing the wings off a beautiful butterfly, and that poetry is simply to be felt. To bring such doubts out into the open and perhaps allay them, Michael Fixler, at Tufts, has an excellent first writing assignment: in about 1,000 words discuss the preferability of experiencing a poem rather than thinking, talk- ing, or writing about it. Is the first possible without the second? If so, then why do we think, talk, and write?

Here are notes on the two poems contained in this section.

182

ROBERT FROST, Design, page 429

"Design" is fruitful to compare in theme with Walt Whitman's
"A Noiseless Patient Spider" (page 234). One could begin by comparing the early versions of the two poems, Whitman's "The Soul,
reaching" and Frost's "In White" (given on pages 235 and 443).
What are the themes of these versions? It is more difficult to tell
from these vaguer, more general statements. In rewriting, both
poets seem not only to have made their details more specific, but
also to have defined their central ideas.
    If you wish to deal with this section in class you might have
students read "Design," then the two student papers about it (pages
429 and 435). What did these writers notice about the poem that you
didn't notice? What did you notice about it that they left out?
    Besides Jarrell's classic explication, many other good dis-
cussions of the poem can be consulted. Elizabeth Drew has a succinct explication in Poetry: A Modern Guide to Its Understanding
and Enjoyment (New York: Norton, 1959), and there is a more detailed
reading by Richard Ohmann in College English, 28 (February 1967),
pp. 359-367.

ABBIE HUSTON EVANS, Wing-Spread, page 436

    The student's evaluation seems just to me. While "Wing-Spread"
is not so vivid a cameo as "Design," nor so troubling in its theme,
and while it contains trite rimes (except for beryl / peril), I
think it a decent poem and admirably terse.
    Insufficiently recognized (like most poets), Evans was born in
1881 and (as far as I know) is still alive at this writing. Her
Collected Poems was published in 1970 by the University of Pittsburgh Press. There are dozens of poems better than "Wing-Spread"
in it.

TOPICS FOR WRITING

    These suggestions for paper assignments supplement the list of
topics on pages 442-444.

Topics for Brief Papers (250-500 words)

    1. A précis (French, from Latin: "to cut short") is a short
abstract or condensation of a literary work that tries to sum up
the work's most essential elements. Although a précis, like a paraphrase, states the poet's thought in the writer's own words, a paraphrase is sometimes as long as the original poem, if not longer. A
précis, while it tends to be much briefer than a poem, also takes
in essentials: theme, subject, tone, character, events (in a narrative poem), and anything else that strikes the writer as important. A précis might range in length from one ample sentence to a

few hundred words (if, say, it were condensing a long play or novel, or a complex longer poem). Here, for instance, is an acceptable précis of Robert Browning's "Soliloquy of the Spanish Cloister":

> The speaker, a monk in a religious community, voices to himself while gardening the bitter grudge he has against Brother Lawrence, one of his fellow monks. He charges Lawrence with boring him with dull talk at meal-time, sporting monogrammed tableware, ogling women, drinking greedily, ignoring rituals (unlike the speaker, who after a meal lays knife and fork in a cross--which seems overly scrupulous). Having vented his grudge by slyly scissoring Lawrence's favorite flowering shrubs, the speaker is now determined to go further, and plots to work Lawrence's damnation. Perhaps he will lure Lawrence into misinter-preting a text in Scripture, or plant a pornographic volume on him. So far gone is the speaker in his hatred that he is even willing to sell his soul to the devil if the devil will carry off Lawrence's; and so proud is the speaker of his own wiles that he thinks he can cheat the devil in the bargain. Vespers ring, ending the meditation, but his terrible grudge seems sure to go on.

As the detailed précis makes clear, Browning's poem contains a chronicle of events and a study in character. The précis also in-dicates the tone of the poem and (another essential) its point of view.

Students might be supplied with a copy of the above material to guide them and be asked to write précis of four or five poems, chosen from a list the instructor compiles of six or eight poems in the Anthology.

2. Pick a short poem rich in figures of speech (Plath's "Metaphors," say, or Burns's "Oh my love is like a red, red rose," or Keats's "On First Looking into Chapman's Homer"). Rewrite it, taking for your model Howard Moss's deliberately bepiddling version of Shakespeare's "Shall I compare thee to a summer's day?" Elimi-nate all figurative language and turn the poem into language as flat and unsuggestive as possible. (Just ignore any rime or rhythm in the original.) Then, in a paragraph, point out those lines in your revised version that seem glaringly worse than the original. In another paragraph, sum up what your barbaric rewrite suggests to you about the nature of poetry.

3. Evaluate a poem, briefly referring to particulars in the poem to support your opinion of it.

4. Take some relatively simple poem (such as Williams's "This Is Just to Say" or Donne's "A Burnt Ship") and write a burlesque critical interpretation of it in which you discover all sorts of symbols, myths, and profundities in the poem that it doesn't con-tain. While allowing your ability to read into a poem to run wild, do not invent anything that you can't somehow support from the text of the poem itself. At the end of your paper, append a sentence or a paragraph summing up what your burlesque indicates about how to read poems, or how not to.

5. Find a poem that you like, one not in this book so it may
be unfamiliar to other members of the class. Insert into it a
passage of five or six lines that you yourself write in imitation
of it. Your object is to lengthen the poem by a bit of forgery
that will go undetected. Type out the whole poem afresh, inserted
lines and all, and have copies duplicated for the others in the
class. Then let them try to tell your forged lines from those of
the original. A successful forgery will be hard to detect, since
you will have imitated the poet's language, handling of form, and
imagery--indeed, the poet's voice.

Topics for More Extensive Papers (600-1,000 words)

1. This is a two-part exercise in analyzing writing for connotations.
    First, analyze a piece of writing whose words very obviously
convey suggestions. In a recent newspaper or magazine, find an
advertisement that tries to surround a product with a certain aura.
For instance, an ad for a new car might describe the car in words
that suggest some powerful jungle animal ("purring power, ready to
leap"). Such language implies that whoever buys the car controls
a savage force, that the car is sleek and beautiful as a panther,
and so on. (Likely hunting grounds for such ads are magazines
printed on slick paper, aimed toward the more affluent: The New
Yorker, Glamour, Playboy, Sports Illustrated, and others.) Clip
or photocopy the ad so that you can turn it in along with your
paper. Circle words in it that seem to you full of suggestions and
explain what the words suggest to you.
    Second, take a more subtle piece of writing: an excellent
poem rich in connotative language. This book abounds in such
poems: among them, Marianne Moore's "The Mind is an Enchanting
Thing" and Shakespeare's pair of sonnets glimpsing spring and
winter, "When daisies pied" and "When icicles hang by the wall."
As you did with the ad, indicate words in the poem that seem to you
especially rich in suggestions and try to state what they suggest.
For an example of such an analysis, see the list of connotations of
words in Blake's "London" (pages 61-63). Your instructor can help
you decide whether to make your analysis in the form of a list or
an essay.
2. Compare or contrast two poems (or compare and contrast
them). Such a paper might be an examination of a theme (or other
element) that you find in both poems. Sample topics:

"Reflections on Fascism in Kumin's 'Woodchucks' and Plath's
'Daddy'"
"Robinson's 'Richard Cory' and Paul Simon's: The Same
Individual?"

For many more pairings of comparable poems, see the back-of-the-
book Anthology, where the note "Compare" after a poem will direct
you to another poem somehow like it (usually in theme).

3. Relate a personal experience of poetry: a brief history of your attempts to read it or to write it; a memoir of your experience in reading poetry aloud; a report of a poetry reading you attended; an account of how reading a poem brought a realization that affected you personally (no instructor-pleasing pieties!); or an account of an effort to foist a favorite poem upon your friends, or to introduce young children to poetry. Don't make up any fabulous experiences or lay claim to profound emotions you haven't had; the result could be blatantly artificial ("How I Read Housman's 'Loveliest of trees' and Found the Meaning of Life"). But if you honestly can sum up what you learned from your experience, then do so, by all means.

4. Write an imitation or a parody, as directed in the "Experiment" on page 245. This topic, and the following topic, may result in a paper of fewer words than the essay topics, but the amount of work required is likely to be slightly more.

(Note: This assignment will be too much of a challenge for some students and not all ought to be required to do it. But those who possess the necessary skill may find themselves viewing the poet's work as if they were insiders.) The instructor has to insist that the student observe the minimal formal requirements of a good imitation. A convincing imitation of, say, Thomas Hardy can hardly be written in Whitmanic free verse. Students may be urged to read whole collections of work in order to soak up a better sense of the poet. This assignment asks much but I have often been surprised by the quality of the results. Honestly attempted, such an exercise requires far more effort from students than the writing of most critical essays, and probably teaches them more.

5. After you have read several ballads (both folk ballads and literary ballads), write a ballad of your own, at least twenty lines long. If you need a subject, consider some event recently in the news: an act of bravery, a wedding that took place despite obstacles, a murder or a catastrophe, a report of spooky or mysterious happenings. Then in a prose paragraph, state what you learned from your reading of traditional or literary ballads that proved useful to you as a ballad composer yourself.

Topics for Long Papers (1,500 words or more)

1. "Concrete Poetry: Vital New Art Form or Visual Trivia?"
2. Leslie Fiedler, the critic and novelist, once wrote an essay in which he pretended to be a critic of the last century. ("A Review of Leaves of Grass and Hiawatha as of 1855," in American Poetry Review, vol. 2, no. 2, March/April 1973.) Writing as if he subscribed to the tastes of that age, Fiedler declared Whitman's book shaggy and shocking, and awarded Professor Longfellow all the praise. If you can steep yourself in the literature of a former age (or recent past year) deeply enough to feel confident, such an essay might be fun to write (and to read). Write about some poem once fashionable, now forgotten; or about some poem once spurned, now esteemed. Your instructor might have some suggestions.

3. Write a study of lyrics by some recent or current popular
songwriter, showing why you believe they deserve the name of poetry.
4. For a month (of some other assigned period of time), keep
a personal journal of your reading of poetry and your thinking about
it. To give direction to your journal, you might confine it to the
work of, say, half a dozen poets who interest you; or you might
concentrate on a theme common to a few poems by various poets.

WRITING A POEM

These notes are provided mainly for the instructor who employs
An Introduction to Poetry in a creative course. Some may be of
interest, however, to anyone who in teaching composition includes
a unit on writing poems. Such an instructor will probably have firm
persuasions about poetry and about the teaching of poets. Instead
of trying to trumpet any persuasions of my own, let me just set
down some hunches that, from teaching poetry workshops, I have come
to feel are mostly true.

In reading a student's poem, you have to look at it with your
mind a blank, reserving judgment for as long as possible. Try to
see what the student is doing, being slow to compare a fledgling
effort to the classics. There's no use in merely reading the poem
and spotting any influences you find in it--"Ha, I see you've been
reading Williams!" You can, however, praise any virtues you discover and you can tell the student firmly, kindly, and honestly any
adverse reactions you feel. Point to anything in the poem that
causes you to respond toward it, or against it. Instead of coldly
damning the poem's faults, you can inquire why the writer said something in such-and-such a way, rather than in some other. You can
ask to have anything you don't understand explained. If a line or
a passage doesn't tell you anything, you can ask the student to
suggest a fresh way of wording it. Perhaps the most valuable service you can perform for a student poet is to be hard to please.
Suggest that the student not settle for the first words that flash
to mind, but reach deeper, go after the word or phrase or line that
will be, not merely adequate, memorable.

The greatest method of teaching poetry writing I have ever
heard of was that of the late John Holmes. Former students at
Tufts remember that Holmes seldom made comments on a poem, but
often would just lay a finger next to a suspect passage and fix the
student with a look of expectancy until the silence became unendurable, and the student began explaining what the passage meant
and how it could have been put better. (I have never made the
Holmes method succeed for me. I can't keep from talking too much.)

Most workshop courses in poetry fall into a classic ritual.
Students duplicate their poems, bring them in, and show them around
to the class. This method of procedure is hard to improve upon.
Some instructors find that the effort of screening the work themselves first and deciding what to spend time on in class makes for

more cogent class sessions, with less time squandered on boring or
inferior material. In general, class sessions won't be any more
lively and valuable than the poems that are on hand. (An exception
was a workshop I once visited years ago at MIT. The poems were
literal, boring stuff, but the quality of the students' impromptu
critical analyses was sensational.) Often a great class discussion
will center around a fine poem with deep faults in it.

The severest challenge for the instructor, incidentally, isn't
a bad poem. A bad poem is easy to deal with; it always gives you
plenty of work to do--passages to delete, purple adjectives to
question. The challenge comes in dealing with a truly surprising,
original, and competent poem. This is risky and sensitive work
because genuine poets usually know what they are doing to a greater
degree than you or any other outsider does; and you don't want to
confuse them with reactions you don't trust. For such rare students,
all a poetry workshop probably does is supply an audience, a little
encouragement, and sometimes even an insight.

There are natural temptations, of course, to which teachers of
poets fall prey. Like coin collectors, they keep wanting to over-
value the talents they have on hand, to convince themselves that a
student is a Gem Mint State poet, when a less personal opinion might
find the student just an average specimen, although uncirculated.
It's better to be too slow than too quick to encourage a student to
seek nationwide publication. It is another temptation, if you have
a class with a competent poet in it, to devote most of each session
to that poet's latest works, causing grumblings of discontent
(sometimes) among the other paying customers. I believe that a
more competent poet deserves more time, but you have to conduct a
class and not a tutorial.

Poetry workshops can become hideously intimate. They are
bound to produce confessional or diary poems that, sometimes behind
the thinnest of fictive screens, confide in painful detail the
writer's sexual, psychic, and religious hangups. I have known
poetry workshops where, by semester's end, the participants feel
toward one another like the members of a hostile therapy group.
That is why I believe in stressing that a poem is not merely the
poet's self-revelation. It usually helps to insist at the start
of the course that poems aren't necessarily to be taken personally.
(See Chapter 2, "The Person in the Poem," if you want any ammuni-
tion.) Everybody will know, of course, that some poets in the
class aren't capable of detached art and that a poem about a seduction may well be blatant autobiography; but believe me, you and
your students will be happier if you can blow the trump in favor of
the Imagination. There is no use in circulating poems in class
anonymously, pretending that nobody knows who wrote them. Somebody
will know and I think that the sooner the members of the class
freely admit their identities, the more easy and relaxed and open
the situation will be. To know each one personally, as soon as you
can, is essential.

As the workshop goes on, I don't always stick to a faithful
conference schedule. Some will need (and wish for) more of your
time than others, but I like to schedule at least one conference

right away, at the beginning of the course. This is a chance to
meet with students in private and get a sense of their needs. I
tell them to bring in a few poems they've already written, if they've
written any. But I make it clear that class sessions will deal only
with brand-new poems. At the end of the course, I program another
such conference (instead of a final exam), sit down with each student, and ask, "Well, where are you now?"

Some students will lean on you for guidance ("What shall I
write about?"); others will spurn all your brilliant suggestions
and want to roar away in their own directions. Fine. I believe in
offering the widest possible latitude in making assignments--but in
having some assignments. Even the most inner-directed poet can
learn something from being expected to move in a new direction.
Having a few assignments will discourage the customers who think
they can get through any number of creative writing courses by using
the same old yellowed sheaf of poems. Encourage revision. Now and
then, suggest a revision as an assignment instead of a new poem.

In "Writing a Poem" I offer a radical suggestion: that the
students memorize excellent poems. Feeling like a curmudgeon for
making this recommendation, I was happy to find some support for it
in the view of Robert Bly, who remarks in Coda, June/July 1981:

> I won't even read a single manuscript now, when I
> visit a university workshop, unless the poet in advance
> agrees to memorize fifty lines of Yeats. At the first
> workshop I visited last fall it cut the number of graduate-
> student writers who wanted to see me from 15 to 2. Next
> year I'm changing that to fifty lines of Beowulf.

Bly may seem unreasonably stern, but he and I agree on the value of
memorization. I believe it helps coax the writing of poetry down
out of the forebrain, helps unite it with the pulse. (Bly, incidentally, has sane things to say in this same article about the
folly of thirsting for publication too soon.)

Although knowing something about any element of poetry may
benefit a poet-in-training, here is a list, chapter by chapter, of
material in An Introduction to Poetry that may be particularly useful in a creative writing class. Certain poems and exercises in
the book may suggest additional writing assignments. For a textbook
wholly devoted to the writing of poetry, see Robert Wallace's excellent Writing Poems (Little, Brown, 1982).

Chapter 1, DONALD FINKEL, Hands, page 7

This fine, humorous poem about poetry may be a springboard for
discussion. What is the relation between a poem and its audience?

Chapter 2, THE PERSON IN THE POEM, page 15

Novice poets often think of their poems as faithful diary
accounts of actual experiences. This section may be useful to

445-462 (text pages)

suggest to them that, in the process of becoming art, the raw
material of a poem may be expected to undergo change.

Chapter 3, DAVID B. AXELROD, Once in a While a Protest Poem, page 38

Assignment: Write a protest poem of your own.

Chapter 5, ABOUT HAIKU, page 75

Assignment: Write some haiku, either original or in imitation
of classic Japanese haiku.

Chapter 5, Experiment: Writing with Images, page 80

A poetry writing assignment with possible examples.

Chapter 6, HOWARD MOSS, Shall I compare thee to a summer's day?
page 85

Assignment: Choosing a different famous poem, write a Moss-
like version of it. Then try to indicate what, in making your
takeoff, was most painful to leave out. (See also George Starbuck's parody "Margaret Are You Drug," page 243.)

Chapter 6, JANE KENYON, The Suitor, 89

Assignment: Write a poem similarly constructed of similes, or
metaphors.

Chapter 7, PAUL SIMON, Richard Cory, page 108

Assignment: In somewhat the fashion of Simon's treatment of
Robinson, take a well-known poem and rewrite it as a song lyric.
Try singing the result to a tune.

Chapter 8, Exercise: Listening to Meaning, page 124

Assignment: After reading these examples, write a brief poem
of your own, heavy with sound effects.

Chapter 8, READING AND HEARING POEMS ALOUD, page 135

Assignment: Ponder this section before reading your own poems
aloud in class.

Chapter 9, <u>METER</u>, page 149

Assignment: After working through this section on your own, write a poem in a meter.

Chapter 10, <u>CLOSED FORM, OPEN FORM</u>

This whole chapter may be of particular value to a poetry writing class. Not only does it analyze some traditional forms, it suggests a rationale for formally open verse and tries to suggest why competent verse is seldom "free."

Assignment: After considering the definition of <u>syllabic verse</u> given in this chapter, carefully read Dylan Thomas's "Fern Hill." Work out the form of Thomas's poem with pencil and paper, then try writing a syllabic poem of your own.

Assignment: Ponder, not too seriously, Wallace Stevens's "Thirteen Ways of Looking at a Blackbird." Then, if the spirit moves you, write a unified series of small poems.

Chapter 11, <u>Experiment: Do It Yourself</u>, page 203

An exercise in making a concrete poem.

Chapter 14, <u>THE POET'S REVISIONS</u>, page 231

This section may help drive home the fact that poets often revise.

Chapter 14, <u>TRANSLATIONS</u>, page 236

Assignment: Consider the translations in this section and decide what you admire or dislike in each of them. Translate a poem of your choice, from any language with which you are familiar or can follow in a bilingual edition.

Chapter 14, <u>PARODY</u>, page 240

Assignment: Read these parodists, comparing their work with the originals. Then, choosing some poet whose work you know thoroughly, write a parody yourself.

Chapter 15, <u>TELLING GOOD FROM BAD</u>

Warning: Although you may care to give something in this chapter a try, this is dangerous matter to introduce into a poetry writing class. Young poets already tend to be self-consciously worried that their work will be laughed at. Save this chapter for late in the course, if you use it at all.

ON INTEGRATING POETRY AND COMPOSITION

How do you teach students to read poetry and, at the same time, to write good prose? Instructors who face this task may find some useful advice in the following article, first published in The English Record, bulletin of the New York State English Council, Winter 1981. It is reprinted here by the kind permission of the author, Irwin Weiser, of the Department of English, Tennessee Technological University.

The Prose Paraphrase:
Integrating Poetry and Composition

Irwin Weiser

Many of us teach composition courses which demand that we not only instruct our students in writing but that we also present literature to them as well. Such courses often frustrate us, since a quarter or a semester seems too brief to allow us to teach fundamentals of composition alone. How are we to integrate the teaching of literature with the teaching of writing? What are we to do with a fat anthology of essays, fiction, poetry, or drama and a rhetoric text and, in some cases, a separate handbook of grammar and usage? Recently, I tried an approach which seemed to provide more integration of reading and writing than I previously had felt I attained in similar courses. The course was the third quarter of a required freshman composition sequence; the departmental course description specifies the teaching of poetry and drama, but also states "English 103 is, however, primarily a composition, not a literature, course. Major emphasis of the course should be on writing." The approach I will describe concerns the study of poetry.

Because this is a writing course, I explained to my students that we would approach poetry primarily as a study of the way writers can use language, and thus our work on denotation and connotation, tone, irony, image, and symbol should help them learn to make conscious language choices when they write. Chapters in X. J. Kennedy's An Introduction to Poetry entitled "Words," "Saying and Suggesting," and "Listening to a Voice" fit nicely with this approach. Further, because this is a writing course, I wanted my students to

have frequent opportunities to write without burying myself under
an even greater number of formal, longish papers than I already required. An appropriate solution seemed to be to have my students
write prose paraphrases of one or two poems from those assigned for
each discussion class.

During the first week of the course, we discussed and practiced
the paraphrase technique, looking first at Kennedy's explanation of
paraphrasing and then at his paraphrase of Housman's "Loveliest of
trees, the cherry now," (page 3). In class, we all paraphrased
Donald Finkel's "Hands" (page 7) and read the paraphrases aloud.
By forcing students to read aloud on the second day of classes and
by deliberately choosing a poem which is more than slightly sexual,
I was able to crack the wall of fear and restraint which often keeps
students tight-lipped throughout the term. By reading my own paraphrase, not among the ablest in the class, I was able to place myself in the position of coinquirer into these poems, most of which
I had not previously taught. This helped establish a classroom
atmosphere similar to that of a creative writing workshop, one con-
ducive to the discussion of both the poetry in the text and the
writing of the students. In fact, while the primary purpose of
assigning the paraphrases was to give my students extra writing
practice, an important additional result was that throughout the
quarter their paraphrases, not the teacher's opinions and interpretations, formed the basis for class discussion. There was rarely a
need for the teacher to explain a poem or a passage: someone, and
frequently several people, had an interpretation which satisfied
most questions and resolved most difficulties.

At the end of this essay are examples of the prose paraphrases
students wrote of Emily Dickinson's "I heard a fly buzz--when I
died." Two of the paraphrases, at 90 and 112 words, are approximately as long as Dickinson's 92-word poem; the 160-word third paraphrase is over 75% longer because this student interpreted as she
paraphrased, explaining, for example, that the narrator willed her
earthly possessions in a futile attempt to hasten death. Such interpretation, while welcome, is not at all necessary, as the two
shorter, yet also successful, paraphrases indicate. In fact, I
had to remind students that paraphrases are not the same as analyses, and that while they might have to interpret a symbol--as these
students variously explained what the fly or the King meant--or un-
weave a metaphor, their major task was to rewrite the poem as clear
prose.

The first paraphrase is perhaps the most straightforward of
this group. The author's voice is nearly inaudible. He has
stripped the poem of its literary qualities--no "Heaves of Storm,"
only "the air before a storm"; no personification; the author is
only present in the choice of the word "sad" to describe the final
buzz of the fly. His paraphrase is a prose rendering of the poem
with no obvious attempt to interpret it.

Paraphrase II seems to ignore the symbolic importance of the
fly, and perhaps in the very casualness of the phrase "and the last
thing I was aware of was this fly and its buzz" suggests the same
insignificance of death from the perspective of the hereafter that

Dickinson does. More interesting is this student's treatment of the willing of the keepsakes: the formal diction of "proper recipients," "standard fashion," and "officially ready to die" suggests death as a ritual. Unexpected interpretations like this appear frequently in the paraphrases, demonstrating the flexibility and richness of language, emphasizing the error in assuming that there is one right way to interpret a poem, and sometimes, when the interpretations are less plausible, leading to discussions of what constitutes valid interpretation and how one finds support for interpretations of what one reads.

The third paraphrase, as I suggested before, offers more interpretation as well as a stronger authorial voice than the previous two. The author adds a simile of her own, "as if the winds had ceased temporarily to catch their breaths," and more obviously than the other students uses the fly as a metaphor for death in her final sentence.

I will not take the space for a thorough analysis of these paraphrases, but I think that they suggest what a teacher might expect from this kind of assignment. Clearly, these three students have read this poem carefully and understand what it says, the first step towards understanding what it means. Small group and classroom discussions would allow us to consider these paraphrases individually and comparatively, to point out their merits and weaknesses, and then to return to the original verse with new perspectives.

Most heartening were the comments of several students during the quarter who told me that they felt more confident about reading poetry than they previously had. Though I doubt that my students are any more ardently devoted to poetry now than they were before the course began, they are not intimidated by verse on the page. They have an approach, a simple heuristic, for dealing with any unfamiliar writing. Ideally, my students will remember and use their ability to paraphrase and their ability to use their paraphrases to understand and evaluate what they read when they come upon a particularly difficult passage in their chemistry or history texts during the next three years or in the quarterly reports or technical manuals or journals they will read when they leave the university and begin their careers.

APPENDIX: SAMPLE PARAPHRASES

Paraphrase I

I heard death coming on. The stillness in the room was like the stillness in the air before a storm. The people around me had wiped their eyes dry, and they held their breaths waiting for that moment when death could be witnessed in the room. I wrote a will which gave away my possessions--that being the only part of me I could give away. A fly then flew between the light and me making a sad, uncertain buzz. My eyesight failed and I could not see to see.

Paraphrase II

I heard a fly buzz as I was about to die. The sound of the
fly broke the quietness in the room which was like the calm before
a storm. The people sitting around waiting for me to die cried
until they could not cry anymore. They began to breathe uneasily
in anticipation of my death when God would come down to the room to
take me away. I had willed all of my valuables to the proper recipients in the standard fashion. I was officially ready to die,
going through the final dramatic moments of my life, and the last
thing I was aware of was this fly and its buzz.

Paraphrase III

I could feel the approach of death just as I could hear the
buzz of an approaching fly. I knew death was buzzing around, but
I did not know when and where it would land. The stillness of death
was like the calmness that exists between storms, as if the winds
had ceased temporarily to catch their breaths.

I was aware of the sorrow in the room. There were those who
had cried because death was near, and they waited for death to
stalk into the room like a king and claim its subject.

I willed all of my earthly possessions, all that could legally
be assigned to a new owner, in an attempt to hasten death. But
there was no way to control death; I was at the mercy of its timing.
And then like the fly that finally lands on its choice place, death
fell upon me, and shut my eyes, and I could no longer see.

In April 1981, Mr. Weiser reported in a letter that, once
again that quarter, he was using the method of poetry paraphrase
in his writing course, and remained pleased with it. "My students,"
he remarked, "no longer treat poems as holy scripts written in some
mystical code, but attack them fearlessly." The course had proved
fun both for them and for him, and he felt he was paying his dues
to both writing and literature.

FURTHER NOTES ON TEACHING POETRY

These notes are offered in response to the wishes of several instructors for additional practical suggestions for teaching poetry. They are, however, mere descriptions of a few strategies that have proved useful in my own teaching. For others, I can neither prescribe nor proscribe.

1. To a greater extent than in teaching prose, the instructor may find it necessary to have poems read aloud. It is best if students do this reading. Since to read a poem aloud effectively requires that the reader understand what is said in it, students will need advance warning so that they can prepare their spoken interpretations. Sometimes I assign particular poems to certain people, or ask each person to take his choice. Some advice on how to read poetry aloud is given in Chapter Eight. I usually suggest only that students beware of waxing overemotionally or rhetorically, and I urge them to read aloud outside of class as often as possible. If the student or the instructor has access to a tape recorder, it may be especially helpful.

2. It is good to recall occasionally that poems may be put back together as well as taken apart. Sometimes I call on a student to read a previously prepared poem, just before opening a discussion of the poem. Then, the discussion over and the poem lying all around in intelligible shreds, I ask the same student to read it over again. It is often startling how the reading improves from the student realizing more clearly what the poet is saying.

3. I believe in asking students to do a certain amount of memorization. Many groan that such rote learning is mindless and grade-schoolish, but it seems to me one way to defeat the intellectualizations that students (and the rest of us) tend to make of poetry. It is also a way to suggest that we do not read a poem primarily for its ideas: to learn a poem by heart is one way to engrave oneself with the sound and weight of it. I ask for twenty or thirty lines at a time, of the student's choice, then have them write the lines out in class. Some students have reported unexpected illuminations. Some people, of course, can't memorize a poem to save their souls, and I try to encourage but not to pressure them. These written memorizations take very little of the instructor's time to check and need not be returned to the students unless there are flagrant lacunae in them.

4. The instructor has to sense when a discussion has gone on long enough. It is a matter of watching each student's face for the

first sign of that fixed set of the mouth. Elizabeth Bishop once wisely declared that, while she was not opposed to all close analysis and criticism, she was against "making poetry monstrous and boring and proceeding to talk the very life out of it." I used to be afraid of classroom silences. Now, I find it helps sometimes to stop a discussion that is getting lost, and say, "Let's all take three minutes and read this poem again and think about it silently." When the discussion resumes, it is usually improved.